The Champlain Canal:
Two Hundred Years of Change

Champlain Canal Anniversary Anthology

Lake Champlain Maritime Museum

Edited by Chris Sabick and Matt Harrison

Anthology Project Manager, Matt Harrison

ONION RIVER PRESS

Burlington, Vermont

Onion River Press
89 Church Street
Burlington, VT 05401
info@onionriverpress.com
www.onionriverpress.com

ISBN: 978-1-966607-36-6

Library of Congress Control Number: 2025923667

Dedicated to all who have appreciated the Champlain Canal
for what it was, what it is, and what it could be.

Contents

The Champlain Canal:
Two Hundred Years of Change

Chris Sabick
Executive Director, Lake Champlain Maritime Museum

The impact of the opening of the Champlain Canal in 1823 is hard to overstate. The establishment of the canal caused dramatic changes to the landscape, communities, industry, commerce, and even the ecology of the Champlain and Hudson Valleys. The Champlain Canal, though distant and little thought-of by many current Champlain Valley residents, has driven huge changes over the last two hundred years. Many stories have been told already, but there will always be many more. This volume is an attempt to examine the canal and its history with a broad and inclusive scope, and to also consider the future of the canal.

Telling the story of a piece of infrastructure, particularly a slow, plodding canal, might encourage a slow and plodding narrative. But canals were built to connect: and connect they did – watersheds, peoples, markets, landscapes, languages, states, and countries were all united by the construction of this narrow strip of water. Even if it seems to have a relatively unseen impact on our world today, the chapters included here aim to deliver the idea that the Champlain Canal remains a vector of change and movement in our world. In the realm of imagination, current ideas about its future still drive conversation and even conflict to this day.

The Erie Canal is fittingly nicknamed "the Mother of Cities" -- the 363-mile canal running east to west from Albany to Buffalo has always been the hero of the story of the New York State Canal System. It led to the growth and development of numerous important cities and towns along its course, spurred a huge amount of change to the landscape of New York, both human and ecological, and played a large part in American history in the 1800s. But the Champlain Canal, its smaller sibling at only 60 miles in length, has never received comparable attention or fame. As Champlain Valley historian Morris Glenn points out, though the Champlain Waterway "gained support from the political and economic leaders of the Northeast, it was viewed as second to New York's Erie or Western Canal and a poor sister to the other Canadian canals." In addition, most histories of the northern canal consider it from the southerly direction, from within New York State. This is entirely appropriate, as the Champlain Canal is a part of the wider state network and built alongside the Erie, but unlike the feeder canals that eventually branched off the main Erie line, the Champlain heads off in a different direction, connecting an entirely unique watershed to the transportation network of New York. To those residents of the Champlain Valley and Quebec, the Champlain Canal rather than the Erie was the great vector for change. We examine the canal (mostly) from this northerly direction, to see what new insights might emerge.

The concept of "change" is a driving force in this historical anthology, which is written from a variety of different disciplines, each looking at the canal from different angles and bodies of evidence. Some chapters are written as traditional history, using mostly textual evidence, maps, and images. Others are from archaeological perspectives, based on work carried out on the bottom of Lake Champlain or along the route of the old canal. A combination is often used by the authors, as in Scott McLaughlin's chapter, which uses many types of historical evidence to try to understand how canal families thought of themselves in relation to other people of the past. And the canal and its legacy is examined from a biological perspective too, which lets us try to understand and imagine how it may change going into the future as it has in the past. Our book is not meant to capture the full history of the Champlain Canal, but just to use the two hundredth anniversary as an opportunity to try to say some new things about its history.

Most of us are looking toward the Champlain Canal from very specific perspectives. Brad Utter, from the New York State Museum, gives the canal its most direct examination. The archaeologists writing here are considering the canal from the perspective of the wrecked or abandoned boats that they study, most resting on the bottom of Lake Champlain, whereas Scott McLaughlin considers the canal to be a vector of movement for a large group of people who traveled through it and far beyond it in the past. Taylor Picard uses archaeology of shipwrecks within Lake Champlain to understand the physical evolution of the original Champlain Canal, while Paul Gates zooms in on very specific instances of the canal's history: landscape change in the area of Fort Edward. Matt Harrison, in Chapter Five, and Meg Modley Gilbertson and Ryan Mitchell, in Chapter Six, collectively consider the canal as an entryway into the larger Lake Champlain watershed, positioned as we are on the northern side of the canal rather than the more typical southern New York perspective. Chapter Six looks into the transition from commercial activity on the Champlain Canal and the Northern Waterway toward today's recreational uses. Modley Gilbertson, in Chapter Six, examines how the canal drives changes to environment in the form of aquatic invasive species both in the past and into the future.

This book is not a narrative of the history of the Champlain Canal. Rather, it is an attempt to gather a diverse set of perspectives from scholars who have varying and unique points of view on the canal and its two-hundred-year history. The canal has always been an imagined connection, from before it was built up through the present. Even as canal families, boats' owners, or local citizens traveled on and through the waters of the Champlain Canal, they imagined what it was and could be in the future. This book is meant to document stories of the canal as it slowly morphed over time but also to contribute to these changes in the future, considering the canal as it is now and imagining how it might appear in years to come. We hope there is something new to discover in these pages for those with a casual interest or canal enthusiasts alike!

CHAPTER 1

The Champlain Canal

_____

Brad Utter
Senior Historian/Curator, New York State Museum

Introduction

> *The advantages which will result from the connection of Lake Erie with the navigable waters of the Hudson by means of a canal, have been so frequently elucidated, and are indeed so obvious to everyone who possesses a correct geographical knowledge of the west, that it has been deemed unnecessary to enumerate them. But, presuming that the benefits to be derived from a similar communication with Lake Champlain, are not fully understood or duly appreciated, the commissioners ask the indulgence of briefly pointing out a few of the most prominent of these benefits.*[1]
>
> Canal Commissioners' Report, March 19, 1817

In many ways this quote from the Canal Commissioners' report to the New York State Legislature, dated March 19, 1817, tells the story of the smaller sibling of the Erie Canal—the Champlain Canal (aka Great Northern

Canal or Northern Canal). The proposed Champlain Canal was not the star of the push for internal improvements. The Erie (aka Great Western or Western Canal) was to connect with the Great Lakes and as a result tap into what seemed at the time to be an endless emporium of potential. Lake Champlain was more of a known commodity and would require a much shorter canal to reach it (roughly sixty-three miles from tidewater). Understandably, the much longer Erie Canal (363 miles long) would gain most of the attention from the public, the press, and legislators. However, the commissioners knew that a reliable water connection between the Hudson River and Lake Champlain would prove to be a very important link in the transportation network of New York State and beyond. Whether it was a compromise to get northern votes or a realization of the importance for the military and commerce to follow, the Champlain Canal was included in the landmark 1817 legislation for the creation of the Erie and Champlain Canals, "An act respecting Navigable Communications, between the great western and northern lakes, and the Atlantic ocean. Passed April 15, 1817."[2]

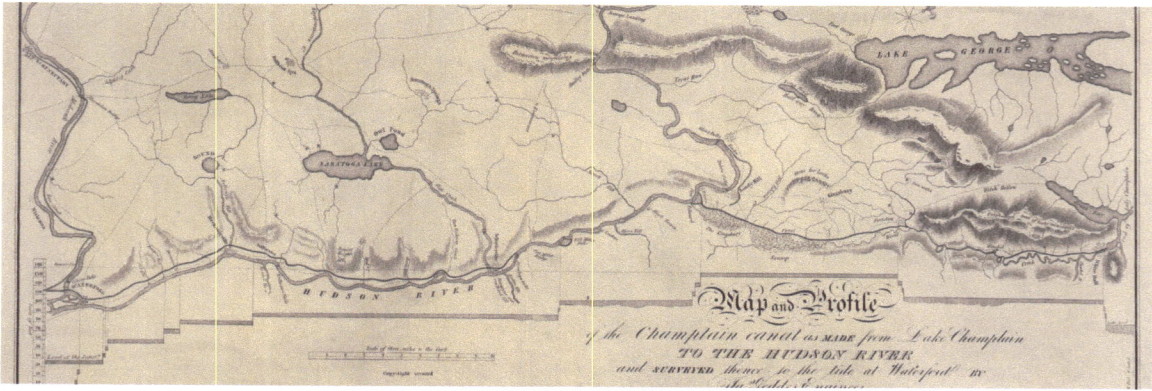

(Figure 1) "Map and profile of the Champlain Canal as made from Lake Champlain to the Hudson River and surveyed thence to the tide at Waterford," 1825.

The call for internal improvements started much earlier and it was a long haul (pun intended) to reach the passing of that important legislation in 1817. For those living beyond the tidewater of the Hudson River, transportation of products in bulk was unreliably slow, difficult, and expensive. In times of war, it was equally difficult to move troops and equipment beyond the tidewater. In 1774, New York provincial governor William Tryon included in his "Report on the Province of New York" a call for two specific canals. He suggested one connecting Fort Stanwix (now Rome) and Wood Creek to open communication with Oneida Lake, and on to Lake Ontario. He also recommended a canal connecting Fort Edward with Lake Champlain to open communication with the St. Lawrence. Tryon went on to say that it was too expensive for the province to fund but "when effected would open a most effective inland navigation, equal perhaps to any as yet known."[3] The Revolutionary War was on the heels of his report, and nothing was done in regard to his proposals.

Areas west of the Appalachian Mountains and north along Lake Champlain did not have easy direct trade routes with the east coast of the United States. In many places commerce was mostly local or found other outlets. George Washington said that for those who were on the frontier, their loyalties would follow commerce, which represented the "cement of interest"[4] which would bind the new nation together. Washington and others suggested that internal improvements to the waterways were the answer to establishing loyalties between settlers on the frontier and the federal government on the coast. For those settlers who lived around Lake Champlain, this theory would be put to the test during the War of 1812.

The mountains provided a large obstacle between the East Coast and the North American interior. The natural barrier limited the flow of commerce, especially bulk products. Canal promotors in New York State noted that the lowest and most complete break in that chain was through the Hudson River Valley, cutting through the Appalachians and the Mohawk Valley which provided a path west separating the Adirondack Mountains and the Alleghany Plateau. These breaks through the mountains made New York State the logical spot for two canals, one to connect through the Mohawk Valley to the Great Lakes and one up the Hudson River Valley to connect to Lake Champlain.

After the Revolution, canal promotors like Christopher Coles, Elkanah Watson, Philip Schuyler, and others saw the same opportunity that Governor Tyron had seen and began campaigning for canals in New York. Improved waterways would tap into the endless resources of the north and west, open land for Euro-American settlement and connect with the existing frontier settlements. Settlement on a large scale could not take place without available land and a transportation network. The land was becoming available for purchase through a series of illegal treaties between the State of New York and Native American tribes (only the federal government can legally negotiate and sign a treaty). Land speculators purchased large swaths of territory to sell to new settlers. However, without a reliable connection to the east for commerce and comfort, the land did not sell as fast as the speculators may have anticipated.

To answer the call for improved waterways, the state legislature incorporated two private businesses to build canals and improve river channels for navigation from tidewater on the Hudson to Lake Champlain, Lake Ontario and Seneca Lake. Land speculators and the State of New York were among those who purchased stock in the two private corporations. The Northern Inlock Navigation Company (NILNC) and the Western Inlock Navigation Company (WILNC) were both chartered by the New York State Legislature in March of 1792.

In the fall of 1792, surveys were conducted for a northern route from Albany to Lake Champlain and a western route from Schenectady to Wood Creek (west of Fort Stanwix/modern-day Rome). Both survey reports are great resources for describing the potential of the canals and the existing conditions of the proposed routes. The report for the northern survey to Lake Champlain predicted that the improvements would lower the expense of transporting produce to market, the tolls would cover the interest on investments, population would increase as a result of the new works, which would in turn produce more commerce and more tolls, so then the company could enlarge and improve the canal, allowing for larger vessels and more growth. The report recommended completing a canal from Waterford to Stillwater first, citing the most benefit to the public. This series of events predicted for the northern route would not be tested, as the NILNC failed to improve any sections of the route and went out of business. The recommendation for the first section of canal was around the most populated area at the time. However, when it came time to build the first section of the Champlain Canal, this recommendation was not followed; in fact, this failure may have served as a lesson learned.

The WILNC completed three short canals and succeeded in improving the waterway from Schenectady to Lake Ontario and Seneca Lake. The high cost of labor, supplies, and maintenance led to a moderate level of success. The WILNC operated until 1820 when the state bought out the company to make way for the Erie Canal. Both efforts gave valuable lessons to the engineers, politicians, and business leaders who would later promote and build the Erie and Champlain Canals. A few of those lessons include: construction and administration of the Erie and Champlain Canals would be too expensive for a private business; the economic and settlement benefits could be tremendous if done correctly; and harnessing the rivers was too difficult and a land-based canal would be the best solution (although this lesson was not followed at first for the Champlain Canal).

Despite the failure of the NILNC and the limited success of the WILNC, communities did slowly grow. By 1800, the Mohawk and upper Hudson Valleys were full of farms and villages and new settlers continued heading farther north and west. Many of the settlers found it easier to trade with markets other than Albany and New York City. Central and western New Yorkers traded with Montreal via the existing rivers and roads and the improved works of the WILNC to get to Lake Ontario. The Susquehanna River provided a route south to Baltimore and most trade on Lake Champlain went north to Montreal.

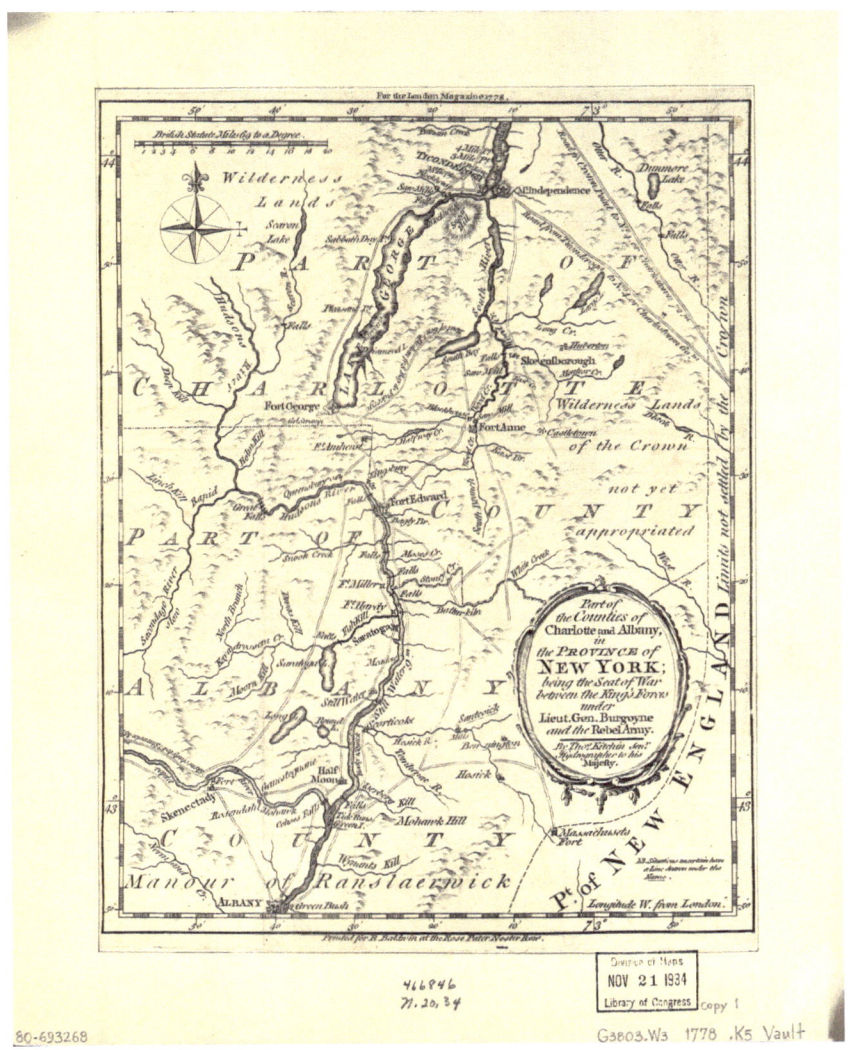

(Figure 2) Map of region from the Revolutionary War period. Note the one road going along the Hudson River, which traverses the eventual route of the Champlain Canal from junction of the upper branch of the Mohawk River to Whitehall. Following this path, you can see all the fortified spots designed to protect the transportation corridor. Highlighting indicates future route of Champlain Canal.

In 1808, the New York State Legislature ordered a survey be made for a canal from the Hudson River to Lake Erie, including a route via Lake Ontario. After the favorable survey was reviewed, a group of canal commissioners were appointed to further examine the possibility of a canal to the west. Primarily focused on the Erie, The Canal Commissioners did not officially mention a canal north to Lake Champlain until 1812, when in closing their report to the legislature they stated that although it was not in their mandate to explore such a route,

> ... a communication, by means of a canal, between Lake Champlain and Hudson's river, is one of those things which are deemed of national importance. It would certainly tend to preserve brotherly affection in the great American family; and the reciprocal advantages which it would procure to New York and Vermont, would strengthen the bands of our union with the eastern states, so conducive to our mutual prosperity.[5]

Those bonds were about to be tested as the War of 1812 raged along the frontier of New York and Lake Champlain. Businessmen living on Lake Champlain had to decide where their loyalties lay, and some went with their commercial ties over their country. Prior to the Champlain Canal, most of the trade along the lake went north to Canada. The war cut that avenue off, at least legally. Some American businessmen turned to treason to maintain their commercial connections and continued trading with partners in Canada.[6]

The war also highlighted the difficulty in getting supplies and troops to the war front. The poor roads and lack of navigable waterways made the process slow and costly. This was not lost on the military leadership, some of whom served in the New York State Legislature. Using their experience, officers like Stephen Van Rensselaer supported internal improvements for national security. Diverting trade from Canada was already being pushed by the Canal Commissioners prior to the war, but afterward it became a more widely shared view among elected officials.

After the war in 1816, the Canal Commissioners reiterated the incalculable benefits from a northern canal. The New York State Legislature responded by assigning the commissioners to come up with an estimate for opening a canal between the navigable Hudson River and Lake Champlain. Their report dated March 19, 1817, started with the statement that started this chapter. The commissioners felt that most people knew the advantages of a canal connecting to the west, so in their report they included an overview of the many advantages of a canal connecting the Hudson with Lake Champlain.

Access to products of the forest was a main selling point for the commissioners. The canal would provide access to vast quantities of lumber, iron ore, marble, surplus agricultural products, pot, and pearl ash. Connection with the Erie Canal would provide access to salt and gypsum for trade from central New York. The canal would lower shipping costs and in general "open new and increasing sources of wealth." In turn, the value of land would go up and, importantly, the new outlet would "divert trade from Lower Canada, and turn to the south, the profits of the trade of Lake Champlain."[7] Further, "by imparting activity and enterprise to agricultural, commercial and mechanical pursuits, it would add to our industry and resources, and thereby augment the substantial wealth and prosperity of the state."[8]

COMMUNICATION.

A reader of the Argus would beg leave, through the medium of that paper, to suggest to the legislature of the state of New-York, one subject for their consideration.

As a very powerful address is soon to be made to them, on the subject of the great western canal, would it not be well for them to advert to the history of the northern inland lock navigation company some years ago incorporated in this state. It is believed that an attention to the journals of that day, would show, that the public were then feasted with high hopes. That by means of that grand project, the country bordering the northern parts of the Hudson and lake Champlain, were soon literally to blossom as the rose, and be transformed into an enchanting paradise—But, sir, an attention to the books of the treasury, it is believed, will shew how much the state profited by their credulity on the subject. Perhaps one of the commissioners appointed on the subject of the memorial alluded to, would be better able than any, to give a history of the rise progress, decline and fall of the great northern canal. If bought wit is the best if at least, behoves the legislature to remember how much they got by it.

I am friendly, sir, to improvements by roads and canals, so far as practicable and so far as the circumstances of the country will warrant. But, sir, I do not believe that great canals are very safe hobbies for great men to ride. Riding such a hobby, "*at the elevation of one hundred and ninety feet above the Cayuga Lake,*" would be very apt to make the head swim.

Yours, &c.

AN INHABITANT OF THE WESTERN DISTRICT.

(**Figure 3**) A "Communication" published in the January 23, 1816, *Albany Argus* warns state leaders to learn the lessons of the failed attempt of the NILNC. They warn that lots of money was spent, big promises were made and yet it did not materialize.

These projects were singular, ambitious, and had lofty moral foundations.

The Canal Commissioners' reports were often reprinted in local newspapers around the state. Sections were reprinted out of state, as this entire process was viewed as important national and international news. Beyond the projected commercial impact, the idea that a state government could take on a project of this magnitude was precedent setting. At the time it was still debated whether a state or the federal government had the authority to construct and operate public works. No financial support was offered from the federal government or other states. The precedent set by the canal projects opened the door for other states to follow suit with public works projects. Today we might take for granted all of the public works projects provided by the state. Prior to the Erie and Champlain Canal project, state governments did not build and operate bridges, roads, and canals. Although a charter from the state was needed, those types of projects were left to businesses or the actual funding and work was organized on a local level.

"An act concerning navigable communications between the great western and northern lakes and the Atlantic ocean," also known as the Canal Bill of 1817, was passed on April 15, 1817. The preamble from the act lays out the intended purposes for the canals:

> *Whereas, navigable communications between Lakes Erie and Champlain, and the Atlantic ocean, by means of canals connected with the Hudson river, will promote agriculture, manufactures and commerce, mitigate the calamities of war, and enhance the blessings of peace, consolidate the union, and advance the prosperity and elevate the character of the United States: And whereas, it is the incumbent duty of the people of this state, to avail themselves of the means which the Almighty has placed in their*

hands for the production of such signal, extensive and lasting benefits to the human race...[9]

Further, the preamble declares that it was fully expected for the states and federal government to pay their fair share to make the mutually beneficial project happen. The commissioners thought that since Ohio and Vermont had the most to gain from this project, they would contribute. But no outside financial support came in from the states or the federal government. New York State went forward with a financial plan involving stocks, lotteries, taxes, and land sales.

Construction of the Champlain Canal

Construction on the Erie started in July of 1817 and that of the Champlain Canal started in November of the same year. But before construction could begin, the state needed to gain ownership of the land where the canals would be built. Agents met with property owners and determined the land values. In most cases the agent would determine that the state did not owe the property owner any money because the canal would enhance the value of the rest of his property. Some owners were not happy and petitioned with the Canal Commissioners for higher values. Either way, the land was taken over by the state in the first large-scale use of eminent domain in the United States.

The commissioners were not authorized to work on the entire length of the proposed canals. First, they had to build a small section in each canal to prove that they could do it and to demonstrate the value. For the Erie Canal they selected a long level between Rome and Utica that would not require any locks. It was decided that connecting Lake Champlain with the Hudson River was the lowest-hanging fruit on the Champlain Canal. Although it was not the easiest section to build, it would produce the quickest commercial results by making a connection for the lumber trade from Lake Champlain to the Hudson River at Fort Edward. Perhaps this decision was based on a lesson learned from the failed 1792 plan of the NILNC, which recommended their first section be a land-based canal to tap into the produce and population of Saratoga County. The section between Whitehall and Fort Edward would utilize Wood Creek and some man-made channels to get to the Hudson River. Log rafts could travel from Lake Champlain via the canal to Fort Edward and continue down the Hudson River.

Geography was key to construction. Both canals were built in a contour style, following the contours of the land formations. When possible, the canal hugged the sides of hills and valleys, utilizing the side of the hill as one side of the canal wall. The construction procedures, methods, and tools were mostly the same between the two canals. Engineers would first lay out the line of the canal to be built. Next, the work was separated into sections to be bid on by contractors. The commissioners kept sections short to encourage residents of moderate means to bid on the work.[10] Contractors who won bids signed detailed contracts that laid out all of the work to be done. Laborers would be hired and overseen by the contractors. This was the first large-scale use of subcontracting by the state. The contractors were not required to turn in records relating to who worked for them, much to the disappointment of modern historians and genealogists. The actual digging was done with axes, shovels, plows, scrapers, wheelbarrows, pickaxes, and black powder when necessary. Engineers would monitor the work as it progressed.

In their March 1817 report, the Canal Commissioners stated that the Champlain Canal was surveyed by Colonel Lewis Garin. This initial survey was enough to demonstrate that the canal would be possible, and in September of the same year James Geddes was made the Chief Engineer of the Champlain Canal and reexamined the route. Geddes had been involved in the canals project since 1808, when he conducted some of the earliest surveys for what became the Erie Canal. Like the other main engineers for the canals, he had no professional training to be a civil engineer. Prior to becoming an engineer, Geddes was involved in the salt industry near modern-day Syracuse and went on to do work as a surveyor, state assemblyman, and judge. After his experiences with the Erie and Champlain Canals, Geddes worked on other canals and served one term in the United States Congress.

The first contract let was to "Messrs. Melancthon Wheeler and Ezra Smith, at twelve and a half cents per cubic yard, except a deep cutting of about thirty rods in length, for which they are to receive eighteen cents."[11] They were to excavate around five miles "immediately south of Whitehall." The work started in the late fall and was paused during the winter. By the end of the next year, twelve miles of canal had been completed and accepted by the engineer.[12]

The original plans called for a canal of 30 feet wide by 3 feet deep, with locks 75 feet long by 10 feet wide. The Canal Commissioners called for that to be enlarged to match the Erie's 40 feet by 4 feet and locks 90 feet by 15 feet in their January 1818 report. The main reasons given were the length of the lumber needed for masts (used in ship building) and the need for boats to be able to traverse both canals without unloading cargo, which would increase shipping costs. The request was quickly approved by the legislature.

The New York canals were finished in stages, and each stage merited celebration. The first official canal boat ride and ceremony took place in late November 1819. The two-day ceremony started with a boat leaving the Hudson River at Fort Edward and going to Whitehall. They returned the next day with three more boats and a band. Along the way they were greeted with large crowds and in Fort Edward and Whitehall cannons were sounded in their honor. The Sandy Hill Times of November 26, 1819, recounted the entire affair and reflected on the moment in saying: "...the occasion was eminently calculated to inspire the mind with the purest and most elevated sentiments: A navigable river opened through forests and morasses – over an extent of country so considerable, and in many places so uneven, and the whole completed in so short a period as to baffle the calculations..." Further, the paper states, "This canal is another proof of the enterprising spirit of our countrymen, and the wonders which can be performed by art and industry, when aided by science and excited by the love of country."[13]

In 1819, the commissioners called for the rest of the canals to be approved. Following the success of the first sections, they stated that "the experiment which has now been made, as a satisfactory test, by which future and more extensive operations may fairly and safely be judged..."[14] The legislature agreed to approve moving forward for both canals on April 7, 1819.[15]

Few of the Canals of Europe extend their benefits beyond the immediate vicinity of their works. But an inspection of the map of this state will shew, that ten times as much territory beyond its northern termination will be benefitted by the Champlain Canal, as exists along its line...[16]

Canal Commissioners' Report, January 31, 1818

Gleaming through the Canal Commissioners' reports, it is clear that the work was done in a hurry, and the commissioners admitted "that mistakes may have occurred."[17] It was a learning process for everyone involved and newspapers were quick to jump on the mistakes and celebrate the successes. Some of the challenges were keeping enough water in the canal, building and maintaining the various dams along the route, and utilizing the Hudson River for part of the channel. On the southern end of the canal, the project included the Troy dam and sloop lock, the Waterford sidecut, the Mohawk River crossing and farther on to the junction with the Erie Canal. Each section provided challenges for the engineers and contractors.

One of the lessons learned by the engineers and Canal Commissioners was that lumber rafts were not great in the canal. These rafts had been the primary mode of transport for lumber on Lake Champlain prior to the canal. But when the first section of the Champlain Canal was opened, the large number of lumber rafts, "frequently upwards of a thousand feet in length,"[18] damaged the canal walls. In response to the frequent damage, the Commissioners decided to make the toll for a lumber raft double that of the toll for lumber on a canal boat. The Commissioners reported that the toll change had the desired effect.

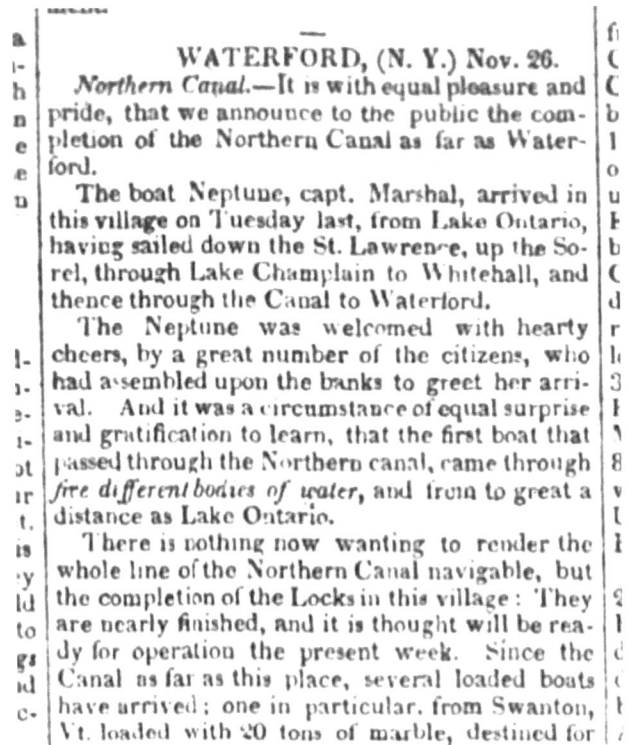

WATERFORD, (N. Y.) Nov. 26.

Northern Canal.—It is with equal pleasure and pride, that we announce to the public the completion of the Northern Canal as far as Waterford.

The boat Neptune, capt. Marshal, arrived in this village on Tuesday last, from Lake Ontario, having sailed down the St. Lawrence, up the Sorel, through Lake Champlain to Whitehall, and thence through the Canal to Waterford.

The Neptune was welcomed with hearty cheers, by a great number of the citizens, who had assembled upon the banks to greet her arrival. And it was a circumstance of equal surprise and gratification to learn, that the first boat that passed through the Northern canal, came through *five different bodies of water*, and from to great a distance as Lake Ontario.

There is nothing now wanting to render the whole line of the Northern Canal navigable, but the completion of the Locks in this village : They are nearly finished, and it is thought will be ready for operation the present week. Since the Canal as far as this place, several loaded boats have arrived ; one in particular, from Swanton, Vt. loaded with 20 tons of marble, destined for

(Figure 4) The *Neptune*, arrived in Waterford loaded with wheat and another boat, from Vermont, carried twenty tons of marble, justifying the fears of some locals who were worried about grain competition. But also demonstrating the ability to have large bulk freight transported on the canal that would have otherwise been too costly to ship overland.

The canal was completed from Whitehall to Waterford by the end of the 1822 boating season. But the entire canal was not declared complete until the dam and sloop lock on the Hudson River at Troy was complete. Various local celebrations took place as major sections opened. DeWitt Clinton himself, then President of the Canal Board, laid the last stone on the sidecut locks in Waterford on November 22, 1822. At the time of the ceremony, the

Neptune, carrying grain, had recently arrived "from Lake Ontario by the St. Lawrence and Sorel rivers and Lake Champlain..." and was welcomed with cheers from the crowd. As outlined in the November 28, 1822, New York Statesmen, the reporter "saw, with great pleasure, packages and boxes, stowed on the banks of' the canal, destined for Whitehall and Peru in Clinton county." Another celebration took place the following September in honor of the opening of the Troy dam and sloop lock.

[From the Waterford Reporter, August 12.]

CHAMPLAIN CANAL NAVIGATION.—The following estimate contains the amount of arrivals at this place on the Champlain canal since the 1st of June :—19,399 bushels wheat . 5148 do rye ; 955 do corn ; 254 bbls. corn meal ; 120 do rye flour ; 20 do pork ; 11 kegs butter ; 16 casks cheese ; 33 tierces beans ; 130 do peas ; 40 tierces salt ; 26 bbls. pot ashes ; 70 hhds. whiskey ; 47 do salted seal skins, from Montreal ; 7 hhds. furs ; 149 tons cement ; 156 kegs nails ; 59 tons iron ; 15 tons marble ; 236,231 cube feet square timber ; 1,730,91 feet boards and plank ; 590,000 shingles ; 316 cords wood ; 46,000 staves. During the same period about 500 tons of merchandize were shipped at this place.

(**Figure 5**) A list of goods shipped on the Champlain Canal between June 1 and August 12, 1823, reprinted in the *Albany Argus*, August 15, 1823.

The largest celebration was reserved for October 8, 1823, in Albany. The event was held to mark the opening of the Erie Canal from Brockport to the Albany basin and the completion of the Champlain Canal. Complete with masonic ceremonies, speeches, and a parade on the land and on the canal into the basin, the celebration was one of the largest events in Albany history to date.

The first boat to ascend Lock 1 in Albany was "the *Maria*, Capt. A. Willey, for Whitehall and Burlington."[19]

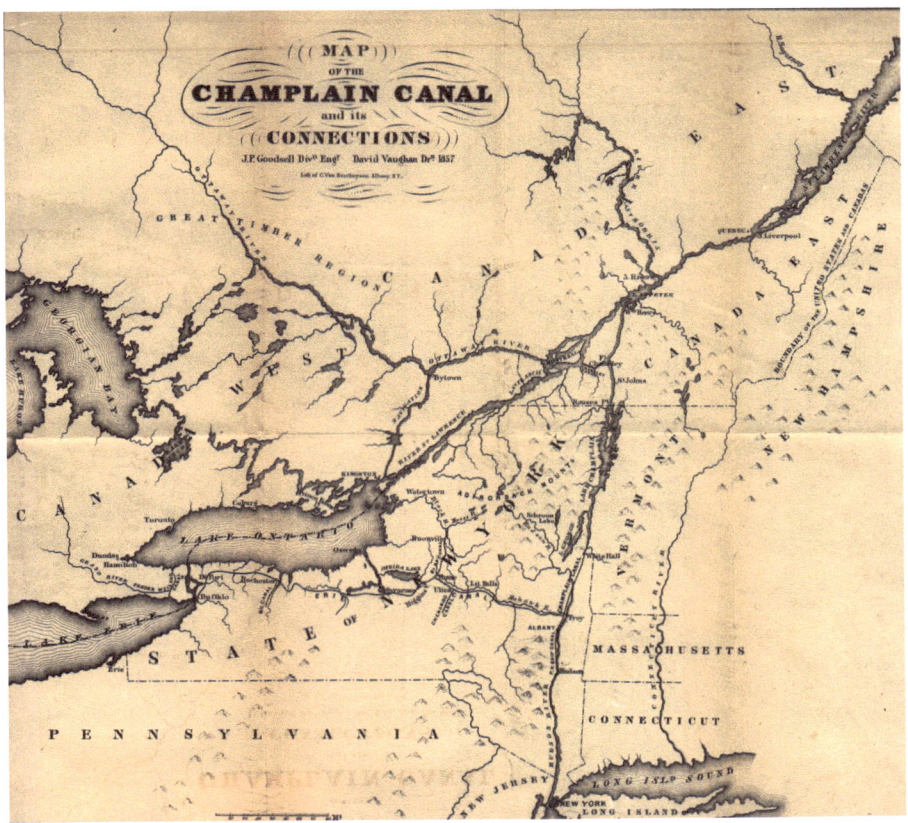

(Figure 6) "Map of the Champlain Canal and its Connections", 1857

The Champlain Canal was part of a larger transportation network of the canals, rivers, lakes and the Atlantic Ocean. It reaching ports from Canada to New York City, and out to Buffalo and the Great Lakes. Many of these routes were at first supplemented by railroads and eventually bypassed by the railroad.

Lake Champlain.—Previous to the opening of the Champlain Canal, there were only about twenty vessels on this lake. Now there are said to be at least 250!

It is stated in the *Vergennes Aurora*, that at the opening of the Champlain Canal, there were only twenty vessels on Lake Champlain —that last year, as near as could be ascertained, there were two hundred and eighteen; and now, the number may be safely calculated at two hundred and fifty! This comes of internal improvements.

(Figures 7 & 8) Newspapers around the country, Canada and even in England ran stories about both canals. Here are two clips about the growth of commerce on Lake Champlain. Top article printed in *The Arkansas Gazette*, April 2, 1828 and the bottom printed in the *Montreal Gazette*, July 21, 1828.

Communities Along the Canal

Following the opening of the Erie Canal, central and western New York experienced a large jump in population. Boom towns formed in areas along the canal where no Euro-Americans had previously lived. Many preexisting towns became cities, all because of the canal and the opportunities it provided. The areas along the Champlain Canal more closely resembled the experience of the Mohawk Valley. By the time the canals opened both regions had established farming communities, with most of the land spoken for, if not improved already. Population growth in both areas did occur but not at the great rate experienced farther west of the Mohawk. Communities along Lake Champlain experienced growth at a similar rate to those along the actual Champlain Canal, with gains of roughly around four hundred to five hundred people every ten years up to 1850, with a few exceptions. Two communities experienced larger growth than the others and they were Plattsburgh and Burlington. In 1820, Plattsburgh had a population of 3,519, in 1830 it went up to 4,832; 1840, 6,416; and in 1850 the population was 10,262. Burlington followed a similar trajectory; 1820, 2,111; 1830, 3,526; 1840, 4,271; and in 1850 the population was 7,585. For comparison, the population in Rochester, New York in 1820 was 1,502 and by 1850 it had jumped to 20,191 people.

Local Economies Prior to the Canal

It is beyond the scope of this work to go too far into details on the experiences of each community along the Champlain Canal and Lake Champlain. Some general observations will help give an idea of the regional economies before and after the Champlain Canal was built.

The southern terminus points of the original Champlain Canal were technically located in two spots: the Troy dam and sloop lock and the junction with the Erie Canal in what was then part of the town of Watervliet, now the city of Cohoes. Both communities benefited from a connection to the Erie and Champlain Canals and experienced tremendous growth in population and industry. Prior to the canals, Cohoes was mostly a farming region. Troy was already a growing town located at the head of tidewater. Available waterpower and Hudson River shipping opportunities helped to establish Troy as an important commercial center on the Hudson prior to the canals.

Waterford was the transportation hub of southern Saratoga County. In general, surplus agricultural products from surrounding towns could be brought south to Waterford for shipment. Waterford, located at the junction of the Mohawk and Hudson Rivers, was at the head of sloop navigation during high water. The community built a large pier out into the Hudson to extend the shipping season and worked with Lansingburgh and Troy to dredge a channel in the Hudson toward Albany. The main roadway heading north from Albany passed through Waterford. The thriving village had a newspaper, numerous inns, taverns, and storefronts to cater to the local and traveling public. Waterford also boasted the first bridge over the navigable Hudson River, built in 1804.

Farther north, and closer to Saratoga Springs, much of the produce found a market catering to the tourist trade in Ballston Spa and Saratoga Springs. Local streams powered saw and grain mills throughout the region. But the main commerce heading south along the upper Hudson was lumber. Trees harvested in the lower Adirondacks would be sent downriver and eventually tied into larger rafts. The rafts would be floated downriver as far as New York City.

As discussed already, much of the commerce along Lake Champlain found an outlet to the north and along the lake itself. Passengers moving between New York and Canada were treated to one of the earliest passenger steamboat lines in America. The Vermont provided service between Whitehall and St. Johns starting in 1809.[20] Waterpower was abundant and multiple mills were active in Whitehall prior to the canal. Whitehall also had a vibrant shipbuilding industry.

CITY OF ALBANY, in the STATE OF NEW YORK

(Figure 9) Lumber raft in the Hudson near Albany, 1827. Note the hut on top of the raft to provide shelter to the crew taking it downriver.

Growing Villages

(**Figure 10**) Village of Waterford, 1841. View looking northeast, with King's power canal in the center and the fourth branch of the Mohawk River on the right.

The canal helped to tie economies together, from local to international. The new "northern route" connected New York City with lower Canada (and beyond). The commercial impacts of the canal were felt differently along the northern route. Multiple factors played into the new commercial reality for the communities. Improving technologies in agriculture, milling, mining, and manufacturing all played an important role. Banking was also integral to commerce. In an effort to promote new business, the state decided to deposit canal toll revenues into small banks along the canal corridors. The Canal Fund enabled banks to loan more cash to those looking for business loans, and in turn that stimulated the economy in areas that otherwise might not have had the ability to extend the loans.[21]

A few communities were based around one main commercial pursuit, such as agricultural surplus or mining, while others became more diversified. The canal enabled industries to grow while physically not near the natural resources they used for production. For example, foundry industries thrived in communities like Waterford, Troy, and Cohoes because they were able to utilize the Champlain Canal to get Adirondack lumber for fuel, molding sand from Saratoga County and iron ore from the mining communities along Lake Champlain. Another example is the pottery industry that grew in Fort Edward, which received clay from places like Long Island and New Jersey and salt from the Syracuse area. Without the canal, this would not have been financially possible.

The canal also brought competition for established commerce, especially in the case of grains. Prior to the canal, established farmers expressed their concerns over being unable to compete with the predicted flood of western grain. By 1826, many farmers in Saratoga and Washington Counties were feeling the predicted pinch and petitioned to have lateral canals built to lower their shipping costs. Greenfield, Galway, Salem, Saratoga Springs, and others petitioned for canals to connect to the Champlain but were unsuccessful. For farmers who did not find a market catering to the springs

(**Figure 11**) Cast-iron stove, Ransom & Co., Albany, New York, 1845. New York State Museum

tourism, the best option was to adapt and switch to perishables. Farmers found a ready market for beef, dairy products, eggs and fruit in the growing cities of Troy, Albany and Schenectady.

The role that Waterford played in shipping local agricultural surplus dwindled as canal boats could load along the course of the canal and bypass Waterford altogether. Local entrepreneurs turned to industry, spurring the economy. In 1828, a new hydropower canal was built along the fourth branch of the Mohawk River that provided year-round waterpower. The new power canal provided for a wide array of industries, from lampblack to fire

(**Figure 12**) 1829 advertisement broadside for King's Power Canal in Waterford.

engines. The new industries created jobs and Waterford adapted to the new commercial environment. Soon, local businesses advertised fast and easy shipping via the Hudson River, Champlain Canal, Erie Canal and the railroad.

Waterpower was an important asset provided by the canal where excess water existed. The state allowed businesses to rent excess canal water through the use of waste weirs to power mills and factories. Factories sprang up along the canal route utilizing the waterpower from the canal and from the Hudson where dams were built for the canal. Eddy Valve in Waterford used waterpower from the original Champlain Canal into the 1960s to power its lights.

Fort Edward also had multiple industries, including various forms of milling, a brewery, a paper mill, and a thriving pottery industry. The potteries took advantage of the canal for transporting clay, salt, and the final product. Customers could buy in bulk and have the pottery shipped on a canal boat. The abundance of wood coming down the Hudson and the canal was utilized for firing the kilns. The pottery business became so large that during the 1870s and 1880s they were only exceeded in output by the potteries in Brooklyn. The pottery business was active in Fort Edward from 1858 to 1942.[22]

Northern view of Whitehall.

(Figure 13) Northern View of Whitehall, engraving, 1842.

On the northern end of the canal, Whitehall enjoyed a monopoly as the entrance and exit to the canal. Various businesses formed to handle the freight and mills utilizing water and steam power. Boat building had a long tradition in Whitehall and continued through the nineteenth century. Steamboat passenger traffic continued to thrive in Whitehall for much of the nineteenth century. In addition to passenger traffic, steam towboats pulled groups of canalboats, tied together, between St. Johns, Canada, and Whitehall. The Northern Transportation Company formed in 1857. They provided towing services on the canal and the lake and grew to control much of the traffic on both.

Communities on the Lake

> ...the commerce of the lake, stimulated to remarkable activity by the completion of the canal and consequent opening of markets, whitened the blue waters with innumerable sails and stirred them into foam by the wheels of many steamboats.[23]

The opening of the Champlain Canal provided a "choice of markets"[24] for communities on Lake Champlain. When international trade regulations cooperated, producers could now send goods north or south and in return could also purchase products and materials from either direction. The iron, lumber, stone, and marble industries grew fast along the shores of the lake. Even when the railroads came, the heavy weight and size of the products of the forest still made the canal a better method for shipping for much of the nineteenth century. Small communities formed around local extraction businesses and their fate often mirrored the success or failure of the company.

(**Figure 14**) Village of Essex, N.Y. Lake Champlain—Whitefield, Edwin, c.1846.

Originally, one of the cited goals of the Canal Commissioners for the Champlain Canal was to direct trade away from Canada and turn it south. However, by the 1840s, the forests around the Lake Champlain were depleting. Communities along the western shore of the lake lobbied the state legislature to build roads into the Adirondacks for access to more timber and mining opportunities. Although some of the roads were subsidized by the state, the successes of these efforts were limited. Thanks to the opening of the Chambly Canal in 1843, and improving relations between the United States and Canada, lumber agents turned to Canadian forests for orders. With coal going north, Canadian lumber went south. Glens Falls was also an outlet for products of the Adirondacks throughout the nineteenth and early twentieth centuries.

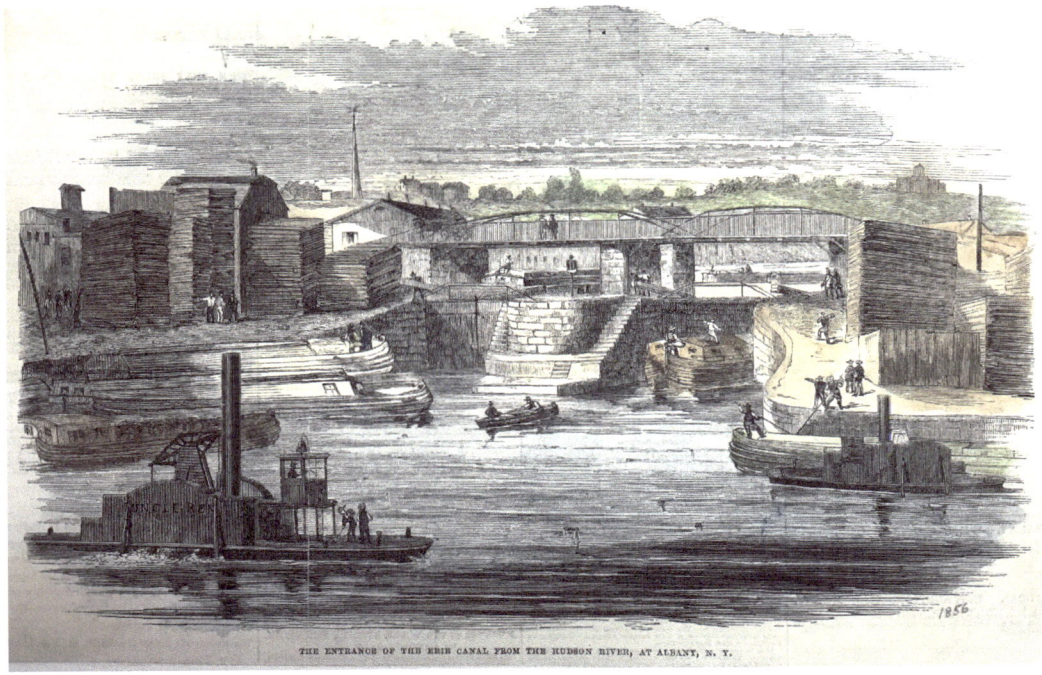

THE ENTRANCE OF THE ERIE CANAL FROM THE HUDSON RIVER, AT ALBANY, N. Y.

(Figure 15) Entrance to the Erie Canal at Albany, note the large piles of lumber, 1856. The Champlain Canal connected with the Erie Canal at Cohoes a few miles north of Albany.

As on the Erie, there was less freight heading away from the tidewater than there was coming toward it. Early on, various consumer products went north, as opposed to the bulk natural resources heading south. Once the D&H Canal opened in 1828, coal become a staple product heading north.

Passenger Traffic

(Figure 16) The Button family (on left) of Waterford enjoy a ride on the Champlain Canal, ca. 1905.

The Champlain Canal supplemented the fashionable northern tour. The northern tour included travel between New York City, Niagara Falls, Montreal, Lakes Champlain and George, and Saratoga Springs. Travelers could take the canal north to the town of Saratoga, see the battlefield, and then take a stagecoach to the Springs. Otherwise, the Champlain Canal was not on the regular route. The recommended route was to go from Saratoga Springs to Lake George and then north on the lake to Ticonderoga, from there using a steamboat to travel north to Montreal. The canal was in competition with stagecoaches heading north from Schenectady and Waterford, and by the mid-1830s, the railroad from Waterford and Troy.

SENTINEL.

SARATOGA SPRINGS, JUNE 25.

THE SPRINGS.

As the warm season advances, the number of strangers resorting to the Springs increases; and present appearances indicate that the company will be more numerous the present year than at any former period. Among the improvements since last season, may be mentioned the enlargement of Union Hall, (see advertisement in to-day's paper) and the internal embellishment of most of the other houses of accommodation. The streets in this village, which have heretofore been unpleasant, in consequence of dust, &c. have also been much improved; and the light sand, which had become so great a nuisance to strangers, is now nearly all covered with clay and gravel.

It may be furthermore gratifying to strangers to be made acquainted with the fact, that the roads from the south to Ballston-Spa and this village, have undergone important repairs, and that the northern canal will very soon be rendered navigable for boats from Schuyler's Ville, (Saratoga) to Whitehall. If to these advantages be added our mineral fountains, and the salubrity of air here enjoyed, we think the watering places of this county present inducements to a resort, which few, if any villages on the continent afford.

(Figure 17) Promotion of the Springs and connection to the new northern canal in the June 6, 1822, issue of the *Saratoga Sentinel*.

Travelers did make use of the canal and there were multiple packet boat lines that serviced the route into the mid-1800s. Packet boats were specifically designed to carry passengers and had regularly scheduled departure and arrival times. The companies would offer various packages for travel on the northern route. For example, an option would be to travel up the Hudson River to Waterford by steamboat, from Waterford to Whitehall in a packet boat, and from Whitehall to St. Johns via steamboat. Of course, one could take a packet boat for just a few miles or the entire length of the canal. By mid-nineteenth century, railroads would take the place of stagecoaches and canal boats as the best way for passenger travel.

Others followed the northern route, north and south. French and Irish immigrants traveled south to find work. French-Canadians were more likely to come into the United States for seasonal or temporary work, with the goal of returning home. Many Irish choose to immigrate to the United States through the northern border. Lumber camps, knitting mills, and more provided opportunities for the new residents.

Like the Erie, the Champlain Canal was also a conduit of information and goods from around the world. Different social movements and popular culture traveled the canal. The Underground Railroad utilized the direct route to Canada. The temperance movement had active groups in communities along the canal. Today, popular architectural styles help date the heyday of communities along the route.

Moving the Freight

Something we might take for granted today when we hit that purchase button online is that numerous businesses are usually involved to make sure that your purchase arrives at your doorstep in a reasonable time. During the nineteenth century, how did a business along the northern route ship its product to New York City? How did they order and receive goods? Like today, usually multiple businesses helped to make it happen. While some businesses had their own boats and crews and made arrangements in-house for shipping, most did not. That is where the forwarding agent came in, especially if you did not require an entire boat. Forwarding agents were not unique to canal commerce, but they were a key component of it. Essentially, they served as the proverbial "middleman." The agents were able to handle a variety of tasks, including ordering, shipping, collecting payment, finding what a customer needed and arranging to have it delivered, sometimes storing it for the customer until needed, and more.

Progress of the Cholera.

The Cincinnati Atlas presents the following facts in regard to the Cholera, during its last visit to the United States—

"Of its progress in the United States, the following facts are worth noticing: It landed at the Quarantine ground of Quebec, from emigrant ships. It passed up the St. Lawrence to Montreal with the emigrants. It passed the Champlain canal in *canal boats*. It went along the Erie canal in *canal boats*. It went along the Lakes in *steamboats*. It broke among the soldiers of Scott's army in steamers. It arrived at Chicago. It passed with them the Upper Mississippi. It reached Louisville in the steamboat Columbus. It ascended the Ohio in steamboats. It arrived at Louisville and Cincinnati: at Cincinnati before Wheeling; at Wheeling before Pittsburgh! Pittsburgh 400 miles by land from Philadelphia: and Cholera arrived at Pittsburg by a circuitous route of 3000 miles! But in that wandering, it pursued steadily the line of *great emigrant and business*.

This fact is not to be got over by any one. It signalizes the progress of Cholera in the United States more than any one thing.

(**Figure 18**) Sometimes the long-distance movement of people on the canal brought unintended consequences. In 1832 and 1849, cholera traveled the canal. Newspapers blamed travellers from Montreal for bringing the disease into America. This article is from the *Alexandria Gazette*, Alexandria, Virginia, January 8, 1849.

Some agents had their own boats, but another avenue was to work with private boat owners to get freight delivered. A private boat owner usually served as captain and businessman of their boat. The typical boat owning captain was male; although some women owned boats it was rare. His family might live on board with his wife filling the position of cook. In addition to the captain and cook, the crew consisted of a steersman and a mule driver. The norm on the Erie Canal was to have two drivers and a second team of mules on board the boat. One team and driver worked while the other rested. After roughly six hours, they switched. However, this was not the normal setup on the Champlain Canal during the 1800s. Most Champlain canal boats did not have a stable on board. A potential reason is the length of the canal vs benefit of the lost space on board. The canal was short when compared to the Erie and without a stable on board the extra space could be utilized for more cargo. Therefore, it was likely more cost-effective to save the cargo space and hire a team. A captain had the choice of hiring a line team and driver that would take the boat as far as the next line barn, where the teams and driver would be swapped out. Another option was to hire a trip team and driver. This method required longer breaks for the team and driver and usually meant spending the night in one place. Long breaks were opportunities to resupply at stores along the route. While looking for a team, the crew could load up with supplies in Whitehall or Waterford before heading out on the lake or Hudson. Waiting to lock through also provided such opportunities. Lock tenders were state employees and were subject to political patronage. They were not above a good bribe, such as a quarter or beer to help a boat lock through quickly.[25] The maintenance boat crew, a.k.a.

the "hurry-up boat," also worked for the state and helped to repair the canal when damages occurred. Breaks in the walls of the canal could mean weeks of being stuck on the bottom of the canal with no water. A long delay could cause the loss of an entire trip for a boat owner.

(**Figure 19**) Many captains tried to time their last run of the season to place them in the area of New York City. Basins filled up with canal boats tied together for the winter. If the captain and his family had nowhere else to go, they stayed on board their boat for the winter. Children could go to school during the winter because the family was not on the move.

Once the canal boat reached either Troy or Albany on the Hudson River or, if heading north, Whitehall, it was time to join a tow. Steam-powered towboats pulled long lines of canal boats and other vessels along Lake Champlain and the Hudson River. The boats in the tow would be lashed together for the ride. This downtime provided opportunities for light repairs, socialization, and laundry for the boat crews. Once the tow had reached its destination, each of the boats would be taken to their specific docks for unloading. The "along-shore-men" were gangs of men who could be hired to help unload boats. Depending on previous arrangements, the captain might be on his own to hire a crew and help unload, or the purchasing company might have a crew ready to unload.

Enlargements

The immediate success of both the Erie and the Champlain Canals led to calls for lateral canals to connect to the main arteries. In 1824, there were multiple petitions to the legislature to form corporations to build private canals to connect with the Champlain, including the Granville Canal Company to go from Granville to Fort Ann. Another was to connect "from the Battenkill, on the line of Vermont, to the navigable waters of the Hudson."[26] An official state survey was conducted in 1824 for a canal from the St. Lawrence at Ogdensburg to Lake Champlain. For various reasons, none of the laterals were built. Another response was to try to bypass the Champlain Canal, as called for in an 1829 newspaper article from The Evening Post (Boston) newspaper. The author complained about the "great depression in business" in that city and cited the Champlain Canal, among other reasons, for the

Dialogue between a *Lock-tender* upon the Northern Canal, and *Farmer P.*

Lock-tender—Well, worthy Sir, our friend Col. Young is once more before the public as a candidate, and as you proved yourself an efficient man at the polls' last fall, I hope to see you again, equally active, at the next election.

Farmer P.—To my regret and mortification, I must admit that I supported Young, as a candidate for governor at the last election, and I must also admit, that the *assurances* which I received from *Young* and *Cramer*, that the damages which I had sustained by the Canal, should be appraised and paid without any delay, induced me to exert myself in his behalf—but Sir, those *assurances* were *deceptive*—a year has elapsed, and *nothing* has been done for my *relief*.

Lock-tender—But, you should recollect Farmer P——, that the duties of Col. Young, have been many and arduous.

Farmer P.—" *Many and arduous,*" indeed—in the first place, much time, labor, and intrigue, were undoubtedly necessary to bring about his nomination as Governor—in the second place ; the time between his nomination and the election of last fall, was diligently devoted to the business of promoting his own election—and in the last place ; the period which has transpired since that time, has been principally occupied by his own private affairs, and a portion of it, has been employed in the work of securing his present nomination for the assembly. Indeed Mr. Lock-tender, the most *arduous* part of the *official duties* of Young, with which I am acquainted, consists in his " quarter day" rides to Albany, for the purpose of receiving a salary of $2000 a year—$500 of which, is paid for *supposed* services as an appraiser, and in that capacity I am yet to learn, that he has ever *earned a farthing*.

Lock-tender—Stop, stop Farmer P—— —don't be too rash—my brother *lock-tender below*, had just before I met you *sent me word*, that *Mr. Cramer* had *told* the lock-tender below him, that Colonel Young had *promised* to meet Mr. Wood, and Mr. Selden, shortly after the election, and go on to appraise the damages.

Farmer P.—Away with your trash— Having last fall relied upon the promises of Young and Cramer, and having been most *egregiously deceived*, I am not to be duped a second time, by *hollow-hearted* *assurances*. Tell your *master*, Young, that I shall *oppose* him, and that for *every* vote which through my instrumentality, he obtained as a candidate for Governor, I pledge myself there shall be *two against him*, as a candidate for the Assembly.

(**Figure 20, left**) Lock tenders gained their positions through political patronage and support letters from local citizens. They were often expected to promote the party in power to keep their jobs, as this "dialogue" printed in the October 25, 1825, *Waterford Reporter* demonstrates. Colonel Young was the canal commissioner in charge of the Champlain Canal. Col. Young was also running for governor and the lock tender wanted the farmer to support Young, but the farmer would not because Commissioner Young is in charge of assessing damages by the canal and he says that Young is not doing his job.

CLOSING OF THE WELLAND CANAL

against American vessels.—The N. Y. Express learns that the Canadian Government has concluded to close the Welland Canal against American vessels. This is a measure which, if persisted in, will inflict a serious blow upon the trade of the lakes, affecting materially the prospects of all the owners of vessels trading in Lake Ontario.

Great excitement exists at *Oswego* and other places connected with the commerce of the lower lakes and river St. Lawrence. This movement is understood to be a retaliation against the United States and the State of New York, in consequence of the former not granting reciprocity of trade, and the latter cutting off Canada from the free use of Lake Champlain and the Champlain Canal.

New York, March 22

(**Figure 21, above**) International trade was not always smooth going, as seen by this article published in the *The Weekly Wisconsin*, Milwaukee, Wisconsin on April 2, 1851.

diversion of trade.[27] Some of the suggestions made to counter that loss were the improvement of the Connecticut River and to build a railroad from Boston to the Hudson River.

Unlike the Erie, the Champlain Canal did not branch off into a series of lateral canals. Other than some short side canals used to connect to industries, the only main lateral canal that was built to supplement the Champlain Canal was the Glens Falls feeder canal. Although not a true lateral in name, the Glens Falls feeder provided water to the summit level of the Champlain and a navigable canal to Glens Falls from Fort Edward. In 1817, Chief Engineer James Geddes felt that the Half Way Brook would provide plenty of water to the summit level for "half a century" unless there was a prolonged drought. The commissioners did follow up by saying that even if that was the case it would still be prudent to build a feeder providing water from the Hudson north of Fort Edward.[28]

Construction of the feeder was approved in 1821, and in 1822, it was decided that the feeder should be made navigable. There were multiple setbacks, including a large dam break, changing the route, and realizing that bed of the canal had to be lined with clay to keep the water in. The enlargement of the feeder for navigation was completed in 1829.[29] In 1836, the legislature approved enlarging the canal and rebuilding the wooden locks with ones of stone. That work was complete in 1839. The enlargement also included sluices that allowed water to bypass the locks in order to have a continuous supply of water to the summit level of the Champlain.[30] More would be done to improve the volume of water that actually made it to the Champlain Canal in the following years.

PLATE II.—LEAKAGE FROM THE GLENS FALLS FEEDER.

(**Figure 22**) Water leaking from the canal bed of the Glens Falls feeder was a constant challenge. Here is a picture from the 1895 Annual Report of the State Engineer and Surveyor showing the water leaking out into the Hudson River. The canal, which is not shown, is on the top of the cliff. Note the large piles of wood on the bank of the canal.

462 - Lumber Yard on Glens Falls Feeder.   9/22/21

450 - Lumber Yard on Glens Falls Feeder   9/22/21

(Figure 23 & 24) In addition to providing a steady water supply, the feeder canal also provided direct access to the lumber coming down the Hudson to Glens Falls. Lumber, lime, and marble were all being shipped from Glens Falls. The navigation on feeder was active into at least the 1920s. Courtesy of the New York State Archives.

The Champlain Canal did not receive the same support as the Erie when it came to enlargements. Although both canals were very successful, the Erie certainly outweighed the Champlain when it came to freight and revenue. In 1835, the state legislature approved the enlargement of the Erie to 70 feet wide at the top, 56 feet wide at the bottom, and 7 feet deep. The Champlain does not appear to have been in the discussion for the same enlargement. The enlargement of the Erie was a slow process, wrapped up in politics and an economic depression. The work began in 1836 and was not declared complete until 1862.

The Champlain Canal was busy and outperforming all of the other canals that connected to the Erie. But the perceived increase in revenue from an enlargement in the 1830s was apparently not enough for the Champlain to be enlarged. After 1853, locks that were rebuilt were made to match the enlarged Erie. However, the channel was still at its 1820s dimensions. On top of that, the canal had not been dredged or "bottomed out" on a regular basis, if at all. When repairs were made, the walls of the canal were raised instead of dredging. So larger locks were a step in the right direction but had minimal impact on traffic because the boats could not be bigger. Multiple legislative efforts were made to enlarge the Champlain, but funding was never enough. Instead, small improvements happened in increments and the canal never truly was at one uniform depth until the barge canal was built.

In addition to efforts to enlarge the Champlain to match the Erie, various efforts were made to promote a ship canal that would connect New York City and Montreal. From 1849 to the 1950s, the federal government and the state government conducted multiple surveys to explore the possibility of bringing ocean-going vessels through the northern route. None of the proposals went very far toward being built.

The lack of maintenance and poor condition of the Champlain Canal coupled with competition from the railroad limited potential commerce on the canal during the last few decades of the nineteenth century. The rest of New York's canal system was in a similar situation. Even the grand Erie was in poor condition and feeling the pinch of the railroads and a lack of funding for upkeep.

Railroad

The introduction of the railroad along the Champlain Canal happened in 1835 when the Rensselaer and Saratoga Railroad was completed from Waterford to Ballston Spa. At first, the road was to provide tourists landing in Troy a connection to the springs. In comparison the first railroad along the Erie Canal corridor, the Mohawk and Hudson Railroad, provided passenger traffic between Albany and Schenectady in 1831, as a supplement to the canal. The railway enabled passengers to bypass a day's worth of travel time in a few hours. Both railroads found success and expanded their lines and other companies joined in. By the mid-1800s, railroads had taken most of the passenger traffic from both canals.

The battle for freight lasted a little longer. An advantage that the Champlain Canal had in this regard was the sheer size and weight of its main cargos. Lumber, iron ore, stone, marble were heavy and easier to ship on the water. The Erie Canal's main cargo of grains had an earlier battle to fight with the railroads. The enlargement of the Erie Canal helped to prolong the competition. However, as locomotives and rails got stronger, the capacity of the Champlain Canal did not grow in a significant way, hampering its ability to compete. The railroads did eventually overtake the bulk of the freight from canals.

Champlain Barge Canal

In response to the growing power of the railroads and the diminishing trade on the canals, the State of New York proposed a barge canal to replace the Erie, Champlain, Oswego and the Cayuga–Seneca Canals. Railroads were gaining a monopoly on freight and freight prices. To combat that and try to regain primacy of trade heading east, a new larger canal was proposed. Governor Theodore Roosevelt would become the champion of the barge canal. Using his political influence, he helped to push the plan to a vote by the general public. Although he would become President of the United States before the referendum was held in 1903, his support for the project was critical to the process. With a majority of votes coming from Buffalo and New York City, the barge canal system was approved in 1903.

Construction of the Champlain Barge Canal started in 1905 and was completed in 1916. The new locks could pass vessels up to 300 feet long, 44 feet wide with a draft of 12 feet. Between Waterford and Fort Edward, the majority of the new channel was in the Hudson River, and a land cut was used from Fort Edward to Whitehall. This is the generation of canal in use today.

New technology played an important role, as the work was done with steam shovels, small-gauge steam trains, specially developed concrete, and a variety of other steam-powered equipment. The majority of manual labor was provided by Italian immigrants, many of whom stayed behind after the work was done.

The Barge Canal system never reached its supporters' predicted "annual traffic of ten million tons"[31] of freight per year. The freight peaked in 1951 with roughly half of what was predicted. In the early years of the Champlain Barge Canal, the main commercial traffic was lumber-based products and iron ore going south and coal going north. Freight traveling south slowly declined and by 1960, most of the commodities moving on the canal were petroleum products heading north. But that too would slowly diminish. In 1961 a special legislative committee produced a report on the Barge Canal in response to a New York State constitutional amendment that would allow the state to transfer ownership to the federal government. The committee did not feel it was part of their mandate to make a recommendation, rather just to present the information. By that time it was clear that commerce on the Barge Canal was declining and the committee explored the other benefits that the canal brought to the state of New York. The main ones were hydro-electric power, industrial use of the water, irrigation, flood control, municipal functions, conservation, and recreation. Looking to those factors, the state legislature felt a strong enough case was made to keep the canals under state ownership.

The primary use, of course, is shipping; it was designed and built for that purpose. But population growth, industrial expansion, scientific discoveries, more leisure time, advanced agricultural processes, all requiring more water in a pure state have made the canal a multi-purpose, invaluable servant of the whole area through which it passes. The uses our people now have for the canal and its waters include water power, flood control, water supply, both industrial and domestic, irrigation, conservation and recreation.

State of New York Report of the Joint Legislative
Committee on the Barge Canal, 1961

The multi-use aspect of the Barge Canal system is still promoted today and although commercial freight has become a rare sight, the canal is alive and well. Communities along the canal have embraced the potential that it provides. Looking to draw in visitors and boaters and improve local quality of life, communities have improved waterfronts, built visitor centers, and built parks along the canal. Boaters from around the world travel the system and visit communities along the way.

Barrel Buoy Channel Marker

(Figure 25) When the barge canal first opened wooden buoys holding kerosene lanterns were used to mark the channel. This buoy was dredged up in 2013 as part of the EPA mandated cleanup of the Hudson River by General Electric (GE) which had dumped industrial pollution into the river.

(Figure 26) Pleasure craft passing a commercial barge while approaching Lock C-1, in 1973. Today it is more common to see pleasure craft instead of commercial vessels on the canal. Communities have been looking back to the water for quality of life and heritage tourism. The new tack has brought the canal back to life, contributing billions of dollars to the state's economy. Courtesy of the New York State Museum.

Conclusion

In the Canal Commissioners' report of March 19, 1817, the commissioners laid out the perceived benefits that would follow from a navigable connection between Lake Champlain and the Hudson River. Looking back now over two hundred years later, those predictions were well calculated. However, a lack of financial support by the state limited the potential of the route. Still, commercial-wise, the canal was a success. The barge canal also fulfilled its role, although not to the levels its projectors may have wanted. Today the barge canal is bringing dollars to communities along its route in new ways and once again proving its value.

Even though, the Champlain Canal is not usually mentioned with the Erie Canal when people today look back at the importance of New York's canal policies, it is clear that the Champlain was an important link in the transportation network. At the time the canals were originally built, the Champlain Canal was not a lateral of the Erie, but rather together they were part of a network. Today, it is the same; all of New York's canals are part of the New York State Barge Canal system.

Endnotes

1   *Laws of the State of New York in Relation to the Erie and Champlain Canals, Together with the Annual Reports of the Canal Commissioners and Other Documents Requisite for a Complete Official History of Those Works. Also, correct Maps Delineating the Routes of the Erie and Champlain Canals and Designating the Lands Through Which They Pass: Volume I,* (E.and E. Hosford, 1825), 287-292.

2   *Laws of the State of New York, Volume I,* 358.

3   John H. Thompson, ed., *Geography of New York State,* (Syracuse University Press, 1966), 136. Chapter by D.W. Meing. Meing cites Tryon's report from "O'Callaghan, Documentary History, I, 737."

4   David Hosack, M.D., F.R.S., *Memoir of De Witt Clinton: With an Appendix, Containing Numerous Documents, Illustrative of the Principal Events of His Life* (J. Seymour, 1829), 278.

5   *Laws of the State of New York, Volume I,* 87.

6   Arthur B. Cohn, *Lake Champlain's Sailing Canal Boats: An Illustrated Journey From Burlington Bay to the Hudson River,* (Lake Champlain Maritime Museum, 2003), 21.

7   *Laws of the State of New York, Volume I,* 289.

8   *Laws of the State of New York, Volume I,* 289.

9   *Laws of the State of New York, Volume I,* 358.

10   *Laws of the State of New York, Volume I,* 371.

11   *Laws of the State of New York, Volume I,* 379, January 31, 1818, Canal Commissioners' Report.

12   *Laws of the State of New York, Volume I,* 417, January 25, 1819, Canal Commissioners' Report.

13   *Geneva Gazette,* December 5, 1819, article reprinted from the *Sandy Hill Times,* November 26, 1819.

14   *Laws of the State of New York, Volume I,* 423.

15   *Laws of the State of New York, Volume I,* 433.

16   *Laws of the State of New York, Volume I,* 381, January 31, 1818 Canal Commissioner's Report,

17   *Laws of the State of New York in Relation to the Erie and Champlain Canals, Together*

with the Annual Reports of the Canal Commissioners and Other Documents Requisite for a Complete Official History of Those Works. Also, correct Maps Delineating the Routes of the Erie and Champlain Canals and Designating the Lands Through Which They Pass: Volume II, (E.and E. Hosford, 1825), 129.

18   *Laws of the State of New York, Volume 2*, 176.

19   Joel Munsell, *Collections on the History of Albany from Its Discovery to the Present Time, with Notices of its Public Institutions, and Biographical Sketches of Citizens Deceased, Vol II*, (J. Munsel, 1867), 448.

20   Cohn, *Lake Champlain's Sailing Canal Boats*, 17.

21   The following four banks from along the northern route received such deposits: Clinton County Bank, Plattsburgh, incorporated in 1836; the Essex County Bank, Keesville, incorporated in 1832; the Bank of Whitehall, incorporated in 1829; and the Saratoga County Bank, in Waterford, incorporated in 1830. (Miller, 1962), Appendix.

22   John L. Scherer, *Art for the People: Decorated Stoneware from the Weitsman Collection*, (RIT Press, 2015), 111-113.

23   Henry P. Smith, ed. *History of Essex County : with illustrations and biographical sketches of some of its prominent men and pioneers*, (D. Mason and Company, 1885), 184.

24   Horatio Gates, ed., *A Gazetteer of the State of New-York: Embracing an Ample Survey and Description of Its Counties, Towns, Cities, Villages, Canals, Mountains, Lakes, Rivers, Creeks, and Natural Topography ... with an Appendix*. (Packard, 1824), 96.

25   Russell Van Dervoort, *Canal Canaries and Other Tough Old Birds*, (CreateSpace Independent Publishing Platform, 2010), 105-107.

26   *Laws of the State of New York, Volume II*, 2281-282.

27   *The Evening Post* (Boston), September 12, 1829, 2.

28   *Laws of the State of New York, Volume I*, 377.

29   Noble E. Whitford, *History of the Canal System of the State of New York: Together with Brief Histories of the United States and Canada*, (Brandow Printing Company, 1906), 418.

30   Whitford, *History of the Canal System*, 421.

31   "State of New York Report of the Joint Legislative Committee on The Barge Canal," (New York State Legislative Committee, 1961), 31.

Figure Citations

(Figure 1) Courtesy of the Lionel Pincus and Princess Firyal Map Division, The New York Public Library Digital Collections.

(Figure 2) Courtesy of the Library of Congress.

(Figure 3) *Albany Argus*, January 23, 1816.

(Figure 4) *Albany Argus*, November 26, 1822, in New York City's *The Evening Post*, November 30, 1822.

(Figure 5) Reprinted in the *Albany Argus*, August 15, 1823.

(Figure 6) "Map of the Champlain Canal and its Connections", 1857.

(Figures 7 & 8) Top article printed in *The Arkansas Gazette*, April 02, 1828 and the bottom printed in *Montreal Gazette*, July 21, 1828.

(Figure 9) Courtesy of the New York State Museum.

(Figure 10) John Warner Barber and Henry Howe, *Containing a General Collection of the Most Interesting Facts, Traditions, Biographical Sketches, Anecdotes, &c., Relating to Its History and Antiquities, with Geographical Descriptions of Every Township in the State*, (S. Tuttle, 1842). Courtesy of the New York State Library, Manuscripts and Special Collections.

(Figure 11) Courtesy of the New York State Museum.

(Figure 12) Courtesy of the New York State Archives.

(Figure 13) Barber and Howe, *Containing a General Collection of the Most Interesting Facts, Traditions, Biographical Sketches, Anecdotes*. Courtesy of the New York State Library, Manuscripts and Special Collections, 974.7 B23a3.

(Figure 14) "Village of Essex, N.Y. Lake Champlain" - Edwin Whitefield, c.1846, Courtesy of the New York State Museum.

(Figure 15) Courtesy of the New York State Museum.

(Figure 16) Courtesy of the New York State Museum.

(Figure 17) *Saratoga Sentinel*, June 6, 1822.

(Figure 18) *Alexandria Gazette*, Alexandria Virginia, January 8, 1849.

(Figure 19) E.J. Meeker, "Laid Up for Winter – Canalboat Colony in Coenties Slip, East River," *Harper's Weekly*, February 16, 1884. Courtesy of the New York State Library.

(Figure 20) *Waterford Reporter*, October 25, 1825.

(Figure 21) *The Weekly Wisconsin*, April 2, 1851.

(Figure 22) 1895 Annual Report of the State Engineer and Surveyor, Plate H, next to page 134.

(Figures 23 & 24) Courtesy of the New York State Archives.

(Figure 25) Courtesy of the New York State Museum.

(Figure 26) Courtesy of the New York State Museum.

Bibliography

Barber, John Warner and Henry Howe. *Containing a General Collection of the Most Interesting Facts, Traditions, Biographical Sketches, Anecdotes, &c., Relating to Its History and Antiquities, with Geographical Descriptions of Every Township in the State*, (S. Tuttle, 1842).

Cohen, Arthur B. *Lake Champlain's Sailing Canal Boats: An Illustrated Journey From Burlington Bay to the Hudson River*. (Lake Champlain Maritime Museum, 2003).

Gates, Horatio. *A Gazetteer of the State of New-York: Embracing an Ample Survey and Description of Its Counties, Towns, Cities, Villages, Canals, Mountains, Lakes, Rivers, Creeks, and Natural Topography*. (B.D. Packard, 1824).

Hosack, David, M.D., F.R.S.. *Memoir of De Witt Clinton: With an Appendix, Containing Numerous Documents*. (J. Seymour, 1829).

Laws of the State of New York in Relation to the Erie and Champlain Canals, Together with the Annual Reports of the Canal Commissioners and Other Documents Requisite for a Complete Official History of Those Works Volume I. (E. and E. Hosford, 1825).

Laws of the State of New York in Relation to the Erie and Champlain Canals, Together with the Annual Reports of the Canal Commissioners and Other Documents Requisite for a Complete Official History of Those Works, Vol II. (E. and E. Hosford, 1825).

Miller, Nathan. *The Enterprise of A Free People: Aspects of Economic Development in New York State during the Canal Period, 1792-1838*. (Cornell University Press, 1962).

Munsell, Joel. *Collections on the History of Albany from Its Discovery to the Present Time, with Notices of its Public Institutions, and Biographical Sketches of Citizens Deceased Vol II*. (Joel Munsell, 1867).

Smith, Henry P., ed. *History of Essex County: with illustrations and biographical sketches of some of its prominent men and pioneers*. (D. Mason and Company, 1885).

"State of New York Report of the Joint Legislative Committee on The Barge Canal." (New York State Legislative Committee, 1961).

Thompson, John H. ed. *Geography of New York State*. (Syracuse University Press, 1966).

Van Dervoort, Russell W.D. *Canal Canaries and Other Tough Old Birds*. (CreateSpace Independent Publishing Platform, 2010).

Whitford, Noble E. 1906. *History of the Canal System of the State of New York: Together with Brief Histories of the United States and Canada*. (Brandow Printing Company, 1906).

CHAPTER 2
Archaeology of Lake Champlain Canal Boats

T. Picard
Staff Archaeologist

The cold dark freshwater of Lake Champlain provides an excellent preservative environment for historic wooden shipwrecks and its bottomlands have become the resting place for hundreds of such vessels. Of all the vessel types found in Lake Champlain, the most common are the remains of canal boats. These wrecks represent vessels from all eras of the Champlain Canal as well as some interesting variations. Canal boats are categorized into five different classes based on their dimensions, which correlate to the dimensions of the canal locks as they change over time. These classes are organized into four periods based on the time between the completion of the section of the canal connecting Fort Edward to Lake Champlain in 1819, the first expansion in 1862, the second expansion in 1873, and the Champlain Barge Canal in 1916. Over the decades, the boats of the Champlain Canal have been of interest to underwater archaeologists working in Lake Champlain. Through their work, there is now a comprehensive understanding of how these unique vessels were designed and built.

The Early Canal Period (1819-1857)

The Early Canal Period, 1819 to 1857, started as one of experimentation and discovery in the design of these early canal boats. One of the challenges faced by canal boat builders was the dimensions of the canal locks. The canal lock is the enclosed space in which the water level can be raised or lowered. By traveling through these locks, a boat is able to move from one body of water to another, even if those bodies of water are not naturally connected and exist at different elevations from each other. Connecting each canal lock is the canal prism, which is a wider channel that boats travel through to reach their desired destinations and is wide enough to allow two canal boats to pass each other in opposite directions. When the Champlain Canal was built, the locks were 90 feet (27.4 meters) long and 15 feet (4.5 meters) wide. The prism was shaped like an inverted trapezoid so that the top had a width of 40 feet (12.2 meters), while the narrower bottom had a width of 26 feet (7.9 meters), as seen in Figure 2. Both the canal lock and canal prism had a depth of 4 feet (1.2 meters)Figures 1 and 2 show comparative images of the sizes of canal locks and prisms through time. These early canal boat builders had to determine which design could best balance the limitation of the canal lock dimensions, carry the largest amount of goods possible, and handle operation on Lake Champlain and the Hudson River. While there were a handful of vessels operating in the completed locks of the Champlain Canal between 1819 and 1823, it was not until the final lock of the canal, which connected it to the Hudson River, was completed that the boat building frenzy started. Many saw economic opportunity in the Champlain Canal, including professional boat builders to businessmen, farmers, and carpenters, and others began constructing their own vessels to grow their businesses. This wide variety of backgrounds is a contributing factor to the variation of boat design.[1]

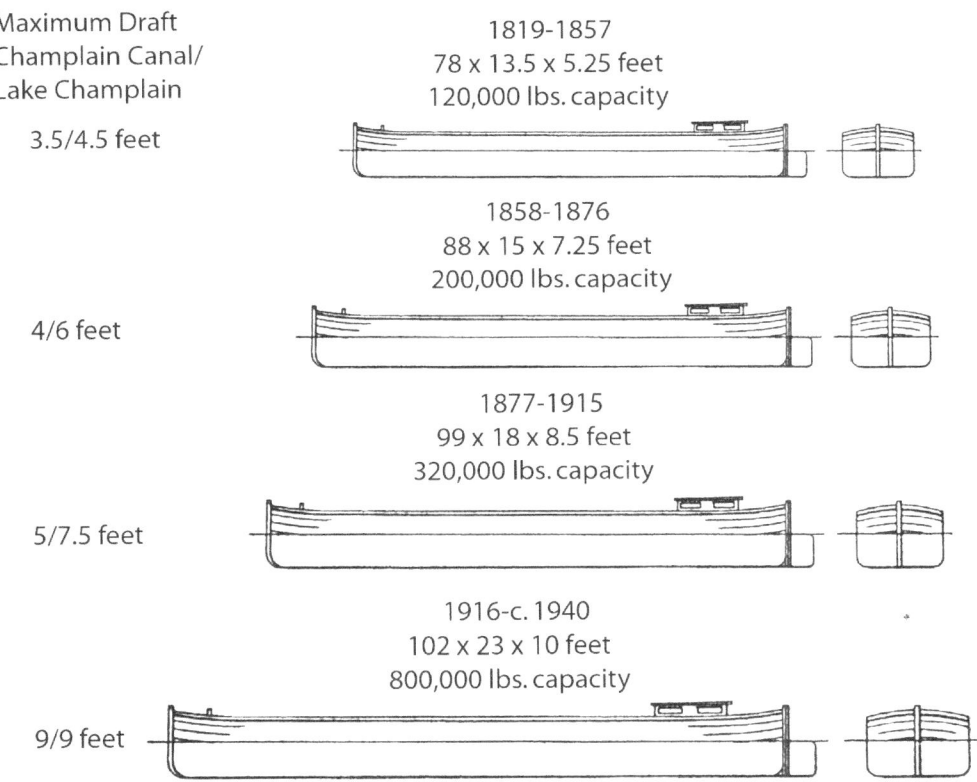

Maximum Draft
Champlain Canal/
Lake Champlain

3.5/4.5 feet

1819-1857
78 x 13.5 x 5.25 feet
120,000 lbs. capacity

4/6 feet

1858-1876
88 x 15 x 7.25 feet
200,000 lbs. capacity

5/7.5 feet

1877-1915
99 x 18 x 8.5 feet
320,000 lbs. capacity

9/9 feet

1916-c. 1940
102 x 23 x 10 feet
800,000 lbs. capacity

(Figure 1) Dimensions of the various classes of canal boats from 1819 to 1940.

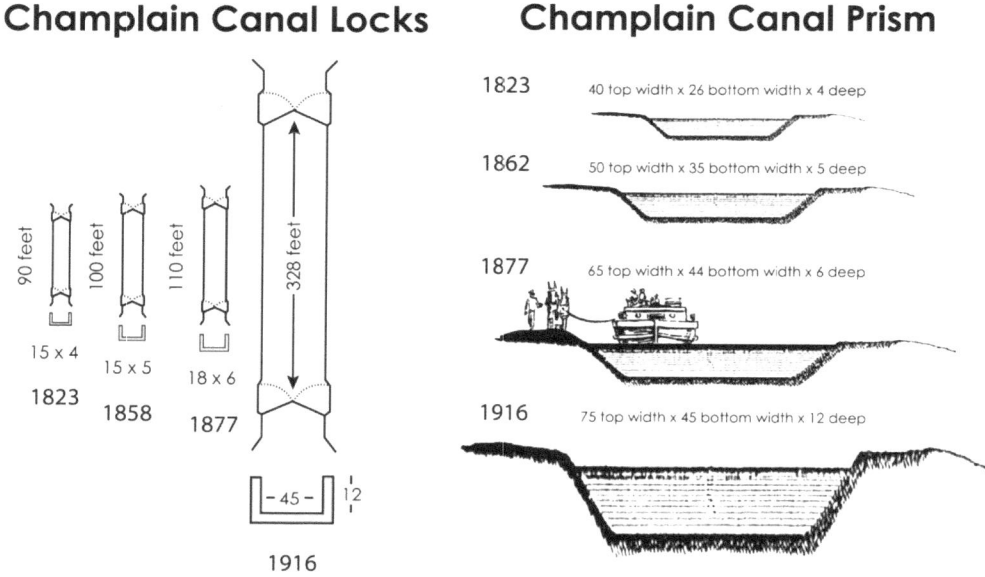

(**Figure 2**) Changes of the Champlain Canal locks during each of the expansions.

During this period, canal boats that operated out of the northern ports of the lake tended to be sailing canal boats, designed similarly to sailing lake sloops or schooners, with masts stepped on deck that could be laid down on the deck while traveling through the canals. The only example of a sailing canal boat from this era that has been found and studied in an archaeological context is the sailing canal schooner *Troy*. *Troy* was launched in 1823 as one of the first generation of sailing canal boats to fulfill the growing demand for transportation on Lake Champlain and through the Champlain Canal. In November 1825, *Troy* was transporting a load of iron ore to the newly established iron furnace in Westport, New York, when it was struck by a winter gale and foundered. At the time of its sinking the schooner was commanded by twenty-five-year-old Jacob Halstead and was crewed by Jacob's thirteen-year-old brother, George, half-brother Jacob Pardee, and two non-related members, Daniel Cannon and John Williams. The bodies of the crew were never found, but a memorial for the Halstead brothers and the tragedy of the schooner *Troy* was placed in the Westport Town Cemetery. John Williams' son Daniel, who was two years old at the time of the sinking, would later write a poem about the loss of his father and his mother's grief.[2]

In 1999, during the Lake Champlain Maritime Museum's (Museum) Lake Champlain Underwater Cultural Resources Survey (Lake Survey) a unique target was identified in the side-scan sonar image. The target was initially dismissed as a geological feature because it projected 30 feet (9.1 meters) off the lake bottom, which is quite unusual for a shipwreck that typically sits upright once it settles. Upon a second review of the side-scan sonar imagery, it was determined that this anomaly should be investigated as it was the only anomaly found in the expected location where *Troy* sank. In August 1999, Arthur Cohn, Director Emeritus of the Museum, executed a complicated deep dive to inspect the anomaly and was able to confirm that the target was the shipwreck site of *Troy*.[3]

During the fall of 1999, the Museum's archaeologists revisited the site to capture video using a remote-operated vehicle (ROV) and get an understanding of the wreck and the reason for it to be standing proud of the lake bottom. Prior to the discovery of the wreck, it was believed that the sinking was caused by the iron ore shifting within the cargo hold during the storm. This was confirmed by the archaeological investigation as thousands of pounds of iron ore had shifted forward to the bow, which would have caused the ship to descend rapidly to the lake bottom bow first and now anchors *Troy* in its current bow down position.[4]

From the 1999 video footage, Kevin Crisman from Texas A&M University's Nautical Archaeology Program was able to create a drawing of the wreck in a perspective view (Figure 3) as well as several pages of notes that document the vessel's construction. Compared to the size of the Champlain Canal locks and the standardized sailing canal boats that would come about in the following decades, *Troy* is a relatively small vessel. *Troy* had an overall length of only 60 feet (18.3 meters), a maximum width of 13 feet 6 inches (4.1 meters), and a depth of 3 feet 6 inches to 4 feet (1.1 to 1.2 meters), as seen in Figure 4. While the dimensions of *Troy* are uncommon, the vessel has revealed key features of canal boats that lasted through the decades and came about during the earliest stage in the development of canal boat design. The first key features are the mast tabernacles, three-sided boxes located on the deck of the vessel at the heel of the mast that allows the mast to be raised when sailing and lowered when being towed. *Troy's* foremast tabernacle is now buried, but its mainmast tabernacle is still visible. The mainmast tabernacle is very similar in design and identical in function to the mast tabernacles found on sailing canal boats of later periods. The second of these features is a centerboard that was essential for a sailing canal boat to maintain stability while under sail. *Troy's* unusual position allowed archaeologists to see the centerboard extended, as it is often pushed up into the centerboard trunk as the vessel settles on the lake bed. *Troy* is one of the oldest shipwrecks in the world that has a centerboard and the wreck's discovery revealed that sailing canal boats on Lake Champlain were among the first to adopt the widespread use of a centerboard.[5]

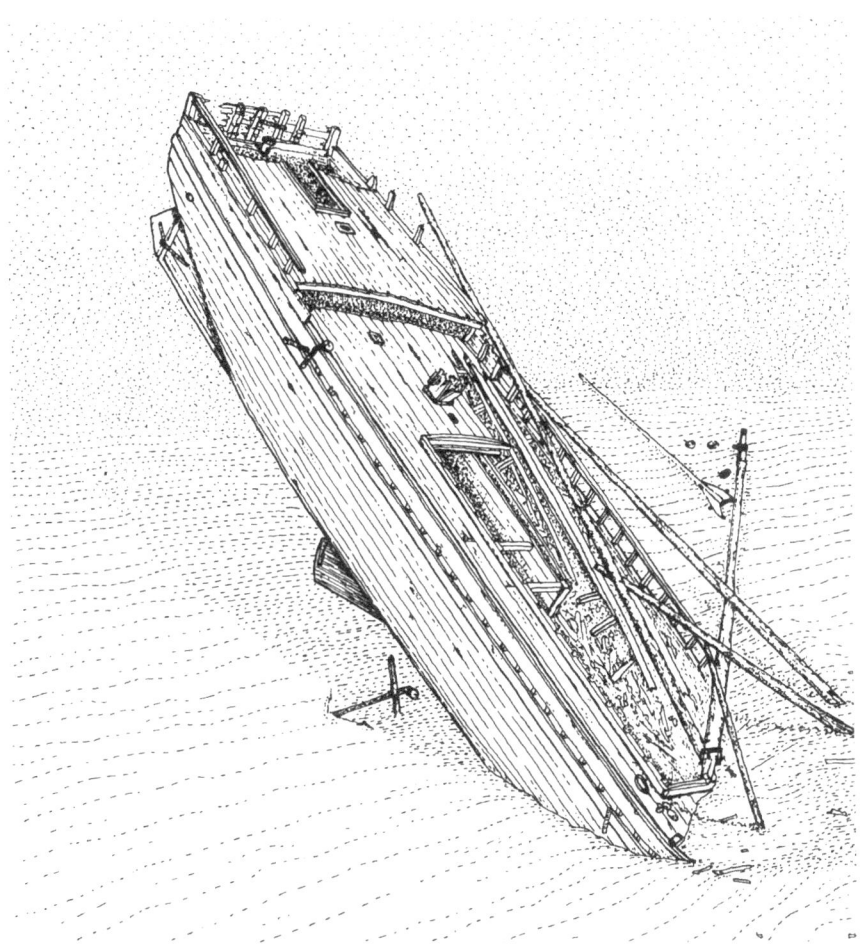

(Figure 3) Wreck of *Troy* from video footage by Kevin Crisman, perspective view.

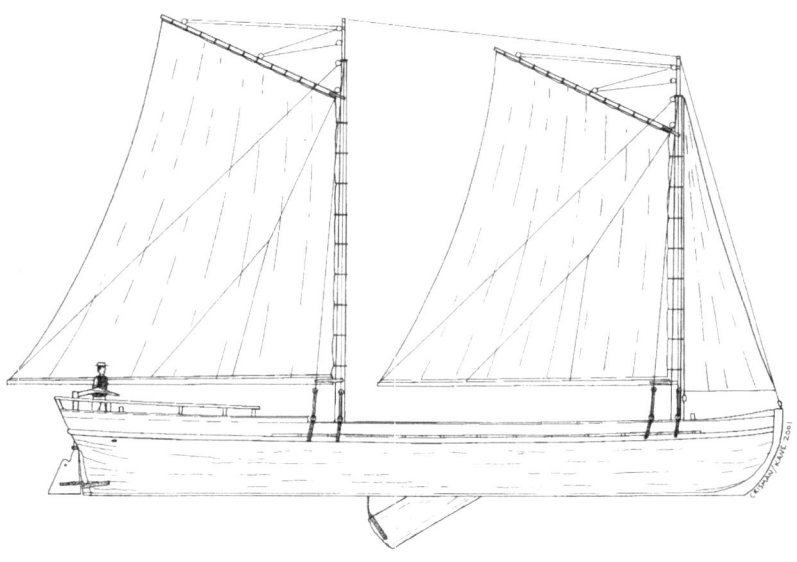

(Figure 4) Profile of *Troy* before it sank in 1825.

The standard canal boat, or a canal boat that was towed by a steamboat (Figure 5), was the more common design for boats that operated out of the south lake ports. The only standard canal boat of the 1823-class found archaeologically in Lake Champlain is the "Stove Boat," later discovered to be the canal boat *Vergennes*. As a standard canal boat *Vergennes* stands apart from its 1823-class sibling *Troy,* as it does not have any of the sailing equipment such as a centerboard or masts. This is because *Vergennes* was designed to be towed by a steamboat so it could focus solely on maximizing cargo space. To accomplish this, the builders used scow construction techniques to remove as many curves as possible. While it is known that *Vergennes* sank while carrying a load of manufactured iron goods, including stoves, cauldrons, and teakettles, the exact details of the cause are unknown. At some point during the vessel's voyage in November of 1853, possibly due to a storm, the cargo shifted to the port side of *Vergennes,* causing the vessel to sink.[6]

(Figure 5) An image of a steam tug pulling a train of standard canal boats on Lake Champlain.

The wreck of *Vergennes* was located by two sport divers in 1990 who went on to report the wreck to archaeologists at the Museum. The underwater archaeology team visited the site that year and began recording the location, orientation, and measurements of the wreck. *Vergennes*, like *Troy*, has an uncommon orientation as the shifting cargo caused the wreck to roll on its port side while sinking. This preliminary work found that the hull's overall length was 80 feet (24.4 meters), had a beam of 12 feet 6 inches (3.8 meters), and a depth of 5 feet 6 inches (1.7 meters). The wreck now rests on its port side on a steep incline, making the site a challenging dive (Figure 6). In 1998, the Museum's archaeology team undertook a more in-depth investigation of *Vergennes* as a part of the Lake Survey for that year. During this investigation, the archaeologists documented the design and construction of *Vergennes* and found that there are many features that would become standard in canal boat design throughout the decades. One of the more interesting discoveries is the lack of a true keel; instead, the vessel was built with a keelson that sits between the hull and ceiling planking alongside multiple sister keelsons (Figure 7). This created a solid flat platform to store cargo within the hull of the canal boat.[7]

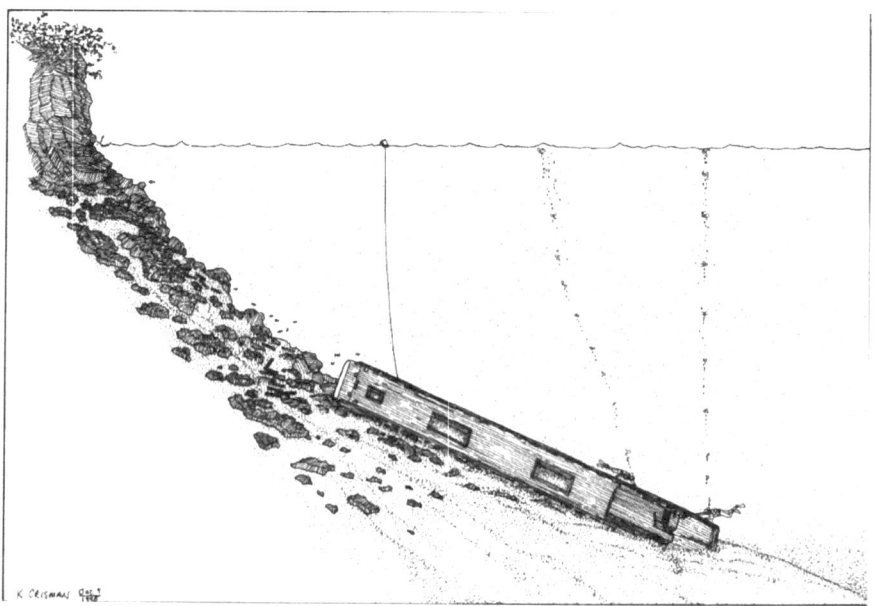

(Figure 6) Drawing of archaeologists documenting the standard canal boat, *Vergennes.*

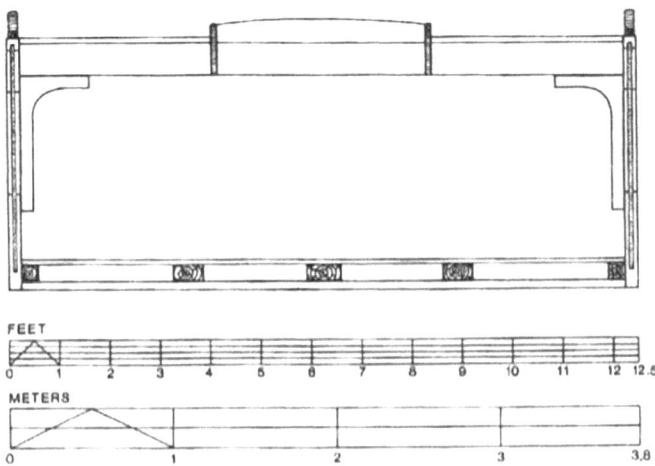

FEET

METERS

(Figure 7) Cross section amidship of *Vergennes.*

Since the vessel was designed to have as few curves as possible, *Vergennes* was built to have a hard chine at a 90° right angle. The hull was built up from the flat bottom starting with attaching the first strakes to a longitudinal timber that was between the hull and ceiling planking known as a chine log, otherwise known as chine-built. The strakes were then built up until they reached the height of the deck, at which point hanging knees would be attached to support the deck beams. This technique eliminated the use of floor timbers and futtocks inside the hull to support the strakes and create latitudinal support. Documentation of *Vergennes'* bow revealed that it was constructed in the same manner as the bottom of the vessel, since the bow was built utilizing the same scow design as the rest of the vessel. The bow has a flat leading edge that rises at a 45° angle from the bottom of the hull with sharp 90° corners where the bow meets the sides of the hull. To create this shape, the keelson and sister keelsons bend upwards or are scarfed to the bottom timbers and are abutted under a trapezoidal transverse timber to form the upper edge of the bow. To create additional support for the bow, a two-piece false stem is fastened to the upper edge of the keelson.[8]

The scow bow such as the one seen on *Vergennes* was immensely popular as it was cheaper to build, since compass timber, which was quite expensive, was not required. The sharp corners of the scow bow generated more wake that caused erosion to the canal banks or created holes when the bow scraped into banks while passing other canal boats, as there was only one foot (0.3 meters) of space between the two passing boats. Finally, when collisions between canal boats happened, the scow bow would often knock a hole in the other vessel that led to it sinking on the spot. This caused traffic in the canals, as boats had to wait to pass the sight of the accident. The New York Canal Board placed regulations into effect as early as 1833 that required scow bows, or any square or sharp cornered bow, to have a semicircular platform in place around the bow to prevent extensive damage to either boat should a collision occur. Canal boats with sharp corner or scow bows that were operating on the canal without a semicircular platform had to pay a five-dollar fine.[9]

The historical record suggests that mounting this semicircular platform may not have been able to prevent these damages, or that the five-dollar fine was not enough to encourage their use, as new regulations were passed in 1846. Stating the damage caused to other canal boats and the canal channel itself, the new regulations outlawed building new canal boats with a scow bow, levied a fee of ten dollars on canal boats that operated with a scow bow to discourage their use. The regulation established that the bow on the canal boats had to have an elliptical or semicircular shape with a curve that was proportional to the beam of the vessel, as seen in Figure 8.[10] While the regulations outlined these strict guidelines for the bow, there was no regulation for using a scow stern; as such future iterations of canal boat design would see a nearly even split between using a molded bow with a scow stern, and a molded bow and molded stern.[11]

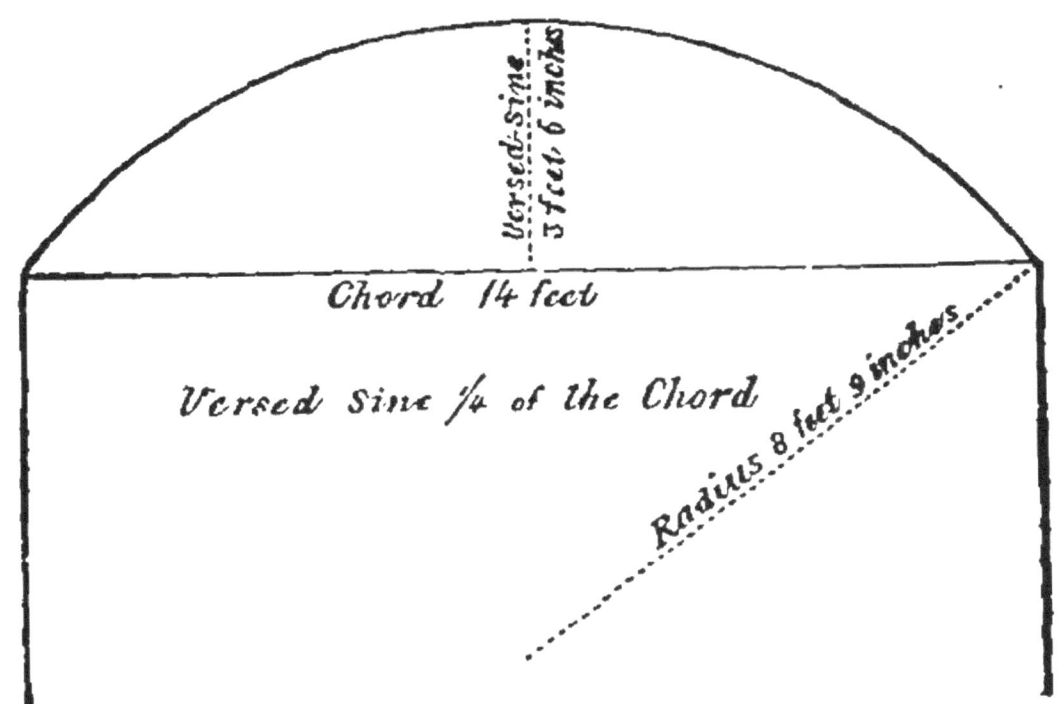

(Figure 8) Diagram from the 1846 laws and regulations showing the semicircular bow required for boats operating on New York canals.

As merchants saw which features worked in their favor to move the most amount of cargo with the greatest amount of success through the era of experimentation, the demand for multiple vessels with similar features increased, which saw a decrease in variability between canal boats of similar types. Eventually merchants would repeatedly order vessels of the same dimensions from boat builders so that by 1841 the range of vessel dimensions had narrowed to a point where archaeologists could place them into their own categories.[12] The development of lines for canal boats helped bring about uniform sizes as well as rigging for the sailing canal boats. [13] This saw the transition from the 1823-class that had dimensions of 48 feet 6 inches to 81 feet (14.8 meters to 24.7 meters) in length, a beam of 13 to 13 feet 6 inches (3.9 meters to 4.1 meters), and a depth of 3 feet 9 inches to 5 feet 3 inches (1.1 meters to 1.6 meters) to the 1841-class that had a length of 73 feet 6 inches to 81 feet (22.4 meters to 24.7 meters), a beam of 12 feet 6 inches to 13 feet 6 inches (3.81 meters to 4.1 meters), and a depth of 3 feet 3 inches to 5 feet 3 inches (0.99 meters to 1.6 meters).[14]

For the sailing canal boats of the 1841-class, sloop rigging ended up becoming the most common type. The historical record reveals that of the one hundred 1841-class sailing canal boats that appear in historical documents, ninety-six were rigged as sloops while only four were rigged as schooners. The archaeology team at the Museum has identified several 1841-class sailing canal boats sites in Lake Champlain, all of which are sloop rigged (Figure 9). One of the most well documented is the Isle La Motte Canal Sloop which has a length of 79 feet 8 inches (24.3 meters), a beam of roughly 13 feet 6 inches (4.1 meters), and an approximate depth of hold of 4 feet (1.2

meters).[15] In comparison to *Troy* the Isle La Motte Canal Sloop is significantly longer but was rigged as a sloop where Troy was rigged as a schooner.[16]

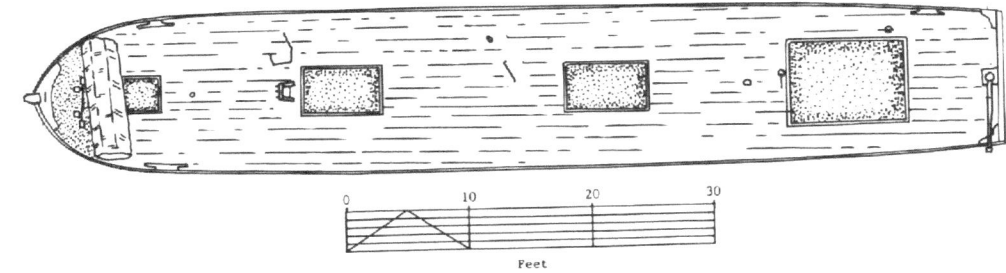

(Figure 9) Plan view drawing of the Isle La Motte sloop.

The Isle La Motte Canal Sloop was the first sail canal boat found in the archaeological record when it was discovered in 1979 by a Canadian-American research team searching for a British sloop from the War of 1812 on a remote sensing survey.[17] The team originally recorded the site as a lake sailing vessel, as sailing canal boats had slipped into obscurity until the discovery of *General Butler*, which had both the characteristics of a sailing vessel and a canal boat. This led archaeologists to reevaluate the Isle La Motte Sloop, which revealed it was a sailing canal boat of a different style.

When archaeologists from the Musuem went to reinvestigate the site, they found documenting the construction of the bottom of the hull quite difficult, due to the presence of the vessel's cargo of heavy marble slabs. The sternpost was the only part of the vessel that could be documented from inside the wreck. The stem of the vessel was recorded from outside of the vessel, as a large marble slab sits on the bow of the deck, making diving inside the bow unsafe. While built before the ban on scow bows, the Isle La Motte Sloop was built with a molded bow and the stem that appears to consist of at least two pieces, a main post which contains the planking rabbet, and a false post attached to the main member's forward edge based on a line in the paint on the stem.[18] *General Butler* shows a similar pattern on its stem that led to the belief that it was made up of two pieces; however, further examination revealed that was not the case, as discussed below.[19] This investigation found that the hull was built using plank-on-frame construction, traditional for lake sailing vessels such as the wreck was first believed to be.

The identity of the vessel is still unknown to archaeologists, but historical research uncovered the cause of the vessel's sink as it was reported by the *Plattsburgh Republican* on September 5, 1846:

> *Accident. – Mr. Daniel Hall, an industrious citizen of this town, who was employed in carrying stone on a small sloop from Gilman's quary [sic] to the new Fort at Rouse's Point, was drowned on the night of the 2d. inst. When within a few miles of Rouses's Point a sudden squall struck his vessel, which was heavily laden, and in endeavoring to throw the anchor over he was caught by the cable, the vessel partly capsized, filled and sunk – taking him down with it. His son and another man who were on board, saved themselves with much difficulty.[20]*

Since the archaeology team was limited in its ability to document the internal structure of the Isle La Motte Canal Sloop, it was difficult to understand the nuances of how these vessels were built. This issue was suddenly and unexpectedly resolved when a second canal sloop was discovered in 1987 by a local sport diver near North Beach in Burlington, which was then investigated by a LCMM archaeologist. The North Beach Wreck, as it later became known, was found to have similar dimensions to the Isle La Motte Wreck but largely broken up and without cargo. This left only the bottom of the wreck, allowing archaeologists the opportunity to study the bottom of a sailing canal sloop. In 1991 LCMM hosted a field school with students from Texas A&M University (TAMU) and University of Vermont (UVM). The preliminary investigation at the start of this field school found that most of the bottom and sides of the vessel were still present, although they had fallen away from the bottom and were buried under a thin layer of sand. The only sections missing were the bow of the boat, the upper works, and the deck.[21]

While recording the wreck, the field crews found a series of iron fasteners that protruded through the sand. Clearing off the sand, they found that the hull was assembled using a technique called edge-fastening. This method uses thick softwood and hardwood planks stacked on top of each other and fastened together by drilling holes through the width of each plank and then driving a drift nail through the holes to join them together. This had been noted on the washboard bulwarks on the Isle La Motte Sloop but had not been seen before to construct the outer hull.[22] The discovery of this new method made this site one of great importance for future research to better understand how canal boats were designed and built. In the following year, the field school focused on exposing more of the hull to understand the details of edge-fastening.[23] The excavation found that between the layers of lake sediments there was a layer of sawdust. The sawdust layer in the sediment has led archaeologists to conclude that the North Beach Wreck must have been deposited in Burlington Bay prior to 1870 when the industry around Burlington Harbor was focused on milling Canadian lumber.[24]

The work on the North Beach Wreck has led archaeologists to better understand the construction methods used to build flat bottom canal boats used throughout Lake Champlain and the Champlain Canal. The core strength of the vessel came from a thick keel that was 75 feet 7 inches (23 meters) long. Since the stem has become disarticulated from the keel, the archaeologists were able to document how it was mounted to the keel. The stem sat on a small two-inch shelf on the top of the keel and was fastened against the forward face of the keel. The stem was reinforced with an apron that attached to the abaft side of the stem and the top of the keel. The remains of the apron are no longer present, but the bolts that held the apron to the keel still remain, and the bolt holes where the apron would have attached are still visible in the stem.[25] The keel at the bow has thirteen notches for floor timbers as well as a rabbet for the bottom planking of the vessel, but only the rabbet remains as the keel transitions into the cargo hold of the vessel. Each one of these floor timbers has a standing knee of futtock fastened to the forward face of the timber. Little of the stern remains, but the keel has nine notches that suggest it was built in the same manner as the bow. Despite this, the sternpost remains in remarkably good condition and was found approximately six feet (1.8 meters) away from the aft end of the keel.[26] The sternpost was attached to the keel with a mortise-and-tenon joint that was fastened with three treenails.[27] The cargo hold of the North Beach

Wreck is entirely chine-built and was supported by two stringers, one on each side of the keel, which ran from after the bow to forward of the stern. A second set of stringers between the keel and the first pair started after the bow and stopped before the centerboard trunk.[28] A portion of a keelson that was between the bow and the forward stanchion of the centerboard truck was found but was heavily deteriorated.[29] The only evidence of a keelson after the centerboard truck are the bolts that would have fastened it to the keel near the stern of the vessel.[30]

While the North Beach Wreck helped reveal much about the new ship construction methods that were being developed, the Pot Ash Canal Boat shows that they may not have been adopted quickly. The Pot Ash Canal Boat is the only 1841-class standard canal boat to be positively identified in Lake Champlain. This vessel is in an advanced state of decay, as only the bow remains intact as the rest of the hull has become disarticulated (Figure 10). Despite this, archaeologists were able to determine that the Pot Ash Canal Boat was an 1841-class, as it has an overall length of 80 feet 2 inches (24.4 meters), although they could not determine the beam of the vessel as the sides have torn away. The deterioration of the hull's sides caused the deck to collapse, which now lies on top of the vessel's cargo of quarried stone. While there are few structural components left to study, a feature that does stand out is that the hull was built using traditional plank-on-frame construction, which could indicate that the edge-fastening method was still not widespread by the time this vessel was constructed.[31]

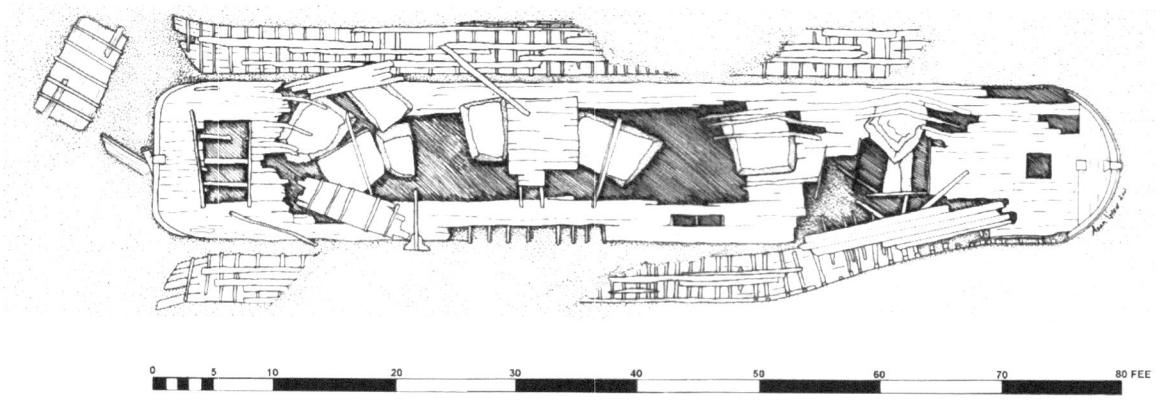

(Figure 10) Plan view of the Pot Ash Point Canal Boat site.

The First Canal Expansion (1858-1872)

The opening of the Champlain Canal was such a success that in 1835 an expansion plan was initiated. This program increased the size of both the canal prism and locks, thus enabling larger vessels to traverse the canal system. The new locks were expanded to 100 feet long (30.5 meters), 15 feet wide (4.6 meters), and a depth of 5 feet (1.5 meters), while the prisms had a top width of 50 feet (15.2 meters), bottom width of 35 feet (10.7 meters), and a depth of 5 feet (1.5 meters). The process was exceedingly slow, as the expansion of locks and dredging of the canal prism was completed only when the existing system failed or needed extensive repairs. This led the expansion to happen in a piecemeal fashion where the expanded locks were completed in 1858, but the canal prism was not completely enlarged until 1862. Meanwhile, the Canadian government completed construction of the Chambly Canal in 1842, which allowed unrestricted access from Lake Champlain to the St. Lawrence River and the Canadian markets to the north by bypassing the rapids of the Richelieu River. With the completion of this portion of the Champlain Waterway, an all-water route, reaching from New York City to the St. Lawrence River, had been realized; however, the delay in expanding the Champlain Canal locks allowed completion of an interconnected railroad network that was able to ship goods faster than canal boats. This left the heavier, less lucrative freight such as coal, stone, iron ore, and lumber to be shipped by canal boat.

Once the entire lock expansion was completed in 1862, canal boat builders began to design vessels to take advantage of the additional carrying capacity, which in turn allowed them to better handle the heavier freight they were shipping. The 1862-class of canal boats was longer, wider, and had a deeper hold. Canal boat dimensions increased to 83 to 87.75 feet (25.3 to 26.8 meters) with an average of 85.5 feet in length, 13 to 15 feet (4 to 4.6 meters) averaging 14.5 feet (4.4 meters) in beam, and depth of hold of 4.5 to 7.5 feet (1.4 to 2.1 meters) averaging 6 feet. (1.8 meters).[32] The combination of the expanded canal locks and shift in freight being shipped by canal boats saw the 1841-class quickly replaced by the new, larger 1862-class. In anticipation of the complete expansion of the Champlain Canal locks, and to take advantage of the locks that had been completed, some ship builders started to use these wider dimensions as early as 1855. The historical record reveals that the canal sloops G. H. Taylor and Rope were built in 1855 and 1857, respectively, using these new dimensions; however, not all ship builders were as quick to adopt these dimensions given the slow pace of the canal expansion. This is seen in the canal sloops Sam, built in 1855, and P. L. Gilbert, built in 1858, which were built using the 1841-class dimensions to make use of the full length of the Champlain Canal.[33] Once the canal expansion was finished in 1862, all canal boats were built using the new dimensions that filled the expanded canal locks.[34]

During this period, sloop rigging remained as the dominant type for the 1862-class of sailing canal boats; however, the historical record suggests that schooners were becoming more common. From the available records of one hundred and three 1862-class sailing boats, twenty of them were schooner rigged. The increase in schooner rigging could be due to the increase in vessel size, or that it had economic value as the two smaller sails has a sail area equal to or greater than sloop rigged canal boats, but required a smaller crew size. This reduced costs and allowed the vessels to charge lower freight rates which helped them compete against alternative methods of shipping, such as the expanding railroad networks.[35] Of the 1862-class sailing canal boat shipwrecks in Lake Champlain, two have been determined to be schooner rigged, *General Butler* and *O.J. Walker*, but the rest have not been determined due to their deteriorated condition.

General Butler was the first sailing canal boat of the 1862-class that was identified in Lake Champlain, when it was discovered at the Burlington Breakwater in 1980 by two sport divers who reported it to the Champlain Maritime Society. The archaeologists from CMS investigated the site and discovered a sailing canal boat, a type of vessel that had been forgotten to history. Through historical research they were able to discover that the wreck was the sailing canal schooner *General Butler* which led to the second investigation of the Isle La Motte Sloop, reclassifying it as an 1841-class sailing canal sloop. CMS researchers were able to identify the wreck from an

1876 newspaper article about *General Butler*. On December 9, 1876, *General Butler* was transporting thirteen marble blocks, weighing approximately thirty tons, from a marble quarry on Isle La Motte to the Burlington Manufacturing Company. Due to the narrow profit margin for marble and given that this would probably be the last shipment before the lake froze over, Captain William Montgomery decided to load twelve of the marble blocks in the hold and placed a thirteenth block on the bow deck.[36] On board, Montgomery had one crewman, his teenage daughter and her friend who were planning to do Christmas shopping in Burlington, and Elisha R. Goodsell, an Isle La Motte quarry owner who was going to Burlington to receive medical treatment for an eye injury. [37]

The weather that day was clear for much of the trip between Isle La Motte and Burlington Harbor, but as *General Butler* approached the north end of Burlington Harbor, a winter storm had set in. While navigating the storm, the steering mechanism failed, and Montgomery ordered a storm anchor to be set to allow him time to chain a tiller to the rudder stock as a temporary fix. As the storm grew in intensity, the canal boat was being pushed to the vessel towards the breakwater, while shredding the sails. In an attempt to avoid this Montgomery ordered the anchor line to be cut, which caused *General Butler* to crash into the breakwater. As the waves repeatedly slammed the vessel into the breakwater, the passengers and crew jumped from the boat onto the breakwater (Figure 11). All made it safely across except Elisha Goodsell who was knocked unconscious when he landed on the breakwater. As Montgomery jumped onto the breakwater, *General Butler* sank below the waves. Burlington residents gathered at the waterfront to watch in horror, including James Wakefield, the town's ship chandler, or a dealer of ship supplies and equipment. Wakefield was a veteran of the British Navy and had prevented a similar disaster at sea. Understanding that action was needed quickly, he commandeered a government rowboat with his son Jack.[38] The two rowed through the storm to reach the breakwater and rescued the stranded shipwreck survivors and brought them back to shore.[39]

(Figure 11) Painting of *General Butler* crashing into the Burlington Breakwater by Ernie Hass, in collections at the Lake Champlain Maritime Museum.

The shipwreck is remarkably intact considering the violent wrecking event and the shallow waters the vessel is sitting in, as the hull, deck, deck features, and sailing equipment are still present (Figure 12). This has led to *General Butler* being one of the most archaeologically investigated shipwrecks in Lake Champlain. The first season of work in 1981 found the tiller was chained to the rudder stock as a jury-rigged control mechanism to control the rudder, which further confirmed the wreck as *General Butler*.[40] Archaeological work in 1983, 1993, and 1995 focused on recording the hull to better understand the construction of sailing canal boats. By excavating around the stem, stern, and centerboard, archaeologists found that the hull is chine-built, but had several unique characteristics.[41] Similar to other canal boats, *General Butler* was built with a keel plank wider than it is thick, and a keelson to reinforce its strength. The keel plank only projects slightly beneath the hull planking of the vessel and does not have a rabbet for the garboard strakes to fit into as seen on traditional keels. Instead, the keel plank acts as a bottom plank and does not provide much in terms of longitudinal strength of the vessel and less for the lateral strength. Despite excavations around the centerboard, archaeologists have not yet been able to determine if the keel plank consists of more than one timber, or how the centerboard is fastened to it.[42]

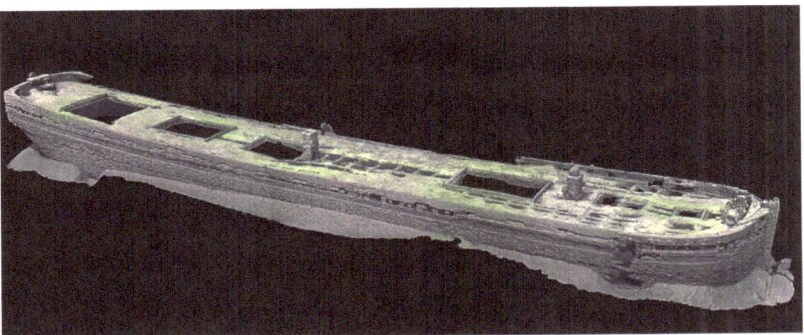

(Figure 12) 3D photogrammetric model of the wreckage of *General Butler* in 2021.

Excavations at the stem and stern revealed that the keel plank narrows at the two ends where it meets the stem and stern, revealing the largest differences between *General Butler* and the North Beach Wreck. The stem is made up of a post and an apron, and the post is butted to the end of the plank without a scarf. To secure the stem post to the keel plank, a flat scarf joins the post to the top and front face of the apron, which runs along the top of the keel plank for the length of 3 feet 7 inches (1.1 meter) and ends at the first floor timber. The apron tapers down from where it meets the first floor timber to the stem post, which continues to narrow down to its front face, giving the vessel a more hydrodynamic shape.[43] This helped provide the strength needed to support the unique bow shape that was first put into regulation in 1846. Since the stern has a more traditional shape, the sternpost is situated on deadwood that sits on the keel plank, as it does on most ships.

While the excavations around the frames were limited, they showed that the length of the vessel was chine-built, though it differed substantially from other documented wrecks such as the North Beach Wreck. *General Butler* was not an edge-fastened hull but instead had twenty-nine floor timbers that were fastened to the keel plank 2 feet (0.6 meters) apart, except at the bow and stern where they were closer and a gap amidship to make room for the centerboard. The frames were all flat and were 13 feet 6 inches (4.1 meters) in length and provided the latitudinal strength for a flat-bottom vessel. A keelson and two sister keelsons were added on top of the floor timbers to provide extra longitudinal strength.[44] On the outboard edges of the frames are the port and starboard chine logs that would allow straight futtocks to be added to create the hard chine of the boat and provided additional longitudinal strength, as they were more than twice as thick as the keel plank.[45] Rather than bolts, nails, and spikes, the floor timbers, chine logs, and futtocks were assembled using mortise-and-tenon joints.[46] Once this shape of the vessel was made, the hull and ceiling planking were added using square iron nails.[47] Although the reason for using plank-on-frame construction is unknown, as it meant a loss of cargo space, the decision to do so may have contributed to the crew and passengers escaping while *General Butler* was battered against the Burlington Breakwater.

While standard canal boats were in operation from the earliest days of the Champlain Canal, they were challenged by the lack of available tugboats to tow them on the open lake. By the 1840s that had changed, as line companies began building steam tugs using a brand-new technology, the propeller. This would add more competition to the sailing canal boats on Lake Champlain which were already challenged by the expanding railroads in the Champlain Valley. By 1866 the number of standard canal boats was almost triple the number of sailing canal boats, both sloops and schooners combined.[48] Today, only a few 1862-class standard canal boats have been found in Lake Champlain, one of the most well known is *L.A. Hall*.

L.A. Hall had been built in Whitehall, New York, in 1867, and measured 85 feet 6 inches (26.1 meters) in length, 14 feet 8 inches (4.5 meters) in beam, with a depth of hold 5 feet 9 inches (1.75 meters). On October 30, 1878, under the command of Captain Kane, the canal boat was in tow behind the steam tug *John F. Winslow*. The canal boat was carrying one hundred tons (90.9 metric tons) of pig iron loaded onto the decks. Around midnight Captain

Kane and his son were jolted awake by a horrible crashing sound. They ran out of the stern cabin to find that a portion of the pig iron had collapsed the deck of the canal boat and punctured the vessel's bottom. Kane and his son escaped only moments before the vessel sank. The wreck of *L.A. Hall* was relocated by the Museum in 1994 using side-scan sonar. The location, depth, and sonar image suggested the wreck was *L.A. Hall*, but video footage taken of the wreckage by a ROV proved it (Figure 13). The video footage showed the piles of pig iron stacked on the deck, and that iron stack amidship had caused the deck and a large portion of the port side hull to collapse under the cargo's weight. Due to the extreme depth of the wreck site, no further archaeological work has been conducted beyond ROV footage.[49]

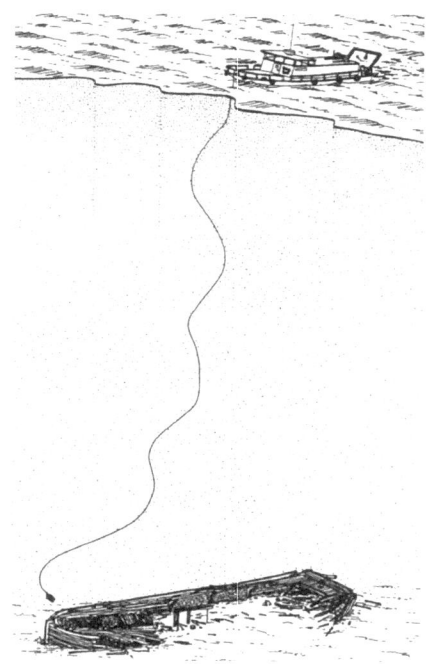

(Figure 13) Drawing of an ROV taking video footage of *L.A. Hall.*

The Second Canal Expansion (1873-1915)

The second expansion came about due to mounting pressure from politicians, boatmen, and shippers calling for New York State to increase the Champlain Canal to match the dimensions of the Erie Canal following its expansion that was finished in 1862. As trade and the local population continued to expand, the nature of industry in the Champlain Valley began to change. When the Champlain Canal opened in 1823, the focus of the Champlain Valley was on extractive industries, but it began to shift to manufactured goods as they became more lucrative due to their growing importance in the mid-nineteenth century. This was driven by the depletion of resources, particularly lumber, in the area and the opening of the Chambly Canal that brought Canadian lumber into the Champlain Valley to be milled. However, the commercial waterway and canal boat freight network faced increased competition throughout the end of the nineteenth century. The first of these threats was the rapidly growing improvements in efficiency and power of the railroads. The second was the discovery of cheaper sources of forestry, mineral, and agricultural products in other regions of the country outside the Northeast. To contend with this competition, pressure mounted to drop the cost of shipping on the Champlain Waterway by increasing the size and carrying capacity of the canals. The demand for reduced shipping cost led to the abandonment of tolls entirely in 1882.

Work to expand the Champlain Canal to match the size of the recently expanded Erie Canal began in 1864, just a few years after the first expansion was completed, and would not be finished until 1873. The Champlain Canal Locks were expanded to be 110 feet long (33.5 meters), 18 feet wide (5.5

meters), and 6 feet (1.8 meters) deep. Once again, ship builders constructed vessels that closely conformed to the enlarged lock dimensions with lengths that ranged from 91.5 to 99 feet (27.9 to 30.2 meters), beams of 15 to 18 feet (4.6 to 5.5 meters), and depth of hold from 6 to 8.5 feet (1.8 to 2.6 meters); however, by the 1870s, the economic advantage of operating a sailing canal boat had been lost to the completion of an all-rail route between New York City and Montreal.[50] This saw almost a complete shift away from sailing canal boats toward standard canal boats. The historical record reveals that at least fifty-three sailing canal sloops had their masts removed and were converted into standard canal boats.[51] The record is less clear on whether these were newer 1873-class vessels, or if they were older vessels that were still operating and needed to reduce their operating costs to make up for their smaller dimensions.

The Sloop Island Canal Boat is one of the best-preserved 1873-class standard canal boats in Lake Champlain and was the subject of an intensive archaeological investigation. The wreck was located by the Lake Survey in 1998, which showed a canal boat sitting completely upright. During a visit after its discovery, archaeologists collected preliminary data by recording video, taking photographs, and taking key measurements. A more detailed investigation took place in 2002 and 2003 as an agreed-upon mitigation for the environmental remediation work that occurred at the Pine Steet Canal Superfund Site.[52] The Sloop Island Canal Boat is estimated to be at least 95 percent intact, along with a substantial number of household-related artifacts of the family that lived on the boat at the time of its sinking. The vessel is 97 feet (29.6 meters) long, 17 feet (5.2 meters) wide and has a depth of 10 feet (3.1 meters). As with the previously mentioned canal boats that were largely intact, the internal structure of the Sloop Island Canal Boat was impossible to document due to the cargo hold being full of coal it was transporting at the time of its sinking.[53] Through the combination of limited excavations around the wreck and documentation of the exposed elements, archaeologists have been able to conclude that the Sloop Island Canal Boat is built with edge-fastened hull strakes.[54] This gives the vessel the classic box shape seen across many of the canal boats that have been found in Lake Champlain.[55] Similar to the North Beach Wreck, this vessel probably has a keel, chine logs, longitudinal stringers, and a keelson.[56] The tips of the stem and futtocks that support the bow are visible at the deck of the boat and show that it was probably constructed in a manner similar to the North Beach Wreck and *General Butler*.[57] While the stern of the Sloop Island Canal Boat is quite unique with an upper transom that curves upwards in the center and overhangs the vertical lower transom, the stern was not accessible to the archaeologists, so the structural assembly is still unclear.[58] The vessel probably has a stern assembly similar to the North Beach Wreck and *General Butler*. The Sloop Island Canal Boat represents the final iteration of wooden canal boat design and reveals which features ended up being the most desirable when building a Champlain Canal boat.

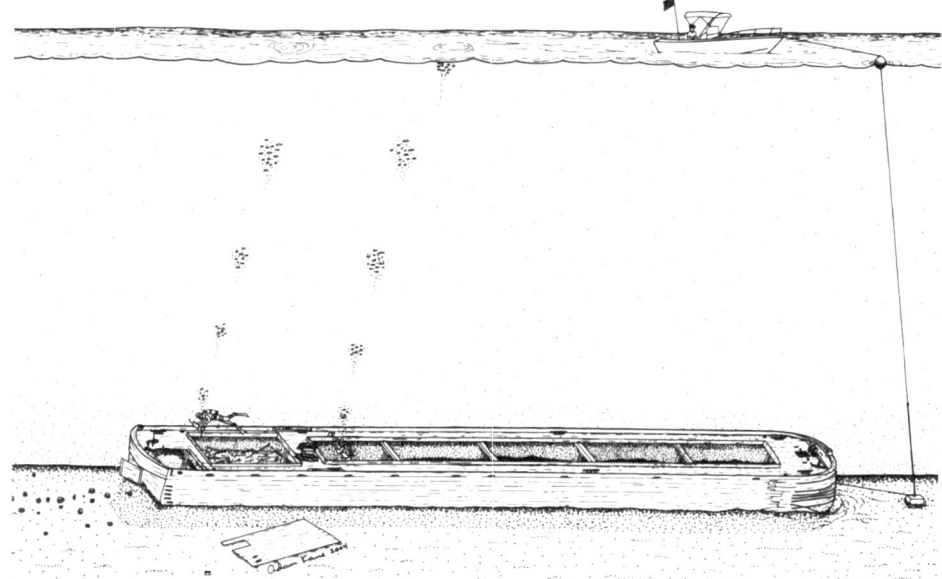

(**Figure 14**) Drawing showing archaeologists working on the Sloop Island Canal Boat.

The Champlain Barge Canal (1916-ca.1940)

In the decades following the completion of the second canal expansion, New York State faced new demands to increase the carrying capacity of the canals. This brought about the final expansion of the Champlain Canal into the New York State Barge Canal from 1903 to 1916, which led to the adoption of steel barges and signaled the eventual end of the wooden canal boat era. The Champlain Barge Canal opened in 1915 as part of the New York State Barge Canal System, replacing the Champlain Canal. It was furnished with concrete locks accommodating vessels 300 feet (91.4 meters) long by 43 feet 6 inches (13.3 meters) wide and drafting less than 12 feet (3.7 meters) of water. Bridges and overhead power and telephone lines limited the vessels to a height of less than 15 feet 6 inches (4.7 meters) at normal water levels. With the opening of the Champlain Barge Canal, the old Champlain Canal boats were no longer economical. Although several new boat designs appeared that could use the larger locks more effectively, the old Champlain Canal boats remained in use alongside these new vessels until the late 1930s. For these reasons the period of significance for old Champlain Canal boats ends in 1940. These wooden canal boats had one large hatch that ran the length of the vessel ending just forward of a crew cabin in the stern. Operation of the vessel was facilitated by a small walkway that ran around the hatch and the cabin. Photographic evidence suggests that these canal boats had flat transoms and lacked a rudder assembly altogether. This class of vessel has not yet been uncovered in Lake Champlain, but archaeologists have an understanding of the design of these vessels by examining the steel hull counterparts, such as *Day Peckinpaugh*.

Conclusion

Through the archaeological study of canal boat wrecks in Lake Champlain, supported by the historical record that is still available, archaeologists have been able to develop a thorough understanding of the canal boats of the Champlain Canal. This study was able to identify the economic pressures of the time as a motivator to expand the dimensions of the canal as well as the size of the boats that operated on it. Additionally, it revealed that there was much experimentation in the early days of designing the canal boats, with features such as the mast tabernacle and centerboard that quickly became standard assets of sailing canal boats. On the other hand, it also revealed that some methods, such as the edge-fastening construction method and choice of rigging, were much slower to take hold. While the edge-fastened standard canal boat appears to be the most common type by the time wooden hull canal boats would no longer operate on the canal, it is the stories of those who lived on these vessels that connect the people of the past to the present.

Endnotes

1   Joseph Cozzi, *The Lake Champlain Sailing Canal Boat*. (Texas A&M University, 2000), 68.

2   Adam I. Kane and Christopher R. Sabick, *Lake Champlain Underwater Cultural Resources Survey Volume IV: 1999 Results and Volume V: 2000 Results* (Lake Champlain Maritime Museum, 2002), 95-97.

3   Kane and Sabick, *Lake Survey 1999 and 2000*, 94-95.

4   Kane and Sabick, *Lake Survey 1999 and 2000*, 97.

5   Kane and Sabick, *Lake Survey 1999 and 2000*, 97-99.

6   Christopher R. Sabick, Anne W. Lessmann, and Scott A. McLaughlin, *Lake Champlain Underwater Cultural Resources Survey Volume II: 1997 Results and Volume III: 1998 Results* (Lake Champlain Maritime Museum, 2000), 134-140.

7   Sabick, et al., *Lake Survey 1997 and 1998*, 134-140.

8   Sabick, et al., *Lake Survey 1997 and 1998*, 134-140.

9   New York State Canal Board, *Rates of Toll, Canal Regulations, and Distances on the New York State Canals; as Established by the Canal Board, the Commissioners of the Canal Fund, and the Canal Commissioners, and in Force on Said Canals on the 15th March, 1833*, (New York State Canal Board, 1833), 11.

10   New York State Canal Board, *Rates of toll, canal regulations, and distances on the New-York State canals; as established by the Canal Board, the Commissioners of the Canal Fund, and the Canal Commissioners, and in force on said canals, 1846*, (New York State Canal Board, 1846), 81.

11   Cozzi, *Lake Champlain Sailing Canal Boats*, 71.

12   Cozzi, *Lake Champlain Sailing Canal Boats*, 72.

13   Cozzi, *Lake Champlain Sailing Canal Boats*, 71.

14   Arthur B, Cohn, *Lake Champlain's Sailing Canal Boats: An Illustrated Journey From Burlington Bay to the Hudson River*, (Lake Champlain Maritime Museum, 2003), 2003, 38-29.

15   Kane and Sabick, *Lake Survey 1999 and 2000*, 151-154.

16   Cozzi, *Lake Champlain Sailing Canal Boats*, 71.

17   Cozzi, *Lake Champlain Sailing Canal Boats*, 95.

18   Kane and Sabick, *Lake Survey 1999 and 2000*, 151.

19   Cozzi, *Lake Champlain Sailing Canal Boats*, 100.

20   *Plattsburgh Republican*, "Accident", September 5, 1846.

21   Cozzi, *Lake Champlain Sailing Canal Boats*, 120.

22   Cozzi, *Lake Champlain Sailing Canal Boats*, 120.

23   Cozzi, *Lake Champlain Sailing Canal Boats*, 122.

24   Cozzi, *Lake Champlain Sailing Canal Boats*, 124.

25   Cozzi, *Lake Champlain Sailing Canal Boats*, 125-126.

26   Cozzi, *Lake Champlain Sailing Canal Boats*, 126-127.

27   Cozzi, *Lake Champlain Sailing Canal Boats*, 126.

28   Cozzi, *Lake Champlain Sailing Canal Boats*, 129.

29   Cozzi, *Lake Champlain Sailing Canal Boats*, 137.

30   Cozzi, *Lake Champlain Sailing Canal Boats*, 137.

31   Kane and Sabick, *Lake Survey 1999 and 2000*, 64.

32   Cozzi, *Lake Champlain Sailing Canal Boats*, 75.

33   Cozzi, *Lake Champlain Sailing Canal Boats*, 76.

34   Cozzi, *Lake Champlain Sailing Canal Boats*, 76.

35   Cozzi, *Lake Champlain Sailing Canal Boats*, 77.

36   Cozzi, *Lake Champlain Sailing Canal Boats*, 152.

37   Cozzi, *Lake Champlain Sailing Canal Boats*, 153.

38   Cozzi, *Lake Champlain Sailing Canal Boats*, 153.

39   Cozzi, *Lake Champlain Sailing Canal Boats*, 155.

40   Cozzi, *Lake Champlain Sailing Canal Boats*, 160.

41   Cozzi, *Lake Champlain Sailing Canal Boats*, 160.

42   Cozzi, *Lake Champlain Sailing Canal Boats*, 162.

43   Cozzi, *Lake Champlain Sailing Canal Boats*, 163.

44   Cozzi, *Lake Champlain Sailing Canal Boats*, 172.

45   Cozzi, *Lake Champlain Sailing Canal Boats*, 168.

46   Cozzi, *Lake Champlain Sailing Canal Boats*, 168.

47   Cozzi, *Lake Champlain Sailing Canal Boats*, 173.

48   Cozzi, *Lake Champlain Sailing Canal Boats*, 79-81.

49   Kane and Sabick, *Lake Survey 1999 and 2000, 60-61.*

50   Cozzi, *Lake Champlain Sailing Canal Boats*, 82.

51   Cozzi, *Lake Champlain Sailing Canal Boats*, 82.

52   Adam I. Kane, Joanne M. Dennis, Scott A. McLaughlin, and Christopher R. Sabick, *Sloop Island Canal Boat Study: Phase III Archaeological Investigation in Connection with the Environmental Remediation of the Pine Street Canal Superfund Site*, (Lake Champlain Maritime Museum, 2010), 4-5.

53   Kane, et al., *Sloop Island Canal Boat Study*, 151.

54   Kane, et al., *Sloop Island Canal Boat Study*, 155.

55   Adam I. Kane, Christopher R. Sabick, Sara Brigadier, *Lake Champlain Underwater Cultural Resources Survey Volume VI: 2001 Results and Volume VII: 2002 Results*, (Lake Champlain Maritime Museum, 2002), 208.

56   Kane, et al., *Sloop Island Canal Boat Study*, 156.

57   Kane, et al., *Sloop Island Canal Boat Study*, 160-161.

58   Kane, et al., *Sloop Island Canal Boat Study*, 166-167.

Figure Citations

(Figure 1): Courtesy of Lake Champlain Maritime Museum collections.

(Figure 2): Courtesy of Lake Champlain Maritime Museum collections.

(Figure 3): From Kane and Sabick, *Lake Survey 1999 and 2000*, 98.

(Figure 4): From Kane and Sabick, *Lake Survey 1999 and 2000*, 100.

(Figure 5): Courtesy of Lake Champlain Maritime Museum collections.

(Figure 6): From Sabick, et al., *Lake Survey 1997 and 1998*, 135.

(Figure 7): From Sabick, et al., *Lake Survey 1997 and 1998*, 136.

(Figure 8): From New York State Canal Board, *Rates of toll, canal regulations, and distances on the New-York State canals; as established by the Canal Board, the Commissioners of the*

Canal Fund, and the Canal Commissioners, and in force on said canals, 1846, (New York, 1846), 81.

(Figure 9): Courtesy of Lake Champlain Maritime Museum collections.

(Figure 10): From Kane and Sabick, *Lake Survey 1999 and 2000*, 65.

(Figure 11): Courtesy of Lake Champlain Maritime Museum collections.

(Figure 12): Courtesy of Lake Champlain Maritime Museum collections.

(Figure 13): From Kane and Sabick, *Lake Survey 1999 and 2000, 61.*

(Figure 14): Courtesy of Lake Champlain Maritime Museum collections.

Bibliography

Cohn, Arthur B. *Lake Champlain's Sailing Canal Boats: An Illustrated Journey From Burlington Bay to the Hudson River*. Lake Champlain Maritime Museum, 2003.

Cozzi, Joseph. *The Lake Champlain Sailing Canal Boat*. Ph.D. Texas A&M University, 2000.

Kane, Adam I., and Christopher R. Sabick. *Lake Champlain Underwater Cultural Resources Survey Volume IV: 1999 Results and Volume V: 2000 Results*. Lake Champlain Maritime Museum, 2002.

Kane, Adam I., Christopher R. Sabick, Sara Brigadier, *Lake Champlain Underwater Cultural Resources Survey Volume VI: 2001 Results and Volume VII: 2002 Results*. Lake Champlain Maritime Museum, 2002.

Kane, Adam I., Joanne M. Dennis, Scott A. McLaughlin, and Christopher R. Sabick, *Sloop Island Canal Boat Study: Phase III Archaeological Investigation in Connection with the Environmental Remediation of the Pine Street Canal Superfund Site*. Lake Champlain Maritime Museum, 2010.

New York State Canal Board, *Rates of Toll, Canal Regulations, and Distances on the New York State Canals; as Established by the Canal Board, the Commissioners of the Canal Fund, and the Canal Commissioners, and in Force on Said Canals on the 15th March, 1833*. New York State Canal Board, 1833.

New York State Canal Board, *Rates of Toll, Canal Regulations, and Distances on the New York State Canals; as Established by the Canal Board, the Commissioners of the Canal Fund, and the Canal Commissioners, and in Force on Said Canals, 1846*. New York State Canal Board, 1846.

Sabick, Christopher R., Anne W. Lessman, and Scott A. McLaughlin. *Lake Champlain Underwater Cultural Resources Survey Volume II: 1997 Results and Volume III: 1998 Results*. Lake Champlain Maritime Museum, 2000.

CHAPTER 3
A Landscape of Change
The Topographical Impact of Human Occupation in the Region of Fort Edward, New York, and the Development of the Champlain Canal

---

Paul Willard Gates
Co-Director of Archaeology, Lake Champlain Maritime Museum

The Champlain Canal was an ambitious artificial waterway project undertaken by the State of New York to connect the Hudson River to Lake Champlain and beyond. The canal, and later the Barge Canal system, represents one of the most significant alterations of the landscape and watershed of the Upper Hudson River. From the initial planning efforts in the late eighteenth century until the augmentation of the system in the twentieth century, the canal system had a significant impact on local communities. Economically, the Champlain Canal was a boon to producers and industrial centers throughout New York State and provided a reliable and efficient means of transportation of both raw materials and manufactured goods. Villages, towns, and cities prospered as a result and rapidly developed infrastructure on and around the waterway.

The Champlain Canal served as a vital lifeline to Fort Edward and countless other towns in New York. It had a major impact on the physical landscape as well as the built environment. The cut and engineered artificial waterway allowed goods and raw materials into newer and previously isolated markets. Geographically, the locations of the Champlain Canal infrastructure were situated primarily along routes close to natural waterways. Fort Edward, for example, is situated along the western bank of the Hudson River in Washington County.

The location of Fort Edward along the Champlain Canal differed from the northern terminus of the canal at Whitehall, New York, as it is along one of the higher inclines of land. This meant that a reliable amount of water was needed to supply the canal at the elevation of Whitehall before the land began to slope downwards. With an artificial waterway in proximity to the Hudson River, it was not uncommon for flooding to occur in and around the Champlain Canal. During the earlier years of the canal, floods were so severe that parts of the canal were often disabled. There was also the problem of water leaking from the canal channel into the ground underneath due to the sandy and rocky consistency of the soil.[1]

Compounding the change in the topography of the terrain even more was the creation of the Barge Canal system in the early twentieth century. The larger system drastically altered the landscape of Fort Edward as deeper and more fortified channels and locks were needed to accommodate bigger, modern vessels. The Champlain Canal was a major feat of engineering and development that radically transformed the landscape of New York. However, the utilization of this canal system does not fully represent the trends of human use and occupation from the prehistoric era to the present. A much larger macrocosmic view of human impact and influence on the New York region tells us just how much the landscape of New York was used and transformed.

While the history on this subject matter is expansive, this chapter will focus on the town and village of Fort Edward as a key area during the development of the canal systems. Furthermore, the significance of the alteration and utilization of Fort Edward is not attributed to the canal alone. Archaeological evidence shows that for thousands of years, the area was used by the ancestors of the Alnôbak (Abenaki), Kanien' kehá:ka (Mohawk), and the Muh-he-conneok (Mohican) peoples. The study of the archaeological remains in the area denotes that Fort Edward was an important center of habitation for prehistoric peoples. The region also provided both natural and food resources and the nearby Hudson River served as a transportation route to other communities. Due to the location on the upper Hudson River, the area was a natural navigable waterway with portages to Lake George and Lake Champlain.

These local waterways provided an important navigation route for prehistoric peoples in the region of Fort Edward. This was essential for transportation, communication, and trade. The archaeological evidence demonstrates this, as traces of human occupation have been found, especially in later prehistoric eras to the contact period with European colonizers, of generational use and occupation of the region. Well into the period of European contact, colonizers also recognized the importance of the Hudson River in Fort Edward as a transportation corridor to the north. Various schemes of land grants from European countries and dubious deals with local Indigenous tribes began in the late seventeenth century to settle the region.

The landscape of Fort Edward slowly began to change during this time from a verdant wilderness dotted with seasonal Indigenous villages to a landscape occupied by permanent European settlements. Changing the landscape even more was the establishment of military fortifications developed by the British in a period of warfare with the French to establish control of the region. Trading posts were also developed along with a rudimentary network of roads for the movement of materials and people between forts and for military expeditions. This trend of developing military installations and support networks continued throughout the eighteenth century, though it declined in an era of peace after the cessation of warfare and hostilities from the American Revolution.

The nineteenth century witnessed continued settlement by Europeans and the town of Fort Edward quickly developed. The trend of using the Hudson River as a transportation route continued, though the falls at Fort Edward and other natural landscape features still posed an impediment. To circumvent these obstacles and allow for uninterrupted navigation through the region to the north and westward, the Champlain and Erie Canals were created. As an artificial waterway, the canals drastically altered the landscape throughout the rest of the nineteenth century and well into the twentieth century. The Champlain Canal ran directly through the middle of the town of Fort Edward and various industries and manufacturing facilities were developed. Fort Edward also served as a port for canal boats transiting through the canal system, with businesses and services to cater to hundreds, if not thousands, of vessels. This dynamic was vastly different from community development along the Erie Canal, where many towns and villages were created after the Erie Canal was finished.

Into the twentieth century, the Champlain Canal system expanded throughout New York State with the construction of the Barge Canal. The town and surrounding area changed yet again with the introduction of this larger canal system, including a junction lock for the new waterway located in Fort Edward. The older and smaller Champlain Canal section was still being used, though the vintage canal boats were no match in cargo capacity and design for the larger, more modern canal boats. Eventually, the older wooden canal boats could no longer compete economically and ceased to be used for commercial purposes. The older Champlain Canal was eventually abandoned, with various channels filled in to make roads and other infrastructure dismantled.

One of the most intriguing and fascinating aspects of the state of New York is the remains of the various sections of the Champlain Canal that still exist and can be seen in towns all over the state. Some of these features, such as canal channels, are unrecognizable, as they have succumbed to development and were filled in and made into roads. Other features are still extant today and have been commemorated through historical markers or incorporated into the public recreation pathways and trails. However, some of these features have not been given their due recognition or are forgotten as they are too far removed from the sightline of everyday life.

The sections of the Champlain Canal that survive today are a testament to the scale and magnitude of the construction efforts undertaken by the engineers, work teams, and artificers of the canal. While much of the history of the Champlain Canal and its construction is covered in Brad Utter's chapter, here we will examine the archaeological and historical remains of the cultural landscape of Fort Edward, New York. The importance of waterborne transportation is highlighted as a primary trend in the use of land from the prehistoric era to first contact with Europeans, and in the modern era. The changes in the topography of the region through time will be explored from era to era, describing the events that caused change and modification to the land. In summary, an assessment of the impact of human occupation in Fort Edward will be conveyed.

The Prehistoric Landscape of Fort Edward

The region of Fort Edward, New York, is part of the ancestral lands of the Alnôbak (Abenaki), Kanien' kehá:ka (Mohawk), and the Muh-he-conneok (Mohican) Indigenous territories of the twenty-first-century Indigenous Nations.[2] Because of the location of the Village and Town of Fort Edward along the Hudson River, it was significant to Indigenous peoples. The Hudson River was used for transportation at Bond Creek by portaging over the rapids to the headwaters of Lake Champlain. *Wahcoloosencoochaleva*, the name that Indigenous peoples called Fort Edward by, meant the "Great Carrying Place."[3] Waterborne transportation along this area was especially important during the seventeenth century when Indigenous peoples were at war with French and Dutch (later English) European colonizers vying to exploit and control areas of New York.

Though before the arrival of Europeans, Fort Edward and the surrounding region were occupied by prehistoric ancestors of Indigenous peoples.

Generally, the prehistoric record of New York State is separated into the Paleoindian, Archaic, Transitional, and Woodland periods. These periods span from approximately ten thousand years before present (B.P.) to about the beginning of the sixteenth century common era (C.E.). The sixteenth century C.E. is referred to as the Contact period. The term Contact is designated as when European colonizers arrived in the New York region, which is attributed to the arrival of Henry Hudson in 1609.[4]

While the archaeological record has revealed remnants of human occupation in the region of Fort Edward dating back to the Paleoindian period, much of the recovered archaeological evidence consisted of isolated finds. Small lithic scatter, or tiny collections of stone tool remains, provides more evidence of the presence of people in the area. Archaeological material relating to an initial, but small-scale, periodic occupation of the area is attributed to the Archaic Period. At this time, the environmental conditions were in the process of stabilizing and prehistoric sites in Fort Edward and beyond were used as seasonal hunting camps. Evidence of lithic projectile points in Washington County, such as the LeCroy Bifurcated Base, Hardaway, Side-Notched, Kirk Corner-Notched, Kanawha Stemmed, and St. Albans Side-Notched points, is representative of lithic tool manufacturing for hunting purposes.[5] While the names of these stone projectiles may be overly technical, they represent various types found in Fort Edward and beyond, suggesting a larger community network.

Given the proximity of Washington County along with the current Village of Fort Edward to the Hudson River, the area must have provided an abundance of food resources for people to use and exploit. Wild animals, nuts, plant roots, and other related edible resources supplied sustenance to peoples as they migrated into the area during favorable environmental conditions and warmer, drier times. Additionally, the Hudson River itself was likely a significant resource for people in the Middle Archaic period. Fish and shellfish collected, processed, and eaten in later precontact periods were probably available for supplementary dietary. The river itself was a resource to provide freshwater as well, perhaps even a transportation corridor for early watercraft such as dugouts and birchbark canoes. However, evidence of these types of watercrafts has not been found in the archaeological record of the immediate vicinity of Fort Edward.

Denser archaeological deposits in Fort Edward suggest a small, but gradual rise in the use and occupation of the region during the Middle Archaic period.[6] Seasonal hunting camps in the area were utilized by small concentrations of people. As the climate reached stabilized levels well into the Late Archaic period, people began occupying more permanent areas of habitation. Evidence shows that staple food crops such as squash and sunflower were domesticated. Variations in diverse types of projectile points found in the area suggest that local groups of people interacted with other groups located farther away. This was likely a purposeful development of distinctive stone tools to express group identity.[7]

The Transitional period and the Woodland period are marked by the continued increase in population levels. With this, the occupation during these eras was more semi-permanent rather than seasonal hunting camps. Evidence of larger-scale cultivation of plants such as maize, beans, squash, fruits, and nuts was found among the material remains of occupied sites.

A variety of faunal species suggests productive hunting practices of animal resources along with an increase in fishing from local waterways such as the Hudson River. Inter-regional lithic points, pottery, food processing materials, and other stone tools show that prehistoric peoples in Fort Edward were continuously efficient in resource extraction and trade.[8]

The Village of Fort Edward During European Settlement

The landscape of the Village of Fort Edward remained unchanged after the end of the prehistoric Woodland Period. Indigenous people still utilized the area for hunting, fishing, plant cultivation, and water-borne transportation. While the area and the larger region of the upper Hudson River was still a verdant wilderness, the arrival of European colonizers in the seventeenth century such as Henry Hudson, along with the Dutch, led to a small but continuous change in the landscape of the area. Historically, land procurement in what is now Fort Edward, and the surrounding counties was conducted through a series of "patents" granted by Dutch governors. Early records of these patents are documented in the New York State Library.

One of the first patents issued for Fort Edward was an individual grant to Reverend Godfredius Dellius, a minister for the Dutch Reformed Church at Albany, New York.[9] Hill notes that the patent was given to the Reverend on September 3, 1696, by Benjamin Fletcher, the colonial governor of New York.[10] However, the patent was obscurely drawn as shown on Figure 1, where the exact boundaries were not marked out. Records also show that a copy of the original patent described the areas as:

a certain track of land lying upon the east side of Hudson's river between the northernmost bounds of Saratoga and the Rock Retsso containing about seventy miles in length and [going backwards into the woods twelve miles from said Hudson's river until it runs into the Woods Creek] and [so far as it goes be it twelve miles more or less from Hudson's river on the east side] and [from said creek by a line twelve miles distant from said river.][11]

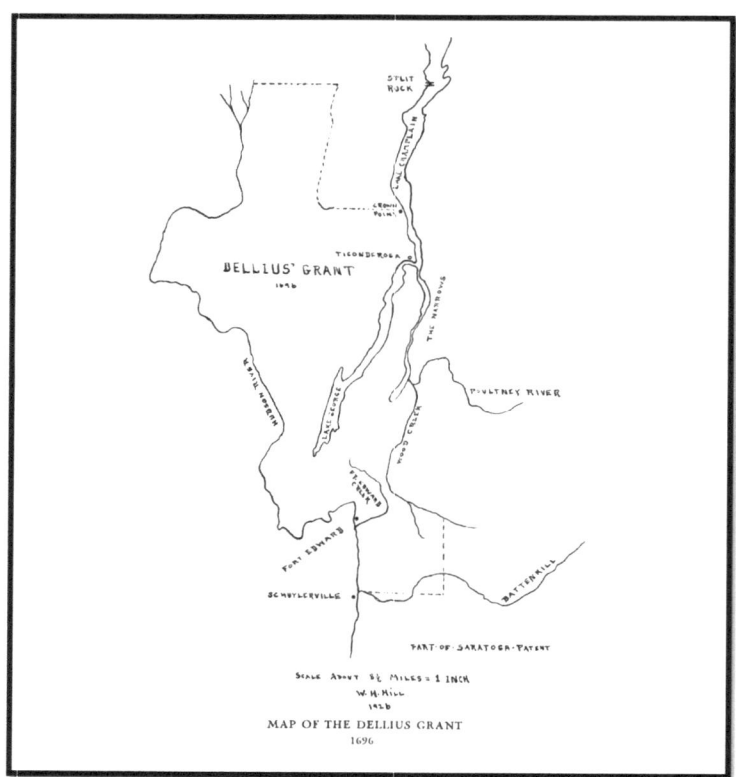

(Figure 1) Map of the Delluis Grant, 1696.

This amount of land was quite substantial. Furthermore, the patent states that all fordings, swamps, lakes, islands in the Hudson River, pastures, lumber, underwood, fields, etc., are included. The quitrent to the Crown, which was a rent paid for land, was to be one racoon skin per year payable "on the feasts day of the annunciation of our Blessed Virgin Mary,"[12]

The Dellius Patent, however, was beset with issues of deceit as Reverend Dellius claimed in 1699 that the land was purchased from the Mohawk tribe. When the governor at the time, the Earl of Belmont, inquired about this with the tribe, their representatives failed to uphold the claim. Suspecting the claim was fraudulent, the Earl of Belmont vacated the patent and claimed that such a large land grant would hinder further settlement of the region.[13] Well into the eighteenth century, various schemes to buy land in the surrounding region from Indigenous peoples continued. Many of these deeds conflicted with previous deeds. Additionally, some deeds such as the Kay-ad-ros-se-ra Patent of August 26, 1702, were suspect in the exact definition of the boundaries of acquired land, which Indigenous tribes claimed were misrepresented.[14]

The system of land granting through patents must have been understood as an alien concept by the Indigenous peoples of the region. Though rudimentary, the maps created to represent ownership and rights to the landscape introduced an additional foreign idea. Complicating the understanding of this system were the dubious methods of European colonizers to manipulate Indigenous tribes to give up their land. If anything, one potential factor of mutual understanding between local tribes and colonizers was the value of the region, given the Hudson River's proximity.

Warfare in the Hudson River Valley at Fort Edward

Even with the various land claims and patents, much of the area of Fort Edward remained uninhabited by European settlers until the start of Queen Anne's War in the beginning of the eighteenth century between France and England. Both countries laid claim to various parts of New York. The outbreak of active warfare between the French, British, and their Indigenous allies led to another change in the landscape and environment of Fort Edward. Due to the large volume of supplies, troops, wagons, cannons, and other provisions needed to sustain both the French and English armies, on-land transportation routes and fortifications were needed to move, provide, and shelter the armies. Well into this period, European military infrastructure and development began to occupy and change the landscape of New York.

During Queen Anne's War, Sir Francis Nicholson of the British military was sent to the Fort Edward area in 1709 to erect a stockade and build a road to Fort Ann.[15] This fortification was named Fort Nicholson after himself and consisted of rude log huts surrounded by palisades. While historical sources are lacking in further information on its development, the defensive work was more of a depot for supplies than a fort.[16] Despite the gaps in the historical record, Fort Nicholson and the cut road leading to Fort Ann along with another developed road leading to Fort Saratoga represented a useful series of land transportation routes and supply depots for the British army and its militias.

Fort Nicholson was only used for a period of several years. In that time, the fortifications served as an essential transportation hub for the movement of British expeditions and material against the French in Canada. In a letter dated September 14th, 1711, from Sir Nicholson to Governor Hunter, Sir Nicholson describes the importance of the fort as a staging area for a planned expedition to capture Quebec, Canada. In his letter, Nicholson states that he has "but fifty wagons and needs fifty more, as well as one hundred and fifty horses, because of the large number of batteaux and the quantity of provisions and stores to be moved."[17]

Batteaux were an important type of watercraft used by both the British and the French during this time. Vessels like these were needed for transport of troops, material, and provisions through Wood Creek, up to Lake George, and finally down Lake Champlain to Canada. Due to the poor conditions of the few established roadways, transport via water was a much more desirable option for the movement of the expedition. However, Sir Nicholson's mission to attack Quebec never transpired due to the loss of supporting British naval forces staged in the St. Lawrence River. Abandoning the prospect, Sir Nicholson traveled to Albany, New York, and destroyed many of the forts along the way, except for Fort Saratoga. After the destruction of Fort Nicholson, Queen Anne's War ended with the Treaty of Utrecht in 1713 and much of the initial British military infrastructure was abandoned.[18]

After the end of Queen Anne's war, a period of peace returned to the region of Fort Edward and the Upper Hudson River. Settlement by Europeans continued in the broader region as both the French and British continued to establish footholds in New York. In 1731, John Henry Lydius, a Dutch trader from Albany, constructed a fur trading post called Lydius House or Fort Lydius.[19] Accounts record that the Lydius House was likely a block type house used in previous construction methods for fortifications, with several outbuildings surrounding it.[20] The Lydius House was an essential trading post in the region and was profitable in selling goods to Indigenous tribes and settlers alike.

Later in the early eighteenth century, the region near Fort Edward experienced continued trends in European settlement with the establishment of the Argyle Patent. The Argyle Patent, as shown in Figure 2, was granted to over one hundred emigrants from Scotland between 1738 and 1739 and in 1740.[21] The scheme allotted a total of 142 "farm lots" consisting of 250 acres each and 142 "town lots" of 25 acres each, with some of the town lots situated along a "street" that ran east to west.[22] A number of these lots were located in the northern section of Fort Edward, with the extension of them from the shoreline of the Hudson River to the eastern boundary of the town of Argyle. While the settlement of the Argyle Patent did not fully succeed due to natural obstacles such as steep terrain, it did represent one of the first organized systems of European land ownership in the area.

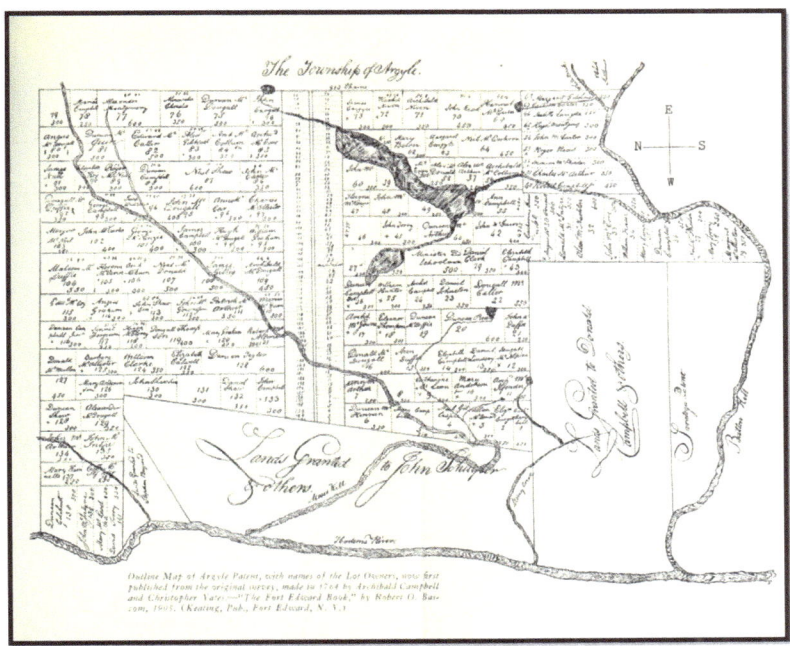

(Figure 2) Outline Map of Argyle Patent, with names of the Lot Owners, first published from the original survey, made in 1764 by Archibald Campbell and Christopher Ya'es.

While the region experienced a brief period of peace in the first half of the eighteenth century, the specter of war once again appeared as hostilities between the English and French renewed. At the start of the French and Indian War (1754-1763), Major General Phineas Lyman of the British Army, constructed a new fort on the site of Fort Nicholson and named it Fort Lyman.[23] The fort was constructed more heavily and reinforced than the earlier fortification. Shaped in as an irregular quadrangular form, the fort was protected to the east and west by the Hudson River and Wood Creek (now known as Fort Edward Creek). In circumference, the fort was 1,560 feet (475.5 meters) with ramparts at height of 16 feet (4.0 meters) with a thickness of 22 feet (6.7 meters).[24]

Major General William Johnson of the British Army later took command of Fort Lyman and changed its name one final time to Fort Edward (Figure 3), on September 21, 1755. This was in honor of Edward Augustus, the Duke of York and Albany, and grandson of George II.[25] Fort Edward quickly proved critical in the French and Indian War, both because of its strategic location and its size. It housed one of the largest British military encampments in the American colonies. It also served as a supply depot and featured the largest concentration of hospitals in northern New York. Sick and injured soldiers were transported there from other military installations. One of the hospitals was a smallpox infirmary, located at the southern end of Rogers Island.

Military activity at Fort Edward declined toward the end of the French and Indian War. Though the construction of the fort was completed at this time, correspondence between British Colonel John Bradstreet and Sir Jeffery Amherst in February 1761 noted that "no unnecessary labor" would be spent that year upon any of the Hudson River barracks.[26] With the end of hostilities, the British garrison at Fort Edward was greatly reduced. Throughout the years of 1761 to 1765, the fort was used primarily as a supply depot for British outposts on Lake Champlain and as a deterrent against Indigenous raiding parties from Canada. However, the garrison at the fort continued to decrease and the fort along with local roads fell into a state of decline. On March 15, 1766, "orders [were] sent to have Fort Edward evacuated," and the fortification was officially abandoned.[27]

During the American Revolution in the latter half of the eighteenth century, Fort Edward was again utilized as a military stronghold. However,

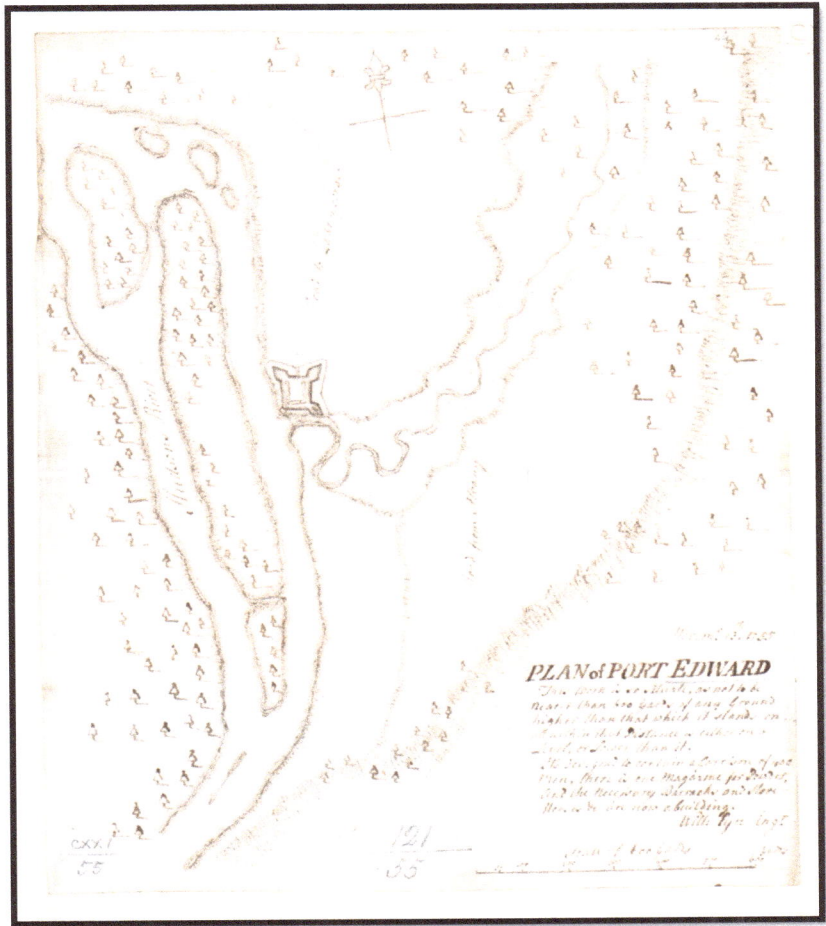

(Figure 3) Plan of Fort Edward, 1755.

during the intervening years of peace, the fort had fallen into disrepair, described even as "razed to the ground"; residents had removed stones for their housing.[28] General Philip Schuyler, commander of the Northern Department, wrote to George Washington that he had often galloped his horse in at one side and out at the other, over the ramparts.[29] The partially dismantled Fort Edward was defenseless. To strengthen the position, several blockhouses were erected on the elevated ground surrounding the fort. However, Schuyler eventually retreated to Saratoga, and Fort Edward came under British occupation. Several months later, Burgoyne's British army was defeated at Saratoga, the "turning point" of the Revolutionary War. The Town of Fort Edward was retaken by Americans October 10, 1777. During the war, the fort itself was little used, and in 1775, the Committee on Safety in Albany ordered any remaining fortifications to be razed.[30]

During the War of 1812, troops stopped at Fort Edward as they bivouacked on their way up to Plattsburgh.[31] There was little other military presence in the immediate area, however. Shortly after the conclusion of hostilities, the community around what had been Fort Edward began to grow as the nation settled into a time of peace and commerce. The town of Fort Edward was created by an act of the New York legislature on April 10, 1818.[32] By now, the fort itself was fully abandoned and left to be developed by citizens of Fort Edward. The fort casemate rooms were filled with sand and houses were built on top of the fort beginning in the mid-1800s.[33]

The Development of the Champlain Canal and the Barge Canal in the Village of Fort Edward

As early as the seventeenth century and back further to pre-Contact eras of habitation by Indigenous peoples, it was clear that the region of Fort Edward was an important part of the navigational channel now referred to as the "Northern Waterway." The natural waterway of the Hudson River was recognized as a transportation route towards Lake Champlain and the St. Lawrence river. However, the landscape in upper New York was difficult, varied in elevation, and had significant obstacles such as rapids and falls. Canals were already employed in Europe for efficient inland transportation through challenging terrain. This technology was envisioned as connecting the region of Fort Edward to natural waterways not only to the north, but also to the Great Lakes region out west.

The initial planning and effort to connect the Hudson River to Lake Champlain with canals began on March 30, 1792, when legislative action proposed the creation of a statewide lock system.[34] During the year, the Northern Inland Lock Navigation Company was contracted to handle the construction along with the Western Inland Lock Navigation Company. The latter was responsible for handling the construction of an artificial waterway from Albany to Ontario, Canada. As a joint business, both companies started construction in 1793.[35] However, the venture ran into financial trouble several years afterwards and no practical work was accomplished on the canal system.[36]

In the early nineteenth century, commissioners for the State of New York revisited the matter of creating a navigable waterway from the Hudson River to the Great Lakes and Lake Champlain. Realizing the importance of using existing natural waterways for transportation, the commissioners began discussing plans and routes for augmenting existing natural waterways in New York with constructed artificial ones. DeWitt Clinton, president of the Canal Commissioners Board, advocated greatly for the creation of a canal system. Clinton submitted his draft plan for the Erie and Champlain Canals, along with the financial pledges of interested New York citizens, estimated costs, and surveyed routes, on February 16, 1816.[37] The plan was approved by the state and represented the first publicly funded canal project in the United States.

A canal system connecting Lake Champlain with the Hudson River was authorized by legislation in 1817, and construction began on the Champlain Canal. Excavations at Fort Edward began on June 10, 1818.[38] By 1822, the canal route was opened from Whitehall to Fort Edward and it was completed to Waterford by 1823.[39] Figure 4 below shows the map and profile of the Champlain Canal at Fort Edward from 1820. This early map of a section of the overall canal shows the canal route connecting to the Hudson River and the area filled with forested regions. Figure 5 depicts a detailed survey of the canal within the boundaries of the Village of Fort Edward.

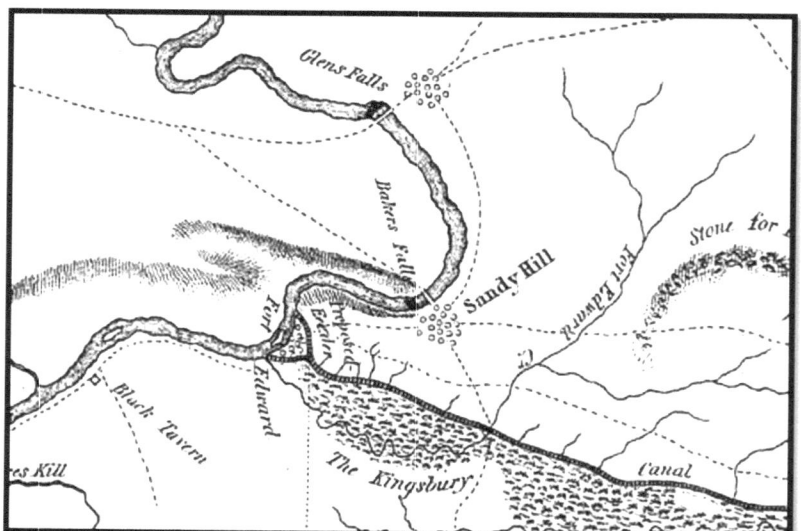

(**Figure 4**) Excerpt from "the Map and profile of the Champlain Canals made from Lake Champlain to the Hudson River and surveyed thence to the tide at Waterford," 1820 Jas Geddes.

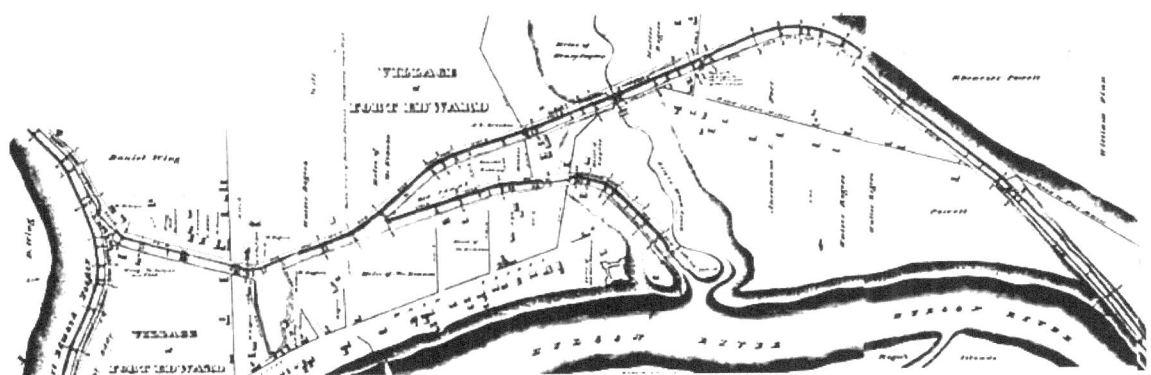

(Figure 5) Excerpt of "Champlain Canal from a survey made in conformity with SEC. IV, ART. I, CHAP. IX, TITLE IX, of the REVISED STATUTES of the State of New York" by E.F Johnson under the supervision of Holmes Hutchinson Esq. Civil Engineers, A.D. 1830.

Initially, the Champlain Canal was designed and built with specific proportions related to the sizes of canal boats in use at the time. The dimensions of the canal prism were 40 feet (12.2 meters) for the top width, 26 feet (7.9 meters) for the bottom width, and 4 feet (1.2 meters) for the depth. The dimensions for the locks were set at 90 feet (27.4 meters) in length, with a width of 15 feet (4.6 meters) and a depth of 5 feet (1.5 meters).[40] The materials used to construct the channels and locks were basic at first, consisting mostly of wood and stone masonry. Conversely, one of the most ingenious uses of canal building material was the introduction of hydraulic cement. This product was a self-hardening and waterproof cement patented by Canvass White, a contractor who worked on the building of the Erie Canal.[41]

Construction of these canal features was done at the expense of the laborers. Before the advent of steam power and heavy equipment such as dredges, excavators, and other machines run by steam, digging the canal was done by hand along with animal-powered equipment. The work would have been demanding and much of it was done by local laborers. Additionally, accidents were common along the construction corridor of the canal where embankments would fail and slide into dug canal prisms and channels. Newspapers and local residents along the entire length of the Champlain and Erie Canals reported accidents that occurred, yet the State of New York did not systematically keep statistics for accidents.[42] The exact number of workers killed or maimed during the construction of the canal system is not known and is a tragic result of the endeavor.

As the Town of Fort Edward developed through the 19th century, it became a central hub for the Champlain Canal. As shown in Figure 6, the town of Fort Edward had drastically changed from a small military post to a thriving community. The falls at Fort Edward, as seen on the lefthand side of the figure along the Hudson River, were developed to an industrial scale for the use of waterpower. The power generated by the Falls was used to operate a sawmill and the mill was referred to as the "Mill Yard."[43] In addition to the sawmill, a clothing mill opened in 1800, then a paper mill in 1832.[44]

Logs destined for the mills were cut down from the forest in the upper Hudson region. By early spring, the timber was floated down to the dam where it was confined by a boom until released for production. The Glens Falls Feeder Canal was established along with the dam at the falls at Fort Edward to augment water levels in the Champlain Canal.[45] The Glens Falls Feeder Canal developed even further to allow navigation of canal boats. The falls at Fort Edward developed even further to include a small port for transferring milled timber to canal boats. As the mills were in operation throughout the nineteenth century, it generated a continuous need for canal boats to ship wood products to faraway markets. One source noted that as many as fifteen canal boats were loaded weekly with products from sawmills.[46]

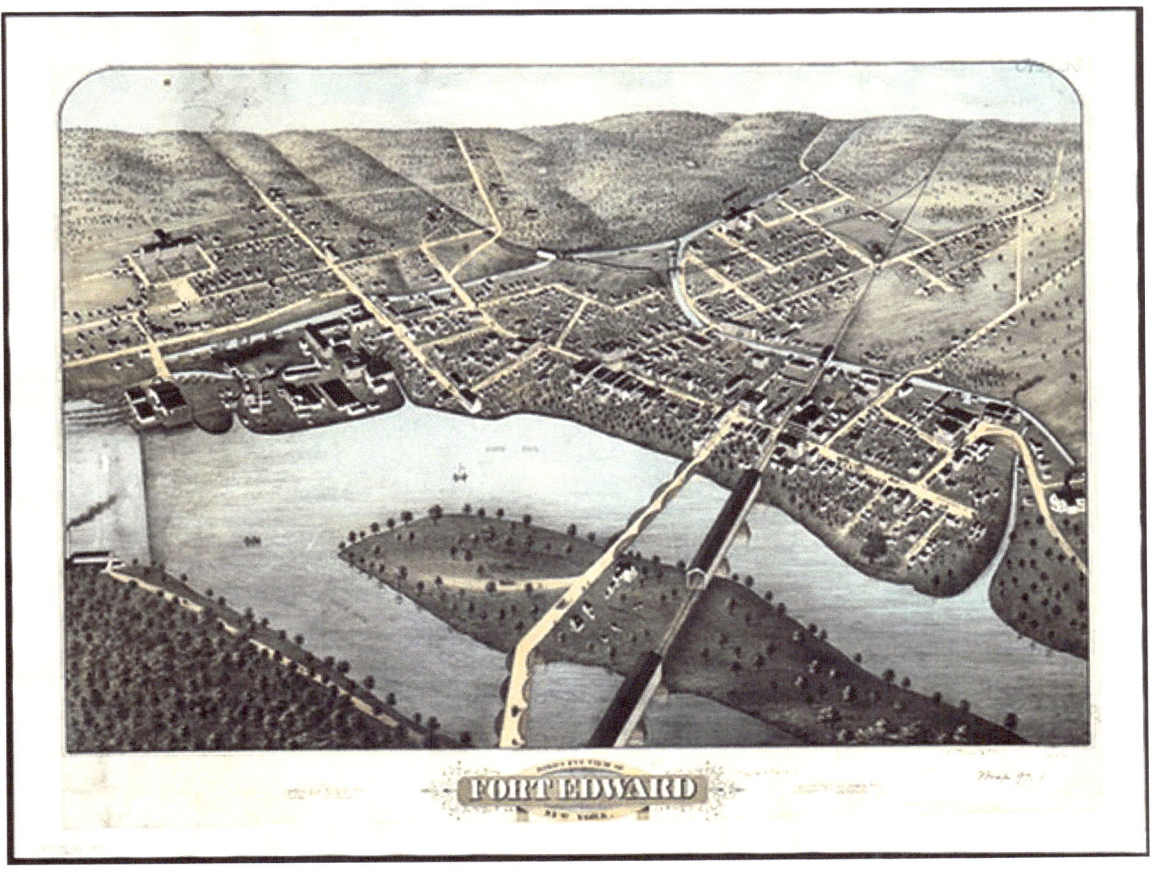

Figure 6. "Bird's Eye View Map of Fort Edward, New York," (H.H. Bailey and Company, 1875).

Other heavy industrial plants developed in Fort Edward with the Champlain Canal serving as a vital shipping corridor for production. In 1850, the Fort Edward Blast Furnace turned iron ore mined from Crown Point and Fort Ann into Bessemer pig iron (some of which was used in the Civil War ironclad *Monitor*) and shipped the iron south to Troy where it was manufactured into plates. The area also had a gristmill, a flour mill, a plaster mill, a sash-blind and door factory, and a broom and match factory.[47] Perhaps Fort Edward's most recognizable export was stoneware. The Fort Edward Pottery Company was opened in 1859 and manufactured clay from New Jersey into jugs, pots, bowls, and pitchers, and sold at markets across the Northeast. Although most of the potters worked with stoneware, only the Hilfinger Brothers produced earthenware pottery from native clay.[48]

Fort Edward prospered as a result of the industrial development propelled by the Champlain Canal. Along the canal route within the town of Fort Edward, smaller businesses developed as well. Boardinghouses, grocery stores, liveries, ports, and small wharves served as important businesses for the people working on the Champlain Canal. In addition to the ports and wharves where canal boats could stop, shop, load and unload cargo, there was also the boatyard of E.P. Heustis "on the canal above the brewery," and a dry-dock at the old lock.[49]. The region grew from a small northern community into a major port of call on an important and lively commercial route.

Toward the middle and the end of the nineteenth century, the Champlain Canal went through several augmentations. The first augmentation of 1835 included the expansion of the canal channel, the locks, and various other canal-related infrastructure.[50] The augmentation of the canal allowed for much larger canal vessels to be both built and used on this system. This gave commercial canals an advantage in terms of load capacity and in competition against older, smaller, obsolete vessels. However, as soon as the secondary expansion of the Champlain Canal was completed, a third and final expansion began in 1864 and was completed in 1877.[51]

The Champlain Canal continued to be successful through the end of the nineteenth century, though it became evident that the canals needed a significant overhaul and expansion. In 1903, enlargement and redevelopment of the Champlain and Erie Canals were approved as part of the Barge Canal Act. The construction of the Barge Canal represents a culmination of the economic growth created by the success of the original Champlain and Erie Canal waterways. As a completely new system, the Barge Canal, more specifically the Champlain section, ran 63 miles from Troy to Whitehall.[52] Construction started in 1906 and was completed by 1916, with the new prism dimensions tabulating at 12 feet (3.5 meters) deep, a surface width of 200 feet (60.9 meters), and 75 feet (22.8 meters) width at the bottom.[53] The locks' measurements themselves were unprecedented, with 12 feet (3.5 meters) of depth, 328 feet (99.9 meters) of length and 45 feet (13.7 meters) of width.[54]

The older section of the Champlain Canal that routed through Fort Edward was still being used during the construction of the new canal system. A junction lock shown in Figure 7 with the new Barge Canal was created at Fort Edward to allow access for vessels of nineteenth century vintage.[55] However, the new and improved barge system allowed much larger vessels clad in steel and propelled with onboard engines to supersede their older wooden-, mule- and rope-towed counterparts. Using all concrete construction with steel, as well as some of the original wooden gates, the improved locks now featured electric gates and water valve systems. With these new advancements in canal technology, the older Champlain Canal eventually fell into disuse, was closed in the 1940s, and was eventually filled in during the 1950s.[56]

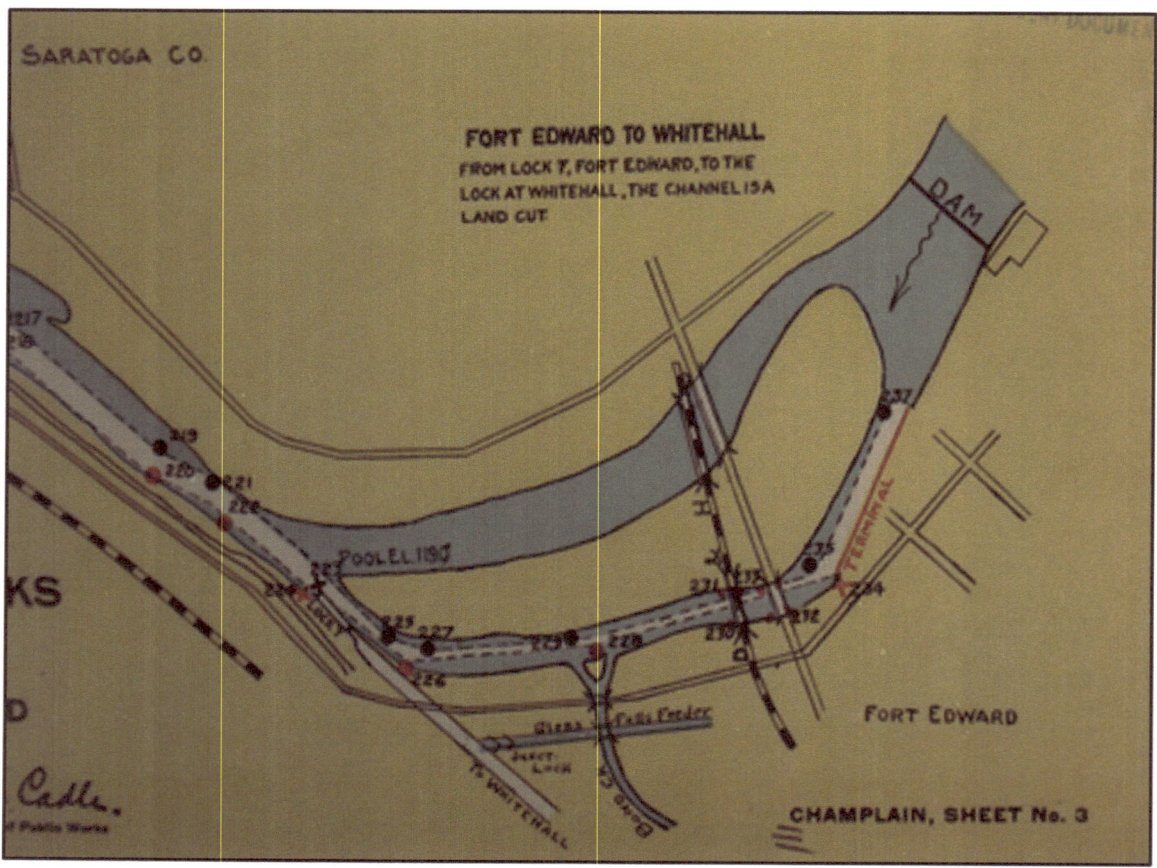

(Figure 7) Excerpt from New York State Department of Public Works, 1922.

Remnants of the Past: Surviving Infrastructure of the Old Champlain Canal

Today, the remains of the older Champlain Canal System are still visible in the landscape of the Town of Fort Edward. Though much of the historic infrastructure is in various states of preservation, it continues to have a presence. Studies conducted by archaeologists and historic preservationists on these features show the impact they had on the scenery and setting of the Town of Fort Edward as a major section of the canal system from the nineteenth century and early twentieth centuries. Studies also show the extent to which the current landscape absorbed the canal channel route and infrastructure into itself. Several sites from the older Champlain Canal are exemplary of this.

The studies were conducted on behalf of the United States Environmental Protection Agency (USEPA), the New York State Department of Environmental Conservation (NYSDEC), the New York State Historic Preservation Offices (NYSHPO), and the Town of Fort Edward for Phase 1 of the Hudson River PCBs Superfund Site Remediation Project. As part of a Memorandum of Agreement among the above entities, stipulations were implemented for data recovery and other mitigative measures as a consequence of unavoidable and adverse effects on significant historic properties located within the dredging corridor of the Hudson River. This report was compiled in accordance with the following stipulation: "A survey of the section of the Champlain Barge Canal in the area of the village of Fort Edward, Washington County, New York, with the purpose of inventory and recordation of structural features of the canal, including locks, feeders, piers, etc. Supplemented by historic documentation (narrative text, historic maps, photographs, drawing, etc.), this report will become available to the public through libraries, museums, state archives, historical societies, and other educational institutions."[57]

As mentioned previously, the construction of the new Barge Canal through Fort Edward included the development of a junction lock connecting to the old Champlain Canal. As shown in Figure 8, the new lock connecting to the older lock involved deep excavation into the soil just off the old canal channel. The figure also exhibits the scale of this part of the Barge Canal construction project along with the type and amount of labor put into it. Figure 9 depicts the junction lock remains from archaeological studies done in 2012. The comparison of historical photographs with modern digital photographs is important, as it highlights the historical landscape of a section of the old Champlain Canal and the changes that ensued after it fell into disuse.

Remarkably, much of the original lock entrance, exit, and walls were in relatively fair condition, with the extant infrastructure measuring approximately 6 feet (1.8 meters) in height and approximately 100 feet (30.4 meters) in length. Some of the original hardware used in the operation of the lock, such as lock door hinges, the recesses for the lock doors, bollards for tying off vessels, and the valve systems for filling and emptying the lock, are still present. The channel of the junction lock is covered with a mix of modern fill and debris, likely burying deeper sections of the junction lock. Graffiti along with crumbling/cracked cement mars most of the surface of the junction lock.

Site 5A-D is a single-arch aqueduct following the canal bed north, passing over Little Wood Creek. This small tributary of the Hudson River was known as Bond Creek or Fort Edward Creek. The extant aqueduct replaced two earlier versions of the structure.[58] The first aqueduct was built in 1827 in order to allow the creek to flow under the canal.[59] The original was replaced in 1837 due to damage from flooding, and a masonry culvert was added a year later. The last version of the aqueduct was built in 1869, with an additional arched culvert built in 1868.[60] It was made out of heavy stone (local quarried dolomite) with concrete abutments on the northern and southern sides. While some of the blocks had shifted from their original orientation, it was still stable and safe for foot traffic. There was a good deal of vegetation and overgrowth around the area, and refuse was scattered throughout the site.

(Figure 8) Construction of junction lock, 1908.

(Figure 9) Profile view of the Fort Edward Junction Lock,1-A, facing North.

(Figure 10) Bond Creek aqueduct, 1900.

(Figure 11) Profile view of single arch aqueduct, Site 5A, facing northeast.

Site 10 is the former canal channel, which, when filled, followed the path of modern-day Canal Street as it ran north/northwest from the intersection of modern Notre Dame Street. A sizable portion of both eastern and western walls was visible and structurally sound. While sections of the retaining walls that were visible seemed stable, there was evidence of decay in some areas. A concrete cap lined both walls. Where exposed, there was less than two feet of wall visible. Much of the canal channel was filled in and paved over.

(Figure 12) Champlain Canal from Notre Dame Street, late nineteenth/early twentieth century.

(Figure 13) Profile view of canal channel, bed, and wall, Site 10, facing north-northeast.

Site 21 is a well-preserved lock located northwest of the intersection of modern-day Culver and McKee Streets. Historical evidence indicates this lock was part of the 1858 expansion of the Champlain Canal.[61] It measured 100 feet (30.480 meters) in length, 15 feet (4.572 meters) wide, and 5 feet (1.524 meters) in depth at that time.[62] The current condition of the lock was similar to what it would have looked like while it was in operation, though it is now overgrown with vegetation and much of the working hardware is missing.

(Figure 14) Champlain Canal from Spruce Street looking north, late nineteenth/early twentieth centuries.

(Figure 15) Profile view of canal channel, bed, and walls, Site 21, facing north.

The 1858 lock was more or less structurally sound, with the exception of the northeastern corner, which is broken and crumbling. Other areas of the walls exhibited mild deterioration and are covered with graffiti. The original doors, gates, and associated mechanisms were not present with the exception of some iron hardware located on the top of the walls. Vegetative growth ran unchecked amid the interior of the lock and along its sides. Along with the modern fill in the lock, there was a significant amount of trash and debris littered all around the area. Towards the northern end of the lock there was a large concrete retaining wall used to cut off this section of the canal. This modern feature was installed when the Champlain Canal went out of use in the 1940s to 1950s.

Impact on Landscape, Environment, and People.

When New York State legislators passed an appropriation bill to fund the building of a navigable waterway connecting the lower Hudson River with Lake Champlain, it created one of the most comprehensive construction projects of the time. It is worth noting that there were no modern machines or equipment available to dig the canal. Work was done by hand. This project drastically changed the local landscape. Where there would have been open land, fields, woodlands, natural waterways, and even cities, towns, and villages, a massive 64-mile canal consisting of 46.5 miles of artificial channel and 17.5 miles of improved river was planned and built instead.

Due to the varying degrees of elevation and changes in the natural landscape, cutting the canal was quite difficult. This presented a problem because the canal never followed a direct path and needed to be within close proximity to a major river (i.e., the Hudson) in order to provide a consistent source of water to maintain the correct level in the canal. The people working used picks, shovels, and wheelbarrows to remove the earth and create the canal prism. One account recalled that only "one set of surveyor's instruments is used, very few engineers are needed." Without heavy dredges, machinery, or the engines to run them, creating the Champlain Canal was intense and backbreaking work which relied solely on the labor of many workers.

This impressive feat created an artificial navigable waterway that allowed vast quantities of goods to be shuttled inland more easily and cost-effectively than by the traditional means of using horse/ox and wagon teams. This waterway also helped give rise to industries along its corridor, such as mills, coal depots, storage houses, etc. The impact of the Champlain included drastic changes not only to the landscape but to the economy as well. The National Park Service described the historical and architectural resources of the town of Moriah, Essex County, New York, as follows:

> In 1824 the opening of the Champlain Canal imparted a new character to the lumbering operations of northern New York State. By 1833, 36 sawmills were operating in Moriah, with Moriah Corners continuing as the civic, commercial, and religious center of the town. The Champlain Canal also sparked interest in the commercial possibilities of the town's iron resources. In 1824, the town's first blast furnace was constructed in the northern section of Port Henry. Ore was procured two miles north of Port Henry at the Cheever Mine. The ore bed sat on what would become

Mineville, six miles inland, were also being explored during the early 1820's. [63]

The Champlain Canal was able to provide a major economic boost not only for a town like Moriah, New York, but for the entire Champlain Valley region. This was especially true for Fort Edward, which experienced tremendous economic growth due to the exponential increase in commerce and trade. Lumber mills and packet services were particularly vibrant along with the transportation of lime, grain, plaster, marble, and other raw materials. In 1823, the receipts from freight moved along the Champlain Canal totaled $26,000.[64] The years of 1866 through 1868 generated $200,000 in tolls, and in the following year the amount of revenue collected had paid for the original expense of the canal, which was $1,000,000.[65] With the amount of money being generated annually, tolls were eliminated in the 1880s.

Conclusion

The Champlain Canal was an ambitious artificial waterway project undertaken by the State of New York to connect the Hudson River to Lake Champlain and beyond. Even the ancestors of prehistoric people recognized the importance of the area as a vital transportation network. The land is culturally significant for the local Indigenous peoples and represented a geographically natural waterway that provided a route to the south along the upper to lower Hudson River. Passage to the north started through the rapids toward Lake George, and led finally Lake Champlain. One can imagine just how vital this corridor was to prehistoric people for communication, passage, and as a link to faraway communities.

European colonization and warfare brought about change in the landscape. Dubious and fraudulent practices of landownership continued to claim land from Indigenous people, which further altered the landscape with the propagation of European settlements in the ensuing pre- and post-war years. The development of military infrastructure such as forts and roads left a lasting legacy in Fort Edward. This expansive network also relied upon the Hudson River as a link to other riverine and lake corridors extending as far as the northeastern Canadian continental shoreline of the Atlantic Ocean.

Fort Edward, like many other towns and cities along major waterways like the Hudson River and the Mohawk River in New York, continued to be utilized for transportation well into the nineteenth century. The introduction of newer European technologies like inland canals caused places like Fort Edward to be radically changed. This Erie and Champlain Canal system represented one of the most significant alterations of the landscape and watershed of the upper Hudson River. The physical cuts made into the Village of Fort Edward and the surrounding region such as Glens Falls allowed for navigation of early canal boats and packet boats to the interior of New York State. This artificial waterway meant that natural transportation routes such as the Hudson River and other major waterways could be avoided, as a fixed route was created to connect the western part of the state toward the Great Lakes.

The success of the Champlain Canal in Fort Edward perpetuated the expansion of the canal system well into the nineteenth century. As the size of the infrastructure increased, so did the development of local industries and manufacturing. Fort Edward served as a port for canal boats transiting through the canal system to facilitate the movement of raw materials and processed goods. Compounding the change in the topography even more was the creation of the Barge Canal system in the early twentieth century. The larger system drastically altered the landscape of Fort Edward as deeper and more fortified channels and locks were needed to accommodate bigger, modern vessels.

Today, vestiges and traces of the older Champlain Canal system are still visible in the landscape of the Town of Fort Edward. Both archaeological and historical research serve as evidence of change in the landscape. Assessing this valuable data through investigations is important for our understanding of landscape changes in the region because it shows the impact of human occupation and the decisions people made to exert control over the natural environment. The scale and size of the older Champlain Canal and the Barge Canal alone are an indication of just how far people went to modify and adapt land to suit their needs. Factors like how we continue to change the landscape and the decisions made in the management of our collective history. Perhaps we will still see these artifacts and relics of the past in the future.

Endnotes

1   Michael LaCross, *A History of the Glens Falls Feeder Canal: Featuring information on the Champlain Canal, the Champlain Barge Canal, and the Fort Edward Feeder Canal* (Feeder Canal Alliance, New York, 2001), 3, 6.

2   "Dispossession of Indigenous Lands Map: Generalized Locations of Indigenous Territories and 21-Century Indigenous Nations," New York State Museum, accessed July 21, 2024, https://nysm.nysed.gov/native-american-heritage-month/indigenous-lands-dispossession-map.

3   William H. Hill, *Old Fort Edward Before 1800* (privately printed, 1929), 8, 63-64.

4   Nancy L. Davis et al., "Cultural Resources Data Recovery and Monitoring Report of the Fort Edward Village Site, Fort Edward Feeder Canal Bridge Site, and Hilfinger Pottery Site, Town and Village of Fort Edward, Washington County, New York," *Cultural Resource Survey Program Series*, no. 8 (2015): 21-25.

5   David Starbuck, *Rangers and Redcoats on the Hudson: Exploring the Past on Rogers Island, the Birthplace of the US Army Rangers* (University Press of New England, 2004), 1.

6   Nancy L. Davis et al., "Cultural Resources Data Recovery and Monitoring Report," iv.

7   Nancy L. Davis et al., "Cultural Resources Data Recovery and Monitoring Report," 22.

8   Nancy L. Davis et al., "Cultural Resources Data Recovery and Monitoring Report," 23-25.

Joel W. Grossman, Lucille L. Johnson, and Dorothy M. Peteet. "The Archaeology of Little Wood Creek: New Chronometric Evidence." *Archaeology of Eastern North America*, no. 42 (2015), 173-174.

9   Robert O. Bascom. *The Fort Edward Book: Containing Some Historical Sketches, with Illustrations, and Family Records*. (J. D. Keating, 1903), 31. Hill, *Old Fort Edward Before 1800*, 12-13.

10   Hill, *Old Fort Edward Before 1800*, 13.

11   Hill, *Old Fort Edward Before 1800*, 13.

12   Hill, *Old Fort Edward Before 1800*, 13.

13   Bascom, *The Fort Edward Book*, 31. Hill, *Old Fort Edward Before 1800*, 14.

14   Hill, *Old Fort Edward Before 1800*, 15.

15   Hill, *Old Fort Edward Before 1800*, 20.

16   Hill, *Old Fort Edward Before 1800*, 20.

17   Hill, *Old Fort Edward Before 1800*, 21.

18   Hill, *Old Fort Edward Before 1800*, 22.

19   Washington County Planning Department, *An Introduction to Historic Resources in Washington County, New York* (Dodge-Graphic Press, 1976), 48.

20   Hill, *Old Fort Edward Before 1800*, 29-30.

21   Bascom, *The Fort Edward Book*, 1903, 35-42. Jennie M. Patten and Andrew Graham, *History of the Somonauk United Presbyterian Church near Sandwich, De Kalb County, Illinois with Ancestral Lines of the Early Members*. (Privately Printed, 1928), 296.

22   Bascom, *The Fort Edward Book*, 35.

23   Crisfield Johnson. *History of Washington Co., New York: With Illustrations and Biographical Sketches of Some of Its Prominent Men and Pioneers*. (Everts & Ensign, 1878), 20.

24   Johnson, *History of Washington Co., New York*, 20.

25   Johnson, *History of Washington Co., New York*, 23. Washington County, *An Introduction to Historic Resources*, 48.

26   Hill, *Old Fort Edward Before 1800*, 243.

27   Hill, *Old Fort Edward Before 1800*, 244.

28   Hill, *Old Fort Edward Before 1800*, 287.

29   Johnson, *History of Washington Co., New York*, 316.

30   Hill, *Old Fort Edward Before 1800*, 287, 327, 333.

31   Anne E. Brislin, *Narratives of Old Fort Edward* (Fort Orange Press, 1962), 38.

32   Bascom, *The Fort Edward Book*, 5.

33   David R. Starbuck, *The Great Warpath: British Military Sites from Albany to Crown Point* (University Press of New England, 1999), 77.

34   Open Library, "State of New-York. An act for establishing and opening lock navigation within the state," Accessed March 4th, 2025, http://openlibrary.org/books/OL18187085M/State_of_New-York._An_act_for_establishing_and_opening_lock_navigation_within_the_state.

35   LaCross, *A History,* 3.

36   LaCross, *A History,* 3.

37   DeWitt Clinton, "Memorial of the Citizens of New York, In Favour of a Canal Navigation between the Great Western Lakes and the Tide-Waters of the Hudson." (paper presented at a meeting for the legislature of the state of New York, Albany, NY February 16th, 1816).

38   Arthur B. Cohn, *Lake Champlain's Sailing Canal Boats: An Illustrated Journey from Burlington Bay to the Hudson River* (LCMM, 2003), 38.

39   Johnson, *History of Washington County,* 318.

40   Cohn, *Lake Champlain's Sailing Canal Boats,* 38.

41   Robert H. Smith, *Clinton's Ditch : The Erie Canal -- 1825 A Short History of the Development of the Erie Canal* (C Books, 2010) 46.

42   Carol Sheriff. *The Artificial River: The Erie Canal and the Paradox of Progress, 1817-1862.* (Straus and Giroux, 1997), 52, 231.

43   Brislin, *Narratives of Old Fort Edward*, 17.

44   Washington County, *An Introduction,* 49.

45   LaCross, *A History,* 4-6.

46   Brislin, *Narratives of Old Fort Edward*, 17.

47   Brislin, *Narratives of Old Fort Edward*, 17.

48   Washington County, *An Introduction,* 49-50.

49   Johnson, *History of Washington County,* 320.

50   Cohn, *Lake Champlain's Sailing Canal Boats*, 40.

51   Cohn, *Lake Champlain's Sailing Canal Boats,* 41.

52   Michele C. McFee, *A Long Haul: The Story of the New York State Barge Canal* (Purple Mountain Press, 1998), 53.

53   LaCross, *A History,* 17.

54   LaCross, *A History,* 17.

55   McFee, *A Long Haul,* 66.

56   Paul Willard Gates, information taken from personal interview with Mr. Bill Munoff

on September 14, 2012.

57   Paul Willard Gates, Alex W. Lehning, Adam I. Kane, Christopher R. Sabick, Sarah Tichonuk, and Joanne Dennis. "A Historic Resources Inventory of the Champlain & Feeder Canal Infrastructure in the Village of Fort Edward, New York," (Lake Champlain Maritime Museum, 2013), 11.

58   LaCross, *A History,* 6.

59   LaCross, *A History,* 6, 9, 12-13.

60   State Engineer and Surveyor's Maps -- Plans for Improvement, Maps Accompanying the Annual Report of the Superintendent of Public Works NYS, New York State Dept. of Public Works Maps, 1868.

61   Cohn, *Lake Champlain Sailing Canal Boats,* 40.

62   Cohn, *Lake Champlain Sailing Canal Boats,* 40.

63   United States Department of the Interior, National Parks Service, "National Register Of Historic Places Multiple Property Documentation Form," Accessed March 5, 2025, http://pdfhost.focus.nps.gov/docs/NRHP/Text/64500457.pdf.

64   LaCross, *A History,* 5.

65   LaCross, *A History,* 5.

Figure Citations

(Figure 1): Courtesy of Hill, 1929.

(Figure 2): First published in Robert O. Bascom, *The Fort Edward Book: Containing Some Historical Sketches, with Illustrations, and Family Records*. (J. D. Keating, 1903). Courtesy of Keating, (Patten and Graham, 1928).

(Figure 3): Courtesy of Eyre, 1755.

(Figure 4): Courtesy of New York Public Library.

(Figure 5): E.F Johnson, Holmes Hutchinson, "Champlain Canal from a survey made in conformity with SEC. IV, ART. I, CHAP. IX, TITLE IX, of the REVISED STATUTES of the State of New York", 1830. Courtesy of New York State Archives.

(Figure 6): Courtesy of H.H. Bailey & Company.

(Figure 7): Courtesy of New York State Archives.

(Figure 8): Courtesy of Old Fort House Museum.

(Figure 9): Courtesy of Lake Champlain Maritime Museum.

(Figure 10): Courtesy of Old Fort House Museum.

(**Figure 11**): Courtesy of Lake Champlain Maritime Museum.

(Figure 12): Courtesy of Old Fort House Museum.

(Figure 13): Courtesy of Lake Champlain Maritime Museum.

(Figure 14): Courtesy of Old Fort House Museum.

(Figure 15): Courtesy of Lake Champlain Maritime Museum.

Bibliography

Bascom, Robert O. *The Fort Edward Book: Containing Some Historical Sketches, with Illustrations, and Family Records.* J. D. Keating, 1903.

Brislin, Anne E. *Narratives of Old Fort Edward*. Fort Orange Press, 1962.

Davis, Nancy L., J. Scott Cardinal, Josalyn Fergusen, Steve Moragne, Martin Pickands, and Joel Ross. "Cultural Resources Data Recovery and Monitoring Report of the Fort Edward Village Site, Fort Edward Feeder Canal Bridge Site, and Hilfinger Pottery Site, Town and Village of Fort Edward, Washington County, New York." *Cultural Resource Survey Program Series*, no. 8 (2015),

State of New York Department of Public Works, Champlain Canal, Northumberland to Whitehall. June 1, 1922. Charles L. Cadle, Superintendent of Public Works. Item Info: (747) [1922] 200-3399 New York State Archives, Manuscripts and Special Collections.

Cohn, Arthur B. *Lake Champlain's Sailing Canal Boats: An Illustrated Journey from Burlington Bay to the Hudson River*. LCMM, 2003.

Eyre, William, active 1755, George, III, King of Great Britain, and King of Great Britain IV George. "PLAN of FORT EDWARD." Map. 1755. Norman B. Leventhal Map & Education Center, Accessed February 28, 2025. https://collections.leventhalmap.org/search/commonwealth:hx11z383t

Gates, Paul Willard, Alex W. Lehning, Adam I. Kane, Christopher R. Sabick, Sarah Tichonuk, and Joanne Dennis. "A Historic Resources Inventory of the Champlain & Feeder Canal Infrastructure in the Village of Fort Edward, New York." Lake Champlain Maritime Museum, 2013.

Lionel Pincus and Princess Firyal Map Division, The New York Public Library. "Map and profile of the Champlain Canal as made from Lake Champlain to the Hudson River and surveyed thence to the tide at Waterford," New York Public Library Digital Collections, Accessed March 1, 2025. https://digitalcollections.nypl.org/items/510d47da-f057-a3d9-e040-e00a18064a99Item Info: (747) 1820 200-3095 New York State Archives, Manuscripts and Special Collection.

Johnson, E.F. and Holmes Hutchinson, Esquire, Civil Engineers. "Champlain Canal from a survey made in conformity with SEC. IV, ART. I, CHAP. IX, TITLE IX, of the REVISED STATUTES of the State of New York by E.F Johnson under the supervision of Holmes Hutchinson Esq. Civil Engineers, A.D. 1830." New York State Library, Albany, N.Y.

Grossman, Joel W., Lucille L. Johnson, and Dorothy M. Peteet. "The Archaeology of Little Wood Creek: New Chronometric Evidence," *Archaeology of Eastern North America*, no. 42 (2015).

Garofalini, Linda. "The Historic and Architectural Resources of the Town of Moriah, Essex County, NY." National Register Of Historic Places Multiple Property Documentation Form." National Register of Historic Places Nomination Form. U.S. Department of the Interior, National Park Service, 1995.

Map and profile of the Champlain Canals made from Lake Champlain to the Hudson River and surveyed thence to the tide at Waterford. Jas Geddes, 1820. Item Info: (747) 1820 200-3095 New York State Archives, Manuscripts and Special Collection.

Hill, William H. *Old Fort Edward Before 1800: An Account of the Historic Ground Now Occupied by the Village of Ft. Edward*. Privately Printed, 1929.

Johnson, Crisfield. *History of Washington Co., New York: With Illustrations and Biographical Sketches of Some of Its Prominent Men and Pioneers.* Everts & Ensign, 1878.

LaCross, Michael. *A History of the Glens Falls Feeder Canal: Featuring information on the Champlain Canal, the Champlain Barge Canal, and the Fort Edward Feeder Canal*. New York: Feeder Canal Alliance, 2001.

McFee, Michele C. *A Long Haul: The Story of the New York State Barge Canal*. Purple Mountain Press. 1998.

Patten, Jennie M., and Andrew Graham. *History of the Somonauk United Presbyterian Church near Sandwich, De Kalb County, Illinois with Ancestral Lines of the Early Members*. Privately Printed, 1928.

Sheriff, Carol. *The Artificial River: The Erie Canal and the Paradox of Progress, 1817-1862.* Farrar,

Straus and Giroux, 1997.

Starbuck, David. *The Great Warpath: British Military Sites from Albany to Crown Point*. University Press of New England, 1999.

Starbuck, David. *Rangers and Redcoats on the Hudson: Exploring the Past on Rogers Island, the Birthplace of the US Army Rangers*. University Press of New England, 2004.

State of New-York. "An Act for Establishing and Opening Lock Navigation Within the State: Passed the 30th of March 1792." Francis Childs and John Swaine, 1792.

Washington County Planning Department. *An Introduction to Historic Resources in Washington County, New York*. Dodge-Graphic Press, 1976.

CHAPTER 4

An Inland Maritime Community: Two Views of the Champlain or Northern Canalers

Scott A. McLaughlin, PhD

Ties That Bind

The life of Champlain or northern canalers was a curious blend of a domestic and nomadic existence from the opening of the Champlain Canal in 1823 until the 1940s. By the second quarter of the nineteenth century, northern canalers consisted of individuals ranging in age from infants to grandparents, setting them apart from other mariners. The northern canalers came from the towns along the Champlain Waterway (i.e., the Champlain Canal and Lake Champlain) and made their home as well as their living on the Northern Waterway (i.e., inland waterways from New York to Quebec) during the navigation season, which occurred annually from May through October. In 1896, author and artist Howard Pyle (1853-1911) described northern canalers as a class of people who had no parallel; their culture was dissimilar to other mariners, as well as to those living in the land communities along the Northern Waterway.[1] Unlike the great expanse of water on which seafarers traveled, there was less than 40 feet (12.2 meters) of water separating the canalers from dry land when in the canals and not 5 miles (8.1 km) when on Lake Champlain or Lake St. Pierre on the St. Lawrence River. The canalers frequently stepped ashore briefly at a canal lock to snub their boat or to buy something at a canal store, but they were as remote from the interests of the villages and hamlets as they were from the woods and fields that they traveled past. The same can be said about the cities to which they delivered cargoes and where they frequently moored during the winter.

Although northern canalers could be found anywhere between New York and Quebec, they remained connected to each other throughout the year. During the winter months from the 1870s to 1940s, a mass of moored canal boats in New York Harbor consisted of hundreds of canalers from throughout the Northeast and included men, women, and children of all ages and with all their belongings and homes about them.[2] Northern canal boat families would seek each other out among the maze of boats located at dozens of piers along the New York and New Jersey shorelines. They would often leave their vessels in port under someone's care and visit fellow northern canalers, traveling by train to wherever their friends might be along the Northern Waterway. Archaeologists and historians have asked, "To whom did the canalers belong?" Were they part of their homeport communities on the Champlain Waterway, the port communities they frequented, or were they a community unto themselves?

The importance of determining the presence and type of community is significant when trying to make comparisons to other communities and when discussing generalizations about human communities. The search for an appropriate definition of community for archaeological and historical use has been discussed in scholarly literature. Some definitions of community necessitate the direct interaction or observation of individuals and groups, but this is impossible for most studies of historic communities, which may no longer exist. These studies begin with the archaeological or material record, which represents only a fraction of the physical resources of past groups. They also have access to other resources such as curated objects, documents, images, standing structures, oral history, and historical landscapes. With this in mind, I selected two recently developed definitions of community for this study, which focus on the physical and imagined community.

The community concept proposed by Anderson, Carter, and Lowe, with its nine criteria, easily corresponds to the material world of archaeologists but would likely continue to support less perceptive readings of the material record, yielding fewer insights into the thought processes of past populations. Their categories are based upon the outcomes of community efforts and do not explore the contested nature of community among its members. This approach also confines the application of the community concept to larger, complex groups as opposed to small, collaborative groups. The alternative community concept selected for this study, proposed by Wood and Judikis, is based on individual or agent actions. It also seeks to link cognitive behavior to community construction and identity. The process of doing so in living groups is complex enough, but, for archaeologists and historians, it may require the use of new methods borrowing from the fields of psychology and cognitive studies. This research is critical to a

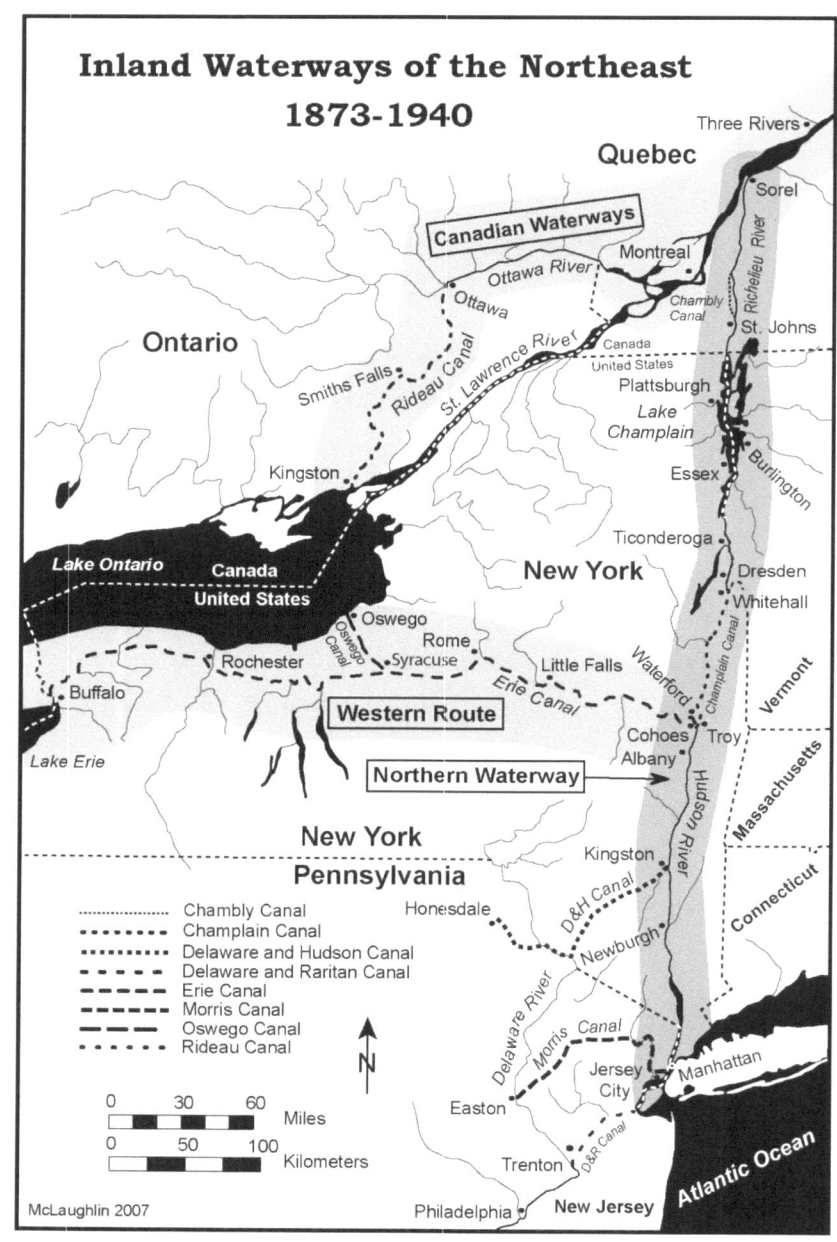

(**Figure 1**) The inland waterways of the Northeast.

historical archaeologist's ability to infer from the material record how people imagined their membership in past communities. Historical archaeologists have the advantage of combining the archaeological record with other historical records, as has been done in this study of the northern canalers, to overcome some of the complexities and issues of searching for individual thoughts, ideas, and emotions of the past.

Based on the use of these two community concepts, this chapter evaluates what we know about the northern canalers against Anderson, Carter, and Lowe's nine characteristics to identify place-based communities, and the six criteria Wood and Judikis used to identify imagined communities.[3] Following a test of each community theory, the chapter reflects upon the application of each to best understand the lives of the northern canalers.

Anderson, Carter, and Lowe—Community as a Social System

According to Anderson, Carter, and Lowe, for a group of people to constitute a community or macro social system, it must have regular interaction and consist of nine linked characteristics, including a shared identity, common history and perceived destiny, unique language and symbols, stratification of its members, shared physical property and locality, unique material culture, kinship and community bonds, group structure, and patterns of behavior. Identification of these nine criteria among the northern canalers is based on their recurrence in numerous households and over time.

Shared Identity

A shared identity within a community fosters unity, belonging, and collaboration, leading to stronger social bonds, increased trust, and improved communication, ultimately benefiting collective action and well-being. Northern canalers developed a shared identity over their 120-year history. Northern canalers led lives of almost constant mobility throughout the navigation season, and this distinguished them from most people living in urban centers and rural communities along the Northern Waterway. Author Vera Connolly (1888-1964) called the northern canalers America's "water gypsies."[4] They were a group unto themselves and were described as "a long-lived lot with a family resemblance among them all, perhaps the result of selection as much as environment." Even though canalers never went to sea, there still was a spiritual kinship between seamen and boatmen. For both, once the water had called them, there was no turning back.[5]

Being a transient population, northern canalers' ideas around their group identity changed depending on where they were and whom they were speaking with about their community associations. In a port on the Champlain Waterway, they identified with their land-based community. However, when discussing their identity with other mariners, they clearly affiliated with the canalers from the Champlain Waterway. Invariably, collective identity for a group, such as this, is expressed in the form of a name that identifies the group. The label that male northern canalers preferred over all others was boatmen, Champlain boatmen, or northern boatmen. They also used the terms canaler, Champlain canaler, northern canaler, or inland seamen to describe themselves, as in the names of their

Northern Boatmen's Transportation Company, Northern Canal Boatmen's Association, and Inland Seamen's Union. The gender-focused labels using "men" did not speak to the shared sense of collective identity of all the canalers on the Champlain Waterway, who consisted of men, women, and children of all ages. Collectively, they were frequently called and referred to themselves as canalers, Champlain canalers, or northern canalers. This sense of identity is best revealed in the writings and oral history of the group's members. These state clearly that the northern canalers shared an occupational identity as well as a way of life and most expressed this identity through their unique canal boat designs, job-related activities, and occupational language. They knew the dangers, joys, and sorrows of life on the Northern Waterway like no one else did and passed this knowledge from one generation to the next over approximately 125 years of service.[6]

Common History and Perceived Destiny

A common history and a shared perceived destiny are essential for community cohesion, fostering a sense of belonging, shared identity, and purpose, which in turn strengthens social bonds and encourages civic engagement. This is most evident in the late-nineteenth-century journals of northern canalers, such as Theodore Declarmont Bartley (1830-1914), Lucy Emeroy Brown (1844-1896), and others. The authors of these journals reflected an understanding that they were a part of a maritime community with a long history of providing service to the region.[7] They also recognized their continuous and sometimes fruitless fight against the weather, ever-changing markets, and sometimes poor management of the canals due to

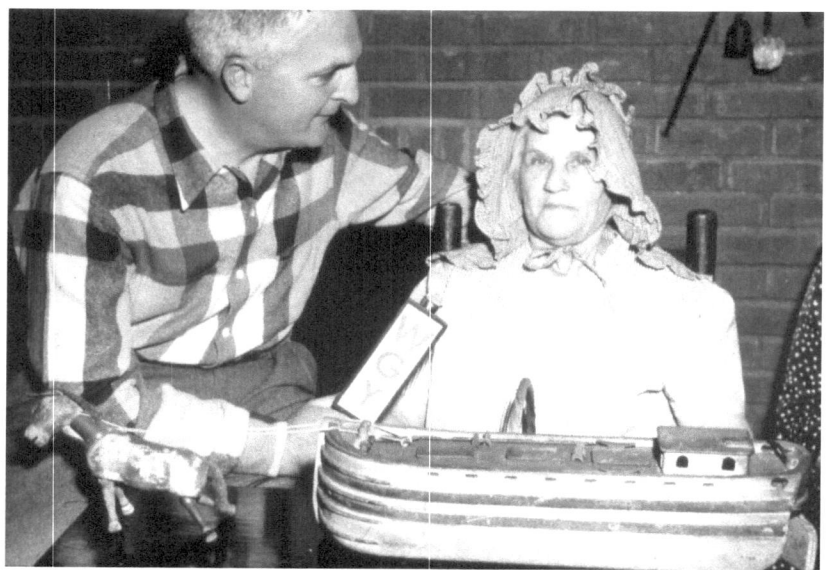

(**Figure 2**) In the early 1960s, Isabella St. Jean Archambault (1878-1965) was interviewed by the radio station WGY (810 AM) of Schenectady, New York about her experiences as a canaler. She holds a northern canal boat toy model made for her children.

(**Figure 3**) At Whitehall, New York, canal boats on the left, waiting for a lake tow; canal boats at right, waiting for a canal tow during the late nineteenth century.

a complex bureaucracy involving two nations, several states and provinces, and numerous port towns and cities. Their collective understanding of the future encouraged many canalers to rally for reforms and resulted in the development of the Northern Boatmen's Transportation Company (established in 1883 and later called the Northern Canal Boatmen's Association) and their Inland Seamen's Union (established in 1903 and granted a charter by the American Federation of Labor), supporting their way of life. Their shared history is most prominently exhibited in the histories of northern canal boat life written by canalers Frank Godfrey (1891-1977), Fred Godfrey (1906-1972), and Martha Juckett (1890-1958), as well as the oral histories collected from canalers, such as Cora Archambault (1904-2006) and Evamay Wilkins (1920-2006).[8]

(**Figure 4**) Lake Champlain schooner-rigged sailing canal boat and two northern standard or unrigged canal boats.

Unique Language and Symbols

The language and symbols used by the northern canalers were fundamental to their identity, acting as tools for communication, cultural transmission, and the creation of shared meaning and social cohesion. An important example of the use of language by the northern canalers is what they called their vessels, which were their home and place of business. Before the construction of the New York State Barge Canal System, they only called their vessels "canal boats." After construction began on the Champlain Barge Canal, the public, officials, and the media called them barges, to the annoyance of many northern canalers. The word "barge" seemed to the northern canalers to diminish their importance in the maritime world. Barges were traditionally roughly built work vessels that received little attention and had little value. The canalers already had to contend with mariners that believed the canal was not the most challenging environment for a mariner. Canalers knew otherwise.

The northern canalers were a part of a large group of inland mariners within eastern Canada and the eastern United States who used similar material culture and processes. However, they stood out among other canalers due to their unique bilingual capabilities, occupational vocabulary, place names, and use of symbols. Many northern canalers were of French-Canadian descent and spoke French in the household as their primary language and English among their neighbors. Between the 1870s and 1940s, most of the northern canalers, especially those of the Champlain Valley, were families with French-Canadian heritage. In the early 1920s, author and artist Joe Duncan Gleason (1881-1959) claimed, "As Ohio produced presidents, so

Champlain, [New York,] a town of but eighteen hundred inhabitants, which yet boasts of two hundred and twenty-five barges [canal boats], one to every eight people, is the port of hail of the [northern] canal boat captain."[9] Those canalers not raised speaking French acquired it as they transacted business in Quebec with French-speaking merchants, mariners, and others. The need for both languages seldom occurred among other North American canalers. As a result of their bilingual backgrounds, the occupational vocabulary of the northern canalers was unique, as were many terms given to objects, processes, and geographic features only occurring along the Champlain Waterway, including docks, waterways, hazards to navigation, and landmarks used for lining up courses.

Those who were not canalers might have understood some of their unique usage of language and vocabulary; however, only those who were northern canalers would have had a full understanding of it. Northern canalers also used the language and symbols from a wide variety of cultural and occupational groups along the Northern Waterway because of their trading. The symbols used by northern canalers were embedded in their material culture and stories. Visual cues that helped the northern canalers to recognize one another consisted of the location and size of their cabin trunks, the absence of quarters for tow animals aboard, and the starboard aft location of their cabin chimneys. The construction of the boat's bow, stern, and cabin trunk also indicated where along the Champlain Waterway their vessel was constructed and potentially how much debt they had.

The stories narrated or sung by the northern canalers were filled with lessons and knowledge that were important to them but often no one else.

They refer to people, places, and events that were only known to those operating along the Champlain Waterway. Some of these stories, although entertaining, were designed to help point out the differences between canalers, other mariners, and landsmen. Other stories point out the differences between the northern canalers and the Erie Canal boatmen, who dominated the canal boat trade in the Northeast.

Stratification of Its Members—Differentiation

Members of every community are placed into categories and frequently into a hierarchical structure. Differentiation occurred among the northern canalers in the form of a hierarchical structure that was based upon the ownership of their boats and relationship to the canalers' Northern Boatmen's Transportation Company, later called the Northern Canal Boatmen's Association (established in 1883), Inland Seamen's Union (established in 1903), and the Champlain Waterway's transportation companies. Captains with full ownership of their canal boats had economic choices. These independent operators had three choices: they could join the association or union and use their freight services and tugs on Lake Champlain and mules in the Champlain Canal; they could hire the local transportation companies' tugs and mules and use their freight services; or they could hire teams of horses and mules owned by local farmers and teamsters and find their own freight. Captains whose boats were owned in full or in part by a transportation company were forced to use the company's towing and freight services when available and were instructed not to use the association's or union's services.

Economic and political power among the northern canalers, as in most communities in North America during the era, was held by men, especially the captains who owned their own vessels and had years of experience operating on the Northern Waterway. Social power was determined by their network of friends, relatives, and business partners who lived along the Northern Waterway. It was this network that provided the canalers with the means to survive economic, personal, and household hardships. Prominent independent captains or owner-operators had the most political power. They served as spokesmen for the northern canalers' Inland Seamen's Union and in other political action groups that promoted improvements to the Northern Waterway. These men also presided over the communal gatherings of northern canalers in New York Harbor and other major ports during the winter months.

Men with less experience, or those who worked for a transportation company, did not wield as much social power among the northern canalers. Deckhands and steersmen were generally young, had little experience, and operated the oldest boats on the waterway; thus, they had a lower status in the group. They also lacked a family, which affected their status. The presence of the captain's wife and children aboard was seen as a symbol of social strength. Family men were viewed by those within the group, as well as those outside, as having stronger morals and a better character.

Women played an important part in operations aboard the canal boats but held no political positions within the group. However, that did not prevent women's voices from being heard, as they generally controlled the domestic tasks aboard the canal boat and could use their position as leverage with their husband, father, or other relative who served as the boat's captain. Women and children, at least during the Champlain Canal days (1819-1915), were a necessity for most canal boatmen's success because of the need for free family labor. According to canal boat enrollment documents issued by the U.S. Department of Commerce, women were also owners and captains of canal boats but not in large numbers. Stories of women's equality among men appear in documentary and oral history sources. Nevertheless, women were clearly of unequal status to the majority of boatmen.

Children were an important part of the canal boat household but had little status due to the fact that their weaker strength and minimal experience and knowledge meant fewer contributions. However, it was through observation and practical experience that children gained the necessary skills and wisdom to become equal to adult canalers. Boys in their mid-teens often operated their own boats, making a place for themselves within the adult world of canalers. Teenage girls traveled with their father or another male relative as their cook and deckhand.

Another differentiation within the canalers occurred along religious and ethnic lines. Many northern canalers were Catholic, including canalers of French-Canadian and Irish heritage, and during the nineteenth and early twentieth centuries, they experienced anti-Catholic nativism throughout their travels in the United States. Although some northern canalers observed the Sabbath, many felt the economic pressures to continue working, representing yet another religious distinction among the canalers and between canalers and landsmen.

Shared Physical Property and Locality

Shared physical property and locality are crucial for community building, fostering a sense of belonging, promoting social interaction, and improving overall quality of life for community members by providing spaces for gathering, recreation, and shared experiences. The northern canalers' territory stretched across hundreds of miles of inland waterways, crossed political boundaries, and included dozens of port communities. Despite this large territory, the boundary of the northern canal boat community was in part physical, like that of a village, as it was defined by the heart of their territory, which included their homeports along the Champlain Canal and Lake Champlain. It was in these ports that the northern canalers frequently lived during the offseason, had living and deceased relatives, and owned property.

The vernacular names used for familiar things and places were important elements of the traditional knowledge of the northern canalers. They created unique labels for communities, docks, and waterways that they used. Whitehall, New York, for example, was known as "Mule Town" for its large collection of barns and corrals for the tow mules.[10] Port Kendall in Willsboro, New York, was called "Port Despair" by the canalers, due to its location in a most unprotected spot on the west side of Willsboro Bay. Many of these place names have been lost with the deaths of the last canalers in the late twentieth century.[11] The northern canalers came from the towns near Lake Champlain and the Champlain Canal of upstate New York and western

Vermont. They took pride in the region they came from, claiming their homeports upon the stern and often the bow of their canal boats.

The community's boundary was also based upon the experiences of its members. All northern canalers lived and worked aboard a canal boat on the Northern Waterway, as this was an occupational community. This boundary was a conscious one that helped to form their identity. The northern canalers as well as outsiders recognized that canalers lived a nomadic way of life, and were a unique population, loosely organized, and engaged in common pursuits that were inseparable from the waterways they traveled. However, their way of life was not as fixed as the waterway but instead adapted to the cultural and natural environment through which they traveled regularly. The canalers created and maintained organizations and processes to fulfill their

(Figure 5) Norman Allard (1909-2005) commands his very first canal boat made by his father, Joseph Allard, (1872-1944), of Champlain, New York.

needs.

The physical and experiential boundary of the northern canal boat community was by no means a barrier. The canalers were traders by their very occupation and worked within an international economy, and, as a result, they were very open to exchanges across their community boundary. For example, farm boys were readily available and willing in many ports to work as deckhands, and canalers were just as willing to work as day laborers in the offseason on farms. In addition to the Champlain Canal, the canalers had a close connection to the villages and cities they traded with along the Northern Waterway. The canalers engaged in loading and unloading cargoes, purchasing goods, and interacting with each port's population. Specific docks were affiliated with the northern canalers, as they were more frequently used by them than any other mariners, especially docks that were used for winter mooring.

The northern canal boat community was a social system that was relatively open, and people, ideas, material culture, and processes adopted from the community systems of those they interacted with flowed through its boundary. In fact, there were important economic and social linkages between the northern canal boat community and many other community systems, including major trading ports and the canalers' homeports. It is this exchange between communities that helps to explain how change occurred within the northern canal boat community but also how that change would contribute to the community's dissolution.

Prior to the completion of the Champlain Barge Canal, other canal boats from the Northeast were simply too large or were prohibited by New York

State law from entering the Champlain Canal. As a result, the northern canalers dominated the number of vessels and trade on the Champlain Waterway. With the exception of a small number of tugs and barges, the canal boats were the only vessels to travel the Champlain Canal. Thus, the northern canalers' ties to this waterway were strong, which was especially true for those northern canalers who were a part of the Northern Boatmen's Transportation Company, Northern Canal Boatmen's Association, or Inland Seamen's Union, who owned line mules on the Champlain Canal and tugs on Lake Champlain.

Unique Material Culture

Unique material culture, encompassing the tangible objects and cultural spaces that define a community, is vital for expressing identity, fostering social cohesion, and preserving a community's history, by acting as a powerful tool for understanding and celebrating a community's values and traditions. At the core of the northern canalers' identity was their unique material world, which included the techniques, equipment, and procedures of canal boating on the Northern Waterway. Although the basic system of navigation was well known to canalers all over the Northeast, the distinctive maritime, commercial, and social practices of those along the Northern Waterway were best known by those who traveled the waters regularly. It was this familiarity that separated the northern canalers from other canalers in the Northeast. Certain kinds of traditional knowledge were shared only among northern canalers: the ways the canalers used their tools, responded to their environment, and interacted with others. There were also many related expressive forms: words and gestures used by the canalers, the arrangement of equipment and other objects on their canal boats, and customs practiced there.[12]

Most of the artifacts found in the northern canal boat shipwrecks in Lake Champlain and the Richelieu River are not unique to the northern canalers; however, the nomenclature, function, values, and context differ dramatically from those used by inland mariners or landsmen. It is the quality, quantity, and diversity of objects that are unique due to the accessibility of goods the northern canalers had on their travels and due to their religious, economic, political, and ethnic backgrounds. Few of the objects found aboard a canal boat were crafted by the canalers, but each was obtained, used, maintained, and in some cases discarded by the canalers. These objects are symbols of what was significant to their way of life.

The northern canal boat is the largest piece of material culture that was built for the canalers with their needs, knowledge, and ideals incorporated into its manufacture. Some northern canalers assisted in their vessel's construction, but more frequently only the vessel's finishing touches, such as the finish carpentry, painting, and decoration, were done at the instruction or hand of the canalers. The construction of the northern canal boat, the layout of the cabin, and other features of the northern canal boat made it a distinctive style. Although slight variations can be seen in historic photographs and shipwrecks, the shipwrights and the canalers of the Champlain Canal and Lake Champlain made a conscious effort to create a home and work vessel that stood out from all the rest in the Northeast. The characteristics of the vessel were dictated by choice but also by necessity due to the cargoes they carried, conditions of the waterways they traveled, and the make-up of their crews. Stories of the canalers' pride in their boats appear throughout the oral histories and written sources.

Kinship and Community Bonds

A community's well-being is based on strong kinship and community bonds, which foster social cohesion and cultural continuity, and provide support networks that are essential for individual and collective success. Of the thousands of northern canalers operating between 1820 and 1940, many were related by blood or marriage. Most canalers came from the towns directly along the Champlain Canal and Lake Champlain and, in the greatest numbers, from the largest port towns. This situation increased the likelihood that canalers had kinship ties. Many canalers were Irish or French-Canadian in heritage and by tradition had large, close-knit families that carried on traditional values and practices, which included marrying within their ethnic and religious affiliations. When kinship bonds were not present, northern canalers still felt a community connection based on their shared experiences and material culture. They exhibited this connection by creating organizations and hosting annual dances and parties at the end of the navigation season. The northern canalers also demonstrated their community bonds by adopting and using similar forms of material culture, processes, and language, which formed their distinctive, shared identity.

Despite the hard work, long hours, and the constant exposure to the elements, there was a fascination and a sort of freedom that not only bound some men and women to the canal for life but drew their sons and daughters after them as well.[13] The job of a canal boat captain became an occupation handed down from father to son and in rare cases from father to daughter or mother to son. When times were good for canaling, more households could establish themselves and support children. In contrast, bad times pushed many of these children, upon reaching working age, out of canaling. Success in bringing up children with good prospects in canaling, as well as still having any of them nearby in one's old age, was a rigorous test of ingenuity and good household management by the canal boat families. Ultimately, some children grew up and married other canalers and remained boating, while some married shore sweethearts from their winter hometowns and left the canals for other vocations. One canal boat mother explained the family tradition in canal boating this way: "The children are brought on the boat and don't know nothin' else, and that is the only reason they take up boating." Yet canal boat children had the opportunity to see a great variety of jobs firsthand, from the building of skyscrapers in New York City to farming the rich agricultural fields along the Champlain Canal to working in the sugar factories of Montreal.[14]

Like many canalers, Captain Henry Walrod (1841-1932) of Fort Edward, New York, passed his canal boating business down to his children. His daughter, Alice Etta Walrod (1869-1945), lived in Fort Edward while he was boating and occasionally rode with him as his cook and deckhand. When Henry retired from boating, he left his business to his son Frank Walrod (1891-1977). Alice also returned to boating later in life with her own family. Alice met and married Frederick Herbert Godfrey (1868-1905), a printer

(**Figure 6**) Two northern canal boat households from different homeports clearly resemble each other in material culture and household membership. The boats are the *Robert & Mary* (built in 1888) of Whitehall, New York and *W.N. Sweet* of Chazy, New York.

for the *Fort Edward Advertiser*. The couple had several young sons before Godfrey fell ill and could no longer work as a printer. The Godfrey family then purchased a canal boat, which was run by Alice and the older boys. Alice's husband eventually died aboard the family's boat one night while crossing Lake Champlain on a return trip from Canada. As the three older Godfrey boys reached their late teens, they left their mother and began to operate their own canal boats. Alice remarried canal boatman Emory Brodie (1874-1922). With the opening of the Champlain Barge Canal, the Godfrey boys later switched careers and began working on tugboats, and all eventually became tugboat captains.[15]

The bond among northern canalers was also strengthened through joint ownership of their canal boats. Vessel enrollment records reveal that many northern canalers purchased their vessels in partnership with another canal boatman, who would later be bought out. It is the bonds among northern canalers that encouraged them to protect and assist one another when in need, whether it was protection from bullying by hooligans, coping with the tragic death of a family member, or weathering out a storm together.

Group Structure and Patterns of Behavior

Group structure and patterns of behavior are vital to a community's function, shaping social norms, influencing individual actions, and fostering stability, cooperation, and collective action. At the core of northern canalers' experience were their regular interactions with the natural and cultural environments along the Northern Waterway that shaped the canalers' behavior and worldviews. As a result of their nomadic maritime lifestyle, the culture of the northern canalers took on structural and behavioral elements from the varied groups they encountered along the Northern Waterway. This included a wide spectrum of American and Canadian society, ranging from isolated Canadian logging and mining communities to manufacturing centers like Troy, New York, to multilingual and ethnic cities such as New York City and Quebec City. For over a century, the northern canalers were bound together by their interpretation of the imperatives and traditions of the Northern Waterway.[16]

The specialization of the northern canal boat community, which made it unique, led to its high degree of dependence upon other groups that it encountered. For example, education of the canalers was provided primarily by the household and family during the navigation season but was also influenced by external groups such as religious leaders and formal schools. Attending church and school was limited during the navigation season but not so during the offseason. Another close linkage occurred between the northern canalers and the numerous communities and organizations that controlled the waterways and the mercantile system of the Northeast.

Although the life of the northern canalers can be generalized, it was highly variable in the households' experiences, as they traveled regularly from multicultural, dynamic urban communities, such as New York City, with seemingly unlimited access to goods, entertainment, and cultural interactions, to rural French-Canadian communities along the shores of the Ottawa River where opportunities were limited and the culture was rooted in its French colonial heritage. The variety of interactions is what made the household patterns of behavior less predictable and more unusual compared to those outside of the northern canal boat community. What was more predictable were the processes and material culture associated with operating canal boats along the Northern Waterway. The northern canalers' daily lives were dominated by their work and the group structure was loose due to the nature of their business and lifestyle. For a time, the Northern Boatmen's Transportation Company, Northern Canal Boatmen's Association, Inland Seamen's Union, and other political action groups guided the community; however, the element that had the greatest impact was the household and its members. Unfortunately, at this time, only two canal boat cabins, the Sloop Island canal boat and canal schooner *General Butler*, have been excavated, but further archaeological research is likely to expose greater variability in household behavior.

Regular Interaction

All social systems have processes of socialization and social control that are designed to secure things or achieve goals. Socialization involved the induction of individuals into the northern canal boat community's way of life. This was achieved through regular interaction within the setting of the household, during community gatherings, and at port communities where non-canalers and canalers came into contact. The successful socialization and loose coupling of the canal boat households meant that few social controls were necessary. As canaler Fred Godfrey (1906-1972) pointed out, there were few fights or confrontations in his memory of working on the canals for decades. Most canalers worked towards the same goal of economic success with as few hardships as possible.

The canalers traveled thousands of miles each season on the Northern Waterway, crossing paths with others they knew and making acquaintances with new northern canalers along the way. Socialization was essential to their existence. The northern canalers had nearly continuous interaction in small groups with other community members throughout much of the navigation season, especially when they were being towed by tugs in the open water of the Northern Waterway. At these times, they had the opportunity to enjoy one another's company, create new and solidify old bonds, share knowledge and stories, and reinforce social values, and the use of their material culture, and modes of communication. The opportunity for lengthy interaction occurred during the winter, when the canalers were in ports along the Northern Waterway or at their homeport. Even when in isolated ports, canalers took the opportunity of the quiet winter to visit friends and relatives in other communities, and to share one another's cabins or houses. It was during these moments at the end of the canal season that canalers gathered in celebration of the season's successes and mourned their losses.

Wood and Judikis—Community as a Collaborative Group

Sociologists George Wood, Jr. and Juan Judikis argue that the best way to identify and describe a community is based on six essential criteria: sense of purpose, mutual responsibility, mutual respect, acknowledged interconnectedness, the well-being of members, and the well-being of the community. This definition of community downplays the geography of the community and stresses the collective apparent and imagined psychological needs for community support and identity. In this regard, it fulfills the recent call of archaeologists and historians to search for the uniqueness of communities and their associated attributes, those we today can learn from and even imitate. Northern canalers, as outlined below, appear to fulfill each characteristic of an imagined community identified by Wood and Judikis.

Sense of Purpose

The northern canalers represent a collaborative community, which is one that exists to serve one or more purposes or goals created by a situation or circumstance.[17] Workplace or occupational communities, such as the northern canal boat community, are common examples of collaborative communities and are formed to address the needs surrounding a particular kind of work. The occupational community only exists as long as the work continues to be needed by society. Therefore, the motivation to create the community is the act of collaboration; that is, individuals need to work together towards a common goal(s) or purpose(s) in order to be successful. Since collaborative occupational communities are based upon work-related tasks, they generally have short lifespans and fragile infrastructure. However, some collaborative communities, especially occupational ones, can last for a long time but disintegrate when 1) their purpose loses importance to its members; 2) the members lose track of or strongly disagree on what their community purpose(s) are; or 3) the members strongly disagree on how the community should operate to serve their common needs.

As a community, the northern canalers, for a time during the nineteenth century, were well adapted to working the Northern Waterway. The flexible gender roles, independence of most operators, versatility of canal boats, and loose social structure permitted them to achieve success. However, that success was limited by the canalers' inability to adapt to the dramatic economic and technological changes during the early twentieth century. Cheaper sources of raw materials were transported from the Midwest and railroads were able to carry more material at lower costs year-round. If any lesson is to be learned from this examination of the northern canal boat community, it is that the adaptable community system and not the well-adapted is the most likely to survive. An occupational community such as the northern canal boat community is the most vulnerable community system because, when the need for their service (i.e., their sense of purpose) ends, the community is likely to end as well.

With the completion of the Champlain Barge Canal in 1915, canalers from throughout the Northeast and unmanned steel barges began to appear on the Champlain Waterway. As a result, the northern canal boat community began to collapse and the number of canalers declined as the community lost much of its purpose and identity. With no unifying community purpose, there was no longer a need for community connectedness, and so the community died long before the last northern canalers tied up their vessels for good in the 1940s. Although the northern canal boat community died with the opening of the barge canal system, some canalers had modified their vessels and created new ways of operating to remain a part of the inland maritime system of trade along the Northern Waterway. The labor unions that had served the northern canalers between the 1880s and 1920s depended upon the northern canalers' communal interactions and attitudes, but, once their community collapsed, so did the union's influence on the canalers.

Mutual Responsibility

Mutual responsibility is at the heart of any thriving community, as it fosters a stronger, more resilient, and supportive environment where individuals contribute to the collective well-being, leading to greater unity, shared goals, and a more equitable society. There occurred a mix of individualism, cooperation, and egalitarianism in the northern canal boat community. Canalers, with their exposure to a variety of lifestyles along the Northern Waterway, had a wide array of choices of how to live their lives. For men, their role as canalers was based upon reputation and skill, which was created by individual spirit, dedication, and ingenuity. However, to be successful, canalers had to create cooperative relationships. Canal boats were expensive to purchase and operate and as a result partnerships and loans among canalers were common. Within households, cooperation was necessary to run the household, the business of trading, and the operations of the canal boat. The reliance on individuals in the household to satisfactorily complete their roles and responsibilities was great, as failure to do so put the household at risk of financial ruin and possibly placed individuals at risk of physical harm or even death. This cooperation and sense of responsibility extended beyond the household to other northern canalers and their households. Most canalers were willing to lend others a hand when in need, knowing that they too would need assistance from others from time to time. This situation was frequently the case because of the limited crew size on the canal boats. Maneuvering boats and moving cargo was labor intensive and at times could not be accomplished without assistance. This cooperative effort led to a level of egalitarianism among the northern canalers not seen in other communities along the Northern Waterway. Women, who might have been limited to domestic roles elsewhere, played a greater part in canaling on the Northern Waterway than in most land-based communities. Women owned and operated canal boats and served as crew members of boats. They negotiated trade agreements on their own behalf and on that of their husband, father, or other relative. This level of cooperation and egalitarianism among both men and women within the canal boat community led to a strong sense of mutual responsibility for the safety and success of all northern canalers.

Mutual Respect

Mutual respect is essential for a healthy community because it fosters trust, inclusivity, and cooperation, leading to stronger relationships, reduced conflict, and a more harmonious environment where everyone feels valued and empowered. Canaling on the Northern Waterway was based upon mutual respect; however, that respect was also created by cultural differences and hostilities between northern canalers and others. These differences lie in social class, religion, and misunderstanding of canal boat life. Violent clashes, name calling, and even shunning of northern canalers occurred as they traveled the Northern Waterway. The nomadic lifestyle of the northern canalers during the navigation season brought them negative attention from some and envy from others.

Despite the reactions of outsiders to the northern canalers, and possibly because of this ill treatment, young farmhands and other landsmen often were given opportunities to join the canal boat community regardless of their origins, education, religious beliefs, ethnicity, or marine experience. Mutual respect for others helped preserve the good relationships that were so critical to their economic success. Among the northern canalers were individuals of Native American, African American, French-Canadian, Irish,

English, Dutch, Welsh, Scottish, and other European ancestry. However, the canal boat community remained dominated by those of French-Canadian, Irish, and English heritage, like the towns and cities along the Champlain Waterway, which were the origins of most northern canalers.

Acknowledged Interconnectedness

Acknowledged interconnectedness fosters stronger, more inclusive, and resilient communities by promoting empathy, understanding, and collaboration, ultimately leading to a greater sense of belonging and shared purpose. The northern canal boat community was a network of relationships built upon family ties, friendships, and business connections. This fact was clearly acknowledged by the canalers and was important to their economic success. The interconnectedness of the northern canaler is evident through the community's construction of common symbols, consisting of its material culture, customs, habits, and rituals. These boundary-making features were the result of the social constructs of insiders and outsiders to the northern canalers. These symbols helped to affirm the canalers' imagined identity and belonging to what was a unique maritime community. This interconnectedness is most apparent when comparing their canal boats in historic photographs and shipwrecks. The construction, layout, functions, and processes that were carried out aboard these boats are remarkably similar. However, when compared to canalers from other regions across North America, there appear few similarities. The northern canalers created a distinctive identity that made them stand out from other maritime groups.

Northern canalers had a traditional rule regarding the way in which formal names were given to individual boats. Every canal boat had a name, and no two boats on the Champlain Waterway were permitted to have the same name. Between 1873 and 1940, canal boat owners had by tradition only a small selection of possibilities. Some names were family names, such as that of the owner's mother, father, wife, son, daughter, sister, or brother (e.g., *H. G. Burleigh, Jr.* of Whitehall, named after himself in 1873). Boats owned by their captains often had the name of the captain's wife or some other immediate family member who lived aboard the boat (e.g., *Mollie J. Boles* of Whitehall, named after the wife of Edward C. Boles, 1907). Now and then a canal boat was named after two individuals, usually siblings or couples (e.g., *May & Annie* of Whitehall, 1891).

Other names that were chosen included prominent businessmen or members of their elite families. Frequently, these important families lived in the canal boat's homeport or the hometown of the canal boat owner. The names of these leading families were used as a means to generate trust, support, and business for the canal boat owner. For example, on Saturday afternoon, June 20, 1874, the usual monotony at Essex, New York, was slightly disturbed by the launching of a new canal boat, the *Walter D. Palmer*. The vessel was built by the Essex Manufacturing Company for Captain Moses Adam Knowlton of Essex at a cost of $4,000 ($115,609 1874/2024 Consumer Price Index). The master builder was Abram Winslow, one of the best ship carpenters on Lake Champlain, and the elegant cabin was finished off by carpenter Myron E. Eggleston. By tradition, some of the cabin's furnishings were a present of the vessel's namesake, Walter D. Palmer, a prominent businessman and civic leader in Essex.[18]

The canal boat families crossed paths on the Northern Waterway during the navigation season and caught up on business, community, and family events. If they were in a tow together, canalers walked from boat to boat to visit and play cards. Canaler Evamay Wilkins recalled fondly her childhood days on the canal: "There was always somebody who knew how to play the accordion or the guitar or the fiddle. And the families then...we'd get together and they'd sing. When people would come down in the cabin, my father would recite these poems and tap dance. And we'd serve coffee and cake and it was always one big happy family. I just can't explain it. It was just wonderful, that's all."[19]

Music was an important recreational and educational tool for canalers. "Those gondoliers [canalers]," noted one nineteenth-century newspaper, "seem to be possessed with an unaccountable furor for bugles and French horns, and the whole country is serenaded by them to a painful extent."[20] Many canalers were fine piano, accordion, and violin players. On a still summer night while tied up in port, canalers would gather under an awning and play music, which would float softly out across the water.[21]

Although many of the songs that were sung by northern canalers were not their own, they frequently changed the words of songs to make them relevant to their lives. Many of the songs taught lessons about the history, identity, and pride the northern canalers had for their way of life. The song "Attend, All Ye Drivers" is one of the many bragging songs sung by canalers on the Champlain Waterway and one of the few that is believed to have originated from the region due to the mention of the 1830s northern canal boat company Baker and Walbridge. This song had been sung for sixty years along the Champlain Waterway before being recorded in the 1890s.[22]

Well-being of Members and the Community

The final two characteristics of an imagined community are that all community members must exhibit mutual commitment to the wellbeing of each other and to the well-being and integrity of the community. The well-being of community members and the community as a whole is necessary for a thriving group, fostering a sense of belonging, supporting individuals, and promoting collective action for positive change, ultimately leading to a more resilient and prosperous community. The northern canalers needed each other's assistance throughout the navigation season to do their job safely and efficiently. They also depended upon each other during times of crises. Their willingness to work together and lend assistance when needed by other canalers was out of mutual personal responsibility to the community and its members. This is not to say that all northern canalers felt the same level of responsibility. As illustrated in several stories, there were some "bad apples" in the bunch. By definition these canalers, who had little understanding or feeling of mutual responsibility, were in fact not members of the northern canal boat community but instead remained on the fringe of the community. The number of northern canalers who did not participate as a member of the community was likely very small and consisted of those who did not work long on the Champlain Waterway because cooperative effort was so critical to the nature of their work. An attribute that these outlying canalers likely lacked was mutual respect for other northern canalers or a willingness to accept a certain level of disagreement over opinions or behavior.

Northern canalers demonstrated their interest in and commitment to their identity by fiercely defending their material identity and way of life in spite of dramatic technological and economic changes along the Northern Waterway during the late nineteenth and early twentieth centuries. The canalers continued to pass from one generation to the next their stories, unique vocabulary, and processes that they believed were critical to canaling on the Northern Waterway and essential to their identity. The northern canalers valued their identity in several ways as revealed through different historical sources. The individual and collective value of the canalers can be identified by reviewing the lives of the individual members and their material remains. If the northern canal boat community was a network of relationships, then one value of the collective was the security of a shared identity, which led to cooperative activities and support of each other. However, for the collective, there also came disadvantages. The communal relationships among the northern canalers suppressed, and even denied, individual differences among the northern canalers. Communal relations also set the stage for conflict between insiders and outsiders. This created an isolation or alienation of the northern canalers from other communities. The suppression of difference, isolation, and conflict is related to the northern canalers' value judgment on their way of life compared to others. Often, they believed their way of life and material culture were superior to others. Some outsiders viewed the canal boat way of life as superior to that of those living in urban communities while others treated canalers similar to vagabonds.

Such comparative judgments led to the devaluing or overvaluing of the unique lifeways of the northern canalers.

Due to the different lifestyle of the northern canalers, they were occasionally teased and bullied by residents living along the Champlain Waterway. Some of the indignities suffered by the northern canalers included teenage boys throwing stones at the canal boats as they passed under bridges. The boys would chant, "Canaler, canaler, you'll never get rich for working on Sunday. You'll die in the ditch, you son of a bitch!" People of all ages also came up to the canal boat cabins and stared into the windows. Although they strongly protested being stared at like an animal in a zoo, most northern canalers were welcoming when they were asked politely by inquisitive people to show them through their cabin.[23]

On occasion, when a northern canaler was unjustly harmed, the community swiftly came to his or her aid. Just after supper one evening in Chambly, a young northern boatman from a northbound tow was attacked by four drunken French-Canadian men while he was in town. The young boatman managed to get away and run back to the canal boat tow, where he told everyone about his scuffle in town. In less than ten minutes, thirty northern boatmen were on their way into town, and shortly thereafter they taught the attackers a lesson about the brotherhood of canal boatmen. Needless to say, no canal boatmen were ever bothered in Chambly after that, at least for a while.[24]

Members of the northern canal boat community supported one another in times of need and assisted other canalers who infrequently worked on the Northern Waterway. One such example comes from the small town of

Louiseville, Quebec, located about 4 miles (6.4 kilometers) up a small winding river that is about halfway between Sorel and Three Rivers, Quebec. Small tugs towed light canal boats from Sorel, to Louiseville where they loaded 4-foot (1.2 meters) pulpwood for paper mills in New York State. About 1911 or 1912, an elderly couple with an old northern canal boat was bound for Sorel after loading pulpwood at Louiseville. Among the many boats in their tow were four boats owned and operated by Fred (1875-1952) and Charles Gates (1868-1930) of Champlain, New York. Although the elderly couple was new to all the northern canalers, they had apparently operated canal boats before, for they understood well the operations of boating. During the trip from Louiseville to Sorel, the couple's old boat was leaking badly, so the Gates brothers helped to pump it out. While still on Lake St. Peter in the St. Lawrence River, a heavy thunderstorm came up suddenly. While pumping his leaky boat, the old captain was struck by lightning and killed instantly. When the tow arrived at Sorel, all the northern canalers went to work pumping and repairing the elderly couple's boat. They also took up a collection that more than covered the captain's burial. The northern canalers then sent the elderly woman, her husband's body, and their belongings home by train. At the widow's request, the Gates brothers took over the couple's canal boat, and after unloading it at Fort Miller, New York, they sold the boat and its freight and sent the money to the woman's home.[25]

A Unique Maritime Community: Summary and Contributions

There is no question that the northern canalers comprised a community unto themselves. When they became a distinctive community is unclear, but it probably occurred by the mid-nineteenth century as their numbers approached a thousand individuals and they developed unique characteristics distinct from other maritime and landed communities in the Northeast. The northern canalers established their own words, skill sets, music, and material culture over nearly thirty years of navigating the inland waterways. At times, their uniqueness was a blessing to the community. For many northern canalers, their way of life was a great source of pride, a source of support when in financial or emotional need, and a source of familiarity and continuity for many families that had long and diverse roots in the canal boat trade. At other times, the distinctive lifestyle of the community put them in conflict with others not familiar with their way of life. Canalers were frequently ridiculed by outsiders and were made to feel inferior to other mariners. Despite the pride and strength of the northern canal boat community, these outside influences tore at the community. Those within the community as well as outsiders came to perceive the lifestyle of the canalers as outdated and inappropriate for families. During the early decades of the twentieth century, canal boat parents forced their children out of the community as a result of outside economic, social, educational, and religious pressures placed on the northern canal boat community.

The northern canal boat community, which was clearly an imagined community, consisted of loose bonds among members but gained its importance through individual commitment. The fluidity of individual involvement resembled those communities of modern society more than their contemporaries in the rural and proto-urban place-based communities of the Champlain Valley, where physical mobility and choice were limited by religious and political systems, and social and economic constraints. The canalers' high physical mobility kept them beyond the reach of many of these barriers, at least during the navigation season.

The community also built upon solidarity in opposition to maritime outsiders to the community, who consisted of canalers from other regions, especially the Erie Canal. After construction of the New York State Barge Canal, Erie Canal boatmen worked on the Northern Waterway, as evident from lock tenders' logbooks and the discovery of several Erie Canal boats sunk on the bottom of Lake Champlain. Additional Erie Canal boats found their way into the Champlain Valley through purchases made by young northern canal boatmen, who were frequently ridiculed for it. Canalers were a specialized form of community; their members had associated lifestyles that were characterized more by individuality and less upon a small, bounded locality or physical place.

The northern canal boat community was a regional community that was complex, spatially extensive, and fluid in its organization, scale, and annual membership. The northern canalers lived a unique lifestyle with an enormously rich culture of values, beliefs, and material culture that was in part a continuum of contemporary life along the Northern Waterway. This lifestyle contained elements representing the many people and places that the northern canalers interacted with in the region, including rural, urban, and maritime peoples. The influence of these communities upon a northern canaler was not one at a time but instead several at the same time and over a canaler's lifetime. The personal identity of canalers was complex, and most canalers likely belonged to multiple communities. Their identities were always in flux with their seasonal transitions from water-based communities to land-based communities. Thus, individual canalers were a product of their collective communities, and the northern canal boat community was a product of the identities of its collective memberships. Archaeologists have paid little attention to the impact and importance of simultaneous memberships in diverse communities.

The northern canalers lived two very different lifestyles throughout the year. During the navigation season, they traveled thousands of miles on the inland waters of the Northeast and participated in the economic and social interactions of communities along the waterways. In the offseason, they became a part of their port community or returned to a land-based community along the Champlain Waterway. As a result of these annual cycles, most northern canalers were members of multiple communities. One such community, their homeport, was clearly displayed on the stern of their boat. Other communities of importance included religious communities and communities related to their ethnic, racial, or social heritage.

The northern canalers were exceptional in several ways: they created their own occupational community and belonged to one or several place-based communities at once. Their dynamic processes of interaction and the space in which this occurred are not typical of most historic communities in the Northeast, many of which were place-based communities. Historical archaeologists are likely to find other parallels when documenting seasonal occupational communities, such as fishing, logging, fur trading, and mining outposts. People flowed in and out of these occupations, creating networks of people, resources, and structures that often spanned great territories and multiple clusters of buildings. Therefore, the concept of a regional imagined community, as outlined by Yaeger, Isbell, and others, is best applied to the northern canalers because it considers the imagined connections of its members within a regional space.

Northern canalers moved independently along the inland waterways for seven months of the year and then returned to land-based homes or boat basins for the remaining five months before beginning the cycle anew. The northern canalers constitute a unique group based on a lifestyle that has few parallels but offers a challenging test of the definition, assumptions, methods, and theories surrounding the study of communities by historical archaeologists and historians.

Appendix A:

(**Figure 7**) Northern canalers unload shipments of potatoes in New York Harbor, relying upon other members of the community to assist.

Most northern canal boatmen appear in the United States census records as boatmen or sailors depending on whether they operated unrigged or sloop and schooner rigged canal boats. U.S. census records do not record northern canal boat women or children as boatmen or sailors. This table should only be used as a general reference to the decline in the number of the northern canalers because the data likely include errors by the census takers or modern transcribers of the census data, such as the inclusion of naval and commercial sailors who were not involved in canal navigation. Northern canalers who were in transit or in Canadian ports at the time of the census are not included in the census data. The table does not include data from New York's Albany, Rensselaer, and Saratoga counties because they border the Erie Canal and Hudson River, which also include the homeports of Erie Canal boatmen. Ports used by northern canalers in these New York counties included Albany, Cohoes, Mechanicville, Rensselaer, Stillwater, Troy, and Waterford. The assumption is that the number of northern canalers in these southern ports (called Estimated Canalers in the table) is equal to those in Washington County, New York, at the northern end of the Champlain Canal. Note that the 1890 U.S. census data is not available.

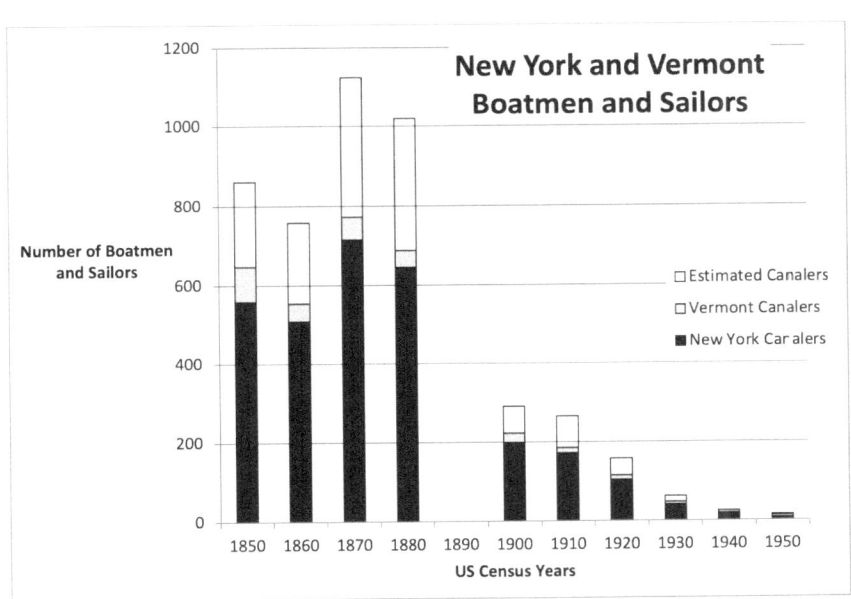

Endnotes

1   Pyle, "Through Inland Waters."; Pyle, "Through Inland Waterways, II."

2   Anonymous, "Bargemen Lend Color to the Harbor," 1926); Anonymous, "Canal-Boat Harbor," 1871); Anonymous, "Canalers' Village: Tow-Path Mariners in Their Winter's Snug Harbor," 1893; Anonymous, "Canalmen in Winter," 1890; Anonymous, "Life on a Canal Boat: Winter Quarters for Many Families," 1898; Anonymous, "On Canalboats," 1898; Levick, 1924.

3   Anderson, Carter and Lowe, 1999; Wood, Jr. and Judikis, 2002.

4   Connolly, 1933.

5   Levick, 1924.

6   F. G. Godfrey, 1965; F. G. Godfrey, *Sailors, Waterways and Tugboats I have Known*, 1993; F. G. Godfrey, *The Champlain Canal: Mules to Tugboats*, 1994; Archambault, 1997; Juckett, 1985.

7   Bellico, *Life on a Canal Boat: The Journals of Theodore D. Bartley*, 1861-1889, 2004.

8   F. H. Godfrey, 1965; F. G. Godfrey, *Sailors, Waterways and Tugboats I have Known*, 1993; F. G. Godfrey, *The Champlain Canal: Mules to Tugboats*, 1994; Archambault, 1997; Juckett, 1985.

9   Gleason, 1922, 18.

10   Morton, 1984.

11   Anonymous, *A Brief History of Commerce on Lake Champlain*, n.d.

12   Taylor 1992, 2.

13   Harlow, *Old Towpaths: The Story of the American Canal Era*, 1926, 341.

14   Bellico, *Sail and Steam in the Mountains*, 2001, 245; F. H. Godfrey, 1965, 10.

15   F. G. Godfrey, *Sailors, Waterways and Tugboats I have Known*, 1993, 111-112.

16   Hill, 1995, 235.

17   Wood, Jr. and Judikis, 2002.

18   Anonymous, "Essex Notes," 1874.

19   McFee, 1998, 152.

20   Harlow, *Old Towpaths: The Story of the American Canal Era*, 1926, 334.

21   F. H. Godfrey, 1965, 11.

22   Hullfish, 1987, 248-249.

23   F. H. Godfrey, 1965, 3.

24   F. H. Godfrey, 1965, 9.

25   F. H. Godfrey, 1965, 23-24.

Figure Citations

All figure are courtesy of the Lake Champlain Maritime Museum Collections, apart from the first and last figures created by the Author.

Bibliography

Anderson, Ralph E., Irl Carter, and Gary R. Lowe. 1999. *Human Behavior in the Social Environment: A Social Systems Approach.* Aldine de Gruyter.

Anonymous. n.d. "A Brief History of Commerce on Lake Champlain." Henry Sheldon Museum of Vermont History.

—."Breaking Up a Tow." *Frank Leslie's Illustrated Newspaper* 71 (1826), 1890.

—."On Canalboats: Where Thousands of People Spend the Winter Months in Comparative Comfort." *Buffalo Commercial,* January 20, 1898.

—."Canalmen in Winter: If They Do Not Enjoy Life, They Would Like to Know Who Does." *Buffalo Courier*, March 11, 1890.

—."Boat Owners on Canal Appoint Traffic Head." *Buffalo News*, April 20, 1923.

—."New Tug Boat: The Unique Occupies a Position on the Lake True to Her Name." *Burlington Free Press*, June 5, 1906.

—."Canal-Boat Harbor." *Frank Leslie's Illustrated Newspaper* 32 (814), 1871.

—."Life on a Canal Boat: Winter Quarters for Many Families." *Daily Arkansas Gazette*, January 22, 1898.

—."Life on a Canalboat." *Essex County Herald*, August 29, 1879.

—."Essex Notes." *Essex County Republican*, June 25, 1874.

—."Life Aboard a Barge in New York Habor." *Literary Digest* 67 (1), 1920.

—."Bargemen Lend Color to the Harbor." *New York Times*, July 18, 1926.

—."Housekeeping on the Canal: What Was Seen Aboard One of These Mastless Ships." *New York Times*, May 7, 1893.

—."River Barge Dwellers Say Life on Shore is Cramping." *New York Times*, July 26, 1925.

—.. "The Tile Club at Whitehall." *New York Times*, July 10, 1879.

—."Canalers' Village: Tow-Path Mariners in Their Winter's Snug Harbor." *Springfield Reporter*, February 3, 1893.

—."The Docks of New York." *Harper's Weekly* 25 (1274), 1881. 351-352.

—."The Tile Club." *Harper's Weekly* 24 (1205), 1880. 72-73, 75.

—."This Hat Always in Style." *Vermont Tribune*, January 17, 1907.

Archambault, Cora, interview by Holly Noordsey and Megan Garrison. Edited by Scott A. McLaughlin. Lake Champlain Maritime Museum, 1997.

Archambault, Cora, interview by Jane Vincent. Edited by Scott A. McLaughlin. Lake Champlain Maritime Museum, 2000.

Barnard, Charles.. "Broken Adrift." *St. Nicholas* 15 (11), 1888: 840-848.

Bellico, Russell Paul. *Chronicles of Lake Champlain: Journeys in War and Peace.* Purple Mountain Press, 1999.

—.*Life on a Canal Boat: The Journals of Theodore D. Bartley, 1861-1889.* Purple Mountain Press, 2004.

—.*Sails and Steam in the Mountains: A Maritime and Military History of Lake George and Lake Champlain.* Revised. Purple Mountain Press, 2001.

Canuto, Marcello A., and Jason Yaeger. *The Archaeology of Communities: A New World Perspective.* Routledge, 2000.

Chester-Kadwell, Mary.. *Early Anglo-Saxon Communities in the Landscape of Norfolk.* BAR British Series 481. Archaeopress, 2009.

Connolly, Vera. "Amerian Water Gypsies." *Delineator* 123 (August) ,1933.

Copeland, Fred Osmon. "Champlain Canal Days." *Vermonter* 46 (8), 1941.

Finch, Roy G. *The Story of the New York Canals: Historical and Commercial Information.* J.B. Lyon, 1925.

Garrity, Richard. *Canal Boatman: My Life on Upstate Waterways.* Syracuse University Press, 1977.

Gleason, J. D. "Barges." *Scribner's Magazine* 72 (1), 1922. 17-25.

Glenn, Morris F. *Glenn's History of Lake Champlain (New York and Vermont).* Vol. 4: Canal Boats. Morris F. Glenn, 1980.

Godfrey, Frank H. "Speech Given Before the Canal Society of New York State." Compiled by Chittenango Landing Canal Boat Museum, 1965.

Godfrey, Fred G. *Sailors, Waterways and Tugboats I Have Known: The New York State Barge Canal System.* Library Research Associates, 1993.

—. *The Champlain Canal: Mules to Tugboats.* Library Research Associates, 1994.

Harlow, Alvin Fay. *Old Towpaths: The Story of the American Canal Era.* D. Appleton and Company, 1926.

—.*When Horses Pulled Boats: A Story of Early Canals.* American Canal and Transportation Center, 1987.

Hill, Ralph Nading. *Lake Champlain: Key to Liberty.* Twentieth Anniversary. Countryman Press, 1995.

Hullfish, William, ed. *The Canaller's Songbook: Words, Music, and Chords to over Thirty Canal Songs.* American Canal and Transportation Center, 1987.

Isbell, William H. "What We Should Be Studying: The 'Imagined Community' and the 'Natural Community'." In *The Archaeology of Communities: A New World Perspective*, edited by Marcello A. Canuto and Jason Yaeger, Routledge, 2000.

Johnson, Clifton. "A Canal-Boat Voyage on the Hudson." *The Outlook* 60 (5), 1898. 304-318.

Juckett, Martha Robbins. *My Canaling Days, 1897-1907.* Historical Society of Whitehall, 1985.

Larkin, F. Daniel. *New York State Canals: A Short History.* Purple Mountain Press, 1999..

Levick, M. B. "The Canal Boats' Winter Sleep Is Over: Soon the Elephantine Fleet Will Leave Coenties Slip for Ports North." *New York Times*, April 13, 1924.

McFee, Michele A. *A Long Haul: The Story of the New York State Barge Canal.* Purple Mountain Press, 1998.

Morton, Doris B. "Garden City." *Whitehall Independent*, April 18, 1984.

—."A Letter from a Little Girl of 1883." *Whitehall Times*, March 3, 1983.

—."Canal Affairs in April, 1880." *Whitehall Times*, April 17, 1980.

O'Hara, John Edward. *Erie's Junior Partner: The Economic and Social Effects of the Champlain*

Canal Upon the Champlain Valley. Columbia University, 1951.

Pyle, Howard. "Through Inland Waters." *Harper's New Monthly Magazine* 92 (552), 1896. 828-839.

Pyle, Howard. "Through Inland Waterways, II." *Harper's New Monthly Magazine* 92 (553) 1896.: 63-75.

Rideing, William H. "The Waterways of New York." *Harper's New Monthly Magazine* 48 (283) 1873: 1-17.

Schachner, Gregson. "Imagining Communities in the Cibola Past." In *Construction of Communities: Agency, Structure, and Identity in the Prehistoric Southwest*, edited by Mark D. Varien and James M. Potter. Altamira Press, 2008.

Springer, Ethel M., and Donald A. Wilson. *Always Know York Pal: Children on the Erie Canal.* Erie Canal Museum, 1993.

Stickler, Charles. "A Birthday Spent on Boats: I Remember." *Poughkeepsie Journal*, October 26, 1979.

Stiles, Fred T. "Tales of Old Canal Days." *North Country Life* 13 (1) 1959.

Taylor, David A. *Documenting Maritime Folklife: An Introductory Guide.* Library of Congress, 1992.

Thompson, Harold W. *Body, Boots, & Britches.* J.B. Lippincott Company, 1940.

Wilkins, Fred H. "Champlain Canal Notes." *Vermonter: The State Magazine* 20 (8), 1915.

Wood, Jr., George S., and Juan C. Judikis. *Conversations on Community Theory.* Purdue University Press, 2002.

Young, James C. "Idyll of the Barge Skipper: His Craft Begins Its Passive Labors While the Captain Busies Himself Loafing." *New York Times*, June 12, 1927.

CHAPTER 5
Commerce to Recreation on the Champlain Waterway

———————————

Matt Harrison
Sailing Programs Manager, Lake Champlain Maritime Museum

Lake Champlain's earliest names reflect the fact that it has always been an important route of northward and southward transportation for humans in the Champlain Valley. Its Haudenosaunee name (Kaniá:tare tsi kahnhokà:ronte) means "the lake that is the door to the country." This description was often repeated by early travelers and touring guides to Lake Champlain, imagining this native heritage of the "North Country."[1] But if the lake was the "gate" into this "North Country" for early outdoor recreation, the Champlain Canal was the first key to that gate, particularly for the widespread water-based recreation that would eventually emerge in the late 1800s.

The goal of this chapter is to document the transformation of the "Northern Waterway," or the waters of the Champlain Canal and its extended influence into the Champlain Valley, from a space of commercial transport into one of recreational or touristic activity. The fact that this waterway knit the Champlain Valley, famous for both its historical value and natural beauty, into the transportation network of the U.S. and Canada, makes the history of Champlain Valley tourism exceptionally important to study. While the lake would always be home to its own local or domestic maritime activity, this chapter argues that the canal was the first element in the growth of perhaps the earliest and most robust "playground" for water recreation in America. Where the Erie Canal was famous for facilitating development and immigration to the west, the Champlain Canal's legacy is outdoor recreation and rural tourism. Connecting watersheds and creating new waterways between regions, the Champlain Canal allowed for the evolution of unique new recreational activities and cultures in the Champlain Valley and nationally.

Transport on the Champlain Canal never focused on passenger transit as it did on the Erie "Western Canal." The Champlain was designed to connect two already-populated areas, not to transport migrants to developing western states as the Erie had. In the first three decades of the canal's life, packet boats delivered passengers between the Hudson River and southern Lake Champlain, meeting regular steamship service on both ends. This would mostly end with the rise of faster and more convenient railroads across the region. The Champlain Canal primarily moved freight. Champlain Canal boats began to accommodate tourists and travelers in a small capacity by the late 1800s, as the novelty of the canal began to grow. By the 1880s, travelogues were published recounting long-distance trips made up and down the Northern Waterway, both aboard canal boats and on small recreational vessels.[2]

American outdoor recreation and tourism begin in earnest in the second half of the 1800s, when urban and middle-class Americans with enough time and money for vacations began taking an interest in the outdoors. The Champlain Valley and its canal linkage played a special role in this era for two reasons. First, boats were key to popularizing outdoor recreation after the Civil War, as the Adirondack Preserve came to be popular with campers and especially canoeists. The most intrepid of these canoeists formed a special tie to the canal, using it to transport their smaller crafts north to the natural playgrounds of Lake Champlain and the Adirondacks. At the same time, the public image of working canal boats evolved a way that made them more welcoming to middle-class tourists. Where sailors and canalers had the patina of hazard or danger in earlier times, the inland waterways became attractive and nostalgic to traveling Americans in the decades after the Civil War.

In his 1891 tourism tract *Lake Champlain and Its Shores*, W.H.H. "Adirondack" Murray predicted that Lake Champlain would become the center of a "Great National Park of the Republic."[3] Written twenty years after Murray's more famous book *Adventures in the Wilderness; or, Camp-Life in the Adirondacks,* Gilded Age guidebooks like these established ideas of environmental conservation and health and stewardship of the outdoors and helped lead to the creation of the Adirondack Forest Preserve in the 1890s.[4] The Champlain Canal underwent a similar change of image to that of the Adirondack wilderness, from "wasted" space to an area with the potential for outdoor health and reinvigoration through recreation. Travelers were soon flocking to the region and the routes they took very often involved all or parts of the Northern Waterway.[5]

Commerce to Recreation—The Northern Transport Network

*...to pass away, in a novel fashion, a few weeks of the summer,
a party of four impecunious women made up an excursion to
Quebec and Montreal; cars and steamboats would have been dusty,
hot and fatiguing, and their speed prevented a full and perfect
enjoyment of the scenery en route, so there was no other way but to
get some good natured canal boat captain to take them along.*[6]

Augusta Woodruf Brown, *Notes of a canal boat trip
taken in the summer of 1895*

The Champlain Canal moved a lot of physical material from its creation in 1823 to today, but it also moved uncountable numbers of people. Much has been made of the passenger-carrying packet boat and its novelty on the early canal systems. Already in 1824, a year after the canal was completed but before the Erie Canal had been fully finished, there were travel guides being published for the tourist on the Champlain Canal, including one by Horatio Gates Stafford titled *A Pocket Guide for the Tourist and Traveller Along the Line of the Canal and Interior Commerce of the State of New-York*.[7] Besides encouraging commercial interactions, the connection of the Hudson and the Champlain watersheds created great opportunities to tour new landscapes for business or pleasure, as shown by the quick development of connecting steamboat traffic on Lake Champlain. In contrast to the dynamic along most of the Erie Canal route, the steamboat lines of Lake Champlain, some of the earliest anywhere, operated in close connection with passenger travel on the Champlain Canal. As long as passenger packet boats operated on the canal (prior to the predominance of railroad travel), steamboats' schedules were aligned to meet them.[8]

By the 1860s, most travelers headed north via the railroads to places like Saratoga, Lake George, and towns on the New York and Vermont sides of Lake Champlain. While steamboats facilitated commerce and business through the valley, the steamboat was always made to represent more than simply commerce. By the late 1800s, ornate "palace steamers" like the *Vermont*, the *Chateaugay*, and the *Ticonderoga* were a major form of recreational travel on Lake Champlain, even as passenger traffic on the Champlain Canal had shifted to rail. The Lake George Steamboat Company recorded that the company always opted for paddlewheel-driven steamers rather than a propeller-driven design because the paddlewheelers could "afford opportunity for lofty construction, grand saloons and imposing cabins which meant so much in steamboat design of the day."[9] Like the railroads, the experience of "palace steamers" was one of elegance and luxury as well as efficiency and technological might.

Surprisingly, interest in luxurious and modern travel went hand in hand with rustic outdoor experiences. Travelers on the decks of steamships enjoyed viewing the natural beauty of the Northern Waterways and "might be photographed on the sun deck of a cruise liner" as they made their way to their rural retreats. But for the most committed recreationists, it was the smaller vessels rather than the steamboat that allowed access to the richness of the "north country." Canoes, a loose term for many small craft at this time, became the famous vehicle of choice in the Adirondack Wilderness

On Deck of the "Vermont"

(Figure 1) Sociable tourists on the deck of the Steamer *Vermont*, 1891.

and along the Northern Waterway.

By this era, most people were not traveling up the Northern Waterway via the canals. But it was partially the rich network of transportation options into the North Country that made it such a suitable space for early outdoor tourism and recreation. A traveler from New York or Boston could knit together a series of routes and roads, including rail, steamship, waterways, and even trekking overland to reach "the north country." As Murray bragged to potential visitors in 1890, the lake's "waters are traversed by steamers that, in size and appointments, are excelled only by the floating palaces of

Long Island Sound, and the railways that touch it at many points enable the tourist to pass, day or night, in any direction."[10]

Two especially interesting travelogues from this era give us an excellent idea of the shape of early tourism on the Champlain Canal, both from the perspective of adventurous middle-class women from New York. The first is an 1892 book called *A Family Canoe Trip* by Florence Waters Snedeker (1857-1893) recounting a long-distance camping trip that the Snedeker family undertook the previous year. Traveling by canoe with their young child up the waterway, the family made their way from New York City to Willsboro, New York, on the western shore of Lake Champlain to attend a convention of the American Canoe Association. Snedeker's writing provides a fascinating perspective into a unique form of recreational activity on the Northern Waterway during this era and shows that the canal route was being utilized directly by recreational vessels even in the 1800s.

The second source, an 1895 manuscript by Augusta Woodruf Brown (1840-1937), provides another fascinating story of early tourism aboard canal boats on the Champlain Canalway, when a group of four women chartered a canal boat to take them from Albany to Canada at a leisurely pace and in "novel fashion," as quoted at the beginning of this section. Augusta Brown, the documentarian of the group, kept a lively and descriptive journal of happenings and impressions while aboard the canal boat *B.M. Bullis*, recording many details of their time as tourists aboard the working canal boats. Brown recounted how easy it was for her party to transfer away from the canal corridor on a whim to see friends in nearby towns, before returning to their "boat home."[11] Compared to railroad or steamboat transport, canal travel was slow, quaint, and allowed time for the tourist to socialize with canal families and locals as well as absorb the landscape at a more leisurely pace.

Touring by the 1890s was becoming mainstream. In 1892, Snedeker assured prospective travelers on the lake that "One will, of course, carry a camera with which to preserve, and to multiply for friends, the delights of the trip." She even recommended the type of camera to carry, a "Henry Clay," which took "5-by-7 pictures."[12] And the Champlain Valley had things to photograph! The historical value of the lake greatly mattered to recreational travelers of the 1800s, who had been raised with patriotic stories of Fort Ticonderoga and the novels of James Fenimore Cooper, set in the region.[13] This history was accessible to people in the form of the fort itself, but also in campfire stories of shipwrecks, colonial treasure, and revolutionary artifacts just below the water's surface.

From its very beginning, this water route offered opportunities for historical tourism. In 1824, Horatio Gates Stafford recorded in *A Pocket Guide for the Tourist and Traveller Along the Line of the Canal and Interior Commerce of the State of New-York* sites of macabre historical note like the "Pine Tree, where Miss M'Crea was killed, in the revolutionary war," located near Fort Edward along the canalway.[14] Howard Pyle recorded that "you find everywhere reminiscences of the past clinging like a green growth about these Northern inland waterways."[15] Later articles from the travelogues of the 1890s record that "one has only to scratch the soil upon which he stands to turn up bullets and grape shot embedded (how long?) in the peaceful bosom of mother earth."[16] These nostalgic but gruesome remembrances were common among lake travelers of the era, especially in close proximity to sites of historical drama like Forts Ticonderoga and Crown Point, Valcour Island, and many more locally known locations. Enthusiasts of American history scoured such sites for artifacts. Later, the exploration of the lake bottom itself in the name of historical discovery and preservation became a major feature of touristic interest in the valley.

Fort Ti, and Grenadier's Battery.

(Figure 2) Sketch by Augusta Brown of "Fort Ti, and Grenadier's Battery" as she passed by in 1895. Historic sites like Fort Ticonderoga were a major draw for early tourists up the Champlain Canal.

The canal continued to be a vector for historical tourism in the twentieth century, in the form of historical materials as well as tourists themselves. In June, 1961, the Smithsonian Institute facilitated the transport by the Champlain Canal of a major historical artifact -- the remains of the Revolutionary War vessel *Philadelphia*, which had been raised from the lake bed in the 1930s and had toured the watershed for thirty years as a historical spectacle. It exited the lake via the canal, bound for Washington, D.C.'s Smithsonian Museum of American History.[17]

It was not only the spectacular environment and geography of the Champlain Valley that evolved thanks to the canal -- the images of boats and canals in the minds of the public were also transforming in a way that benefitted tourism. As recreation on the waterways increased, magazine and travel narratives by journalists and writers like Snedeker, Brown and Howard Pyle painted the American canal boats on the Champlain waterway as novel, picturesque, unique and interesting to Americans with the capacity to tour (already very popular in this region of the country). Where the maritime world had once been dirty and dangerous, it was now shown to be safe and even appealing. Especially as more women gained access or acceptance on the waterway, Victorian ideas of domesticity connected the boats to the popular ideas of the family in new ways, opening up these spaces further for tourism by families.

The Maritime Mystique—Reputations Change

Most people think a canal is a line of black ooze, which crawls at the rear of factories and past the door-yards of scurvy cabins, their refuse on its banks, and their reek in its water. But he who wanders with it knows that a canal is a stream curving to the heart of meadow and wood; that the tow path is a grassy fringe; the heel-path a tangle of clematis, asters, golden-rod; that the white bridges and the clouds and the trees above him look up again from beneath him, so that he floats between; that weirs make falling music; that now he is borne across a brook, now high over the current of a river.[18]

Florence Snedeker, *A Family Canoe Trip*

During their heyday between the 1820s and the 1860s, the reputations of canals and their surrounding areas suffered. People rightly thought of them as dirty, stagnant, sometimes dangerous areas, unlike the newer (and faster) technologies of railroads or steamships. But by the end of the century this reputation began to change. Impressive, large-scale canal projects became international news stories in the late nineteenth century and early twentieth –- the Suez, the Panama, the Chicago Sanitary and Ship Canal. These big projects, combined with nostalgia for the maritime world, began to change the reputation of canals in the eyes of the public.

In the book *A Family Canoe Trip*, Florence Snedeker describes this change in perception, painting a beautiful picture of the Champlain Canal. The above quoted scene of pleasant, inviting, "picturesque" natural beauty fits with the interest in the natural world encouraged by the camping and outdoor movements developing at this time in the North Country. Snedeker and her family hitched rides along the canal, either pulling their canoes aboard obliging canal boats or being pulled along the towpaths themselves by teams of horses. Traveling by water was part of the experience, both rugged and comfortable at the same time. She writes: "we passed a house; a smiling woman ran out, and, with a propriety that savored of genius, waved a teapot in honor of domesticity afloat."[19]

Augusta Brown similarly recalls of her canal trip in 1895 that "Many amusing incidents occur on this sixty-five mile 'walk' to Whitehall. Besides walking on the tow-path, picking berries and flowers, we had evening practice in physical culture, singing by moonlight, and chatting with the passing boatmen and drivers."[20] Her journal portrayed the canal in mysterious, "exotic," and "strange" but not dangerous terms.[21] She encountered people working on canal boats who had adopted the lifestyle because it was slower paced and thought to be "healthful" compared to other forms of labor.[22]

"Loomed around a curve, and came on—slow, inevitable"

"We varied paddling with towing"

(Figures 3.1 & 3.2) Snedeker family canoe being towed along beside a canalboat and along the towpath on the Champlain Canal, 1891.

After her first night on the canal in 1895, Brown awoke to a new view of the unusual space she found herself in:

> *When the sun again shines you all will have disappeared and a new world will unfold for me in that quiet border land of traffic; that seldom visited region, except by canal-boats, mules and small boys on swimming bent; that winding stream with its well trodden tow-path, its countless bridges and mysterious locks.*[23]

As the landscape of the canal underwent a makeover after the Civil War, the boats themselves were also undergoing a reputational change that gave them touristic appeal. A mystique existed about the steamship and the canoe, which were newer modes of travel for Americans. At first, early tourists would not have thought much of the work-a-day canal vessels that plied the canal and lake. But as more and more vessels transitioned to engine power, the picturesque scene of a small sailboat or even a canal boat would eventually fit into the tourist's imagination of the North Country.

Technological change, from sailboats to power-driven vessels, occurred very quickly in the second half of the 1800s. Where sailing vessels had formerly dominated the maritime world along with the unique skills and lifestyles they created, by the end of the century, steam-powered boats had mostly replaced them. This rapid change, acute and visceral for anyone living near major waterways, created nostalgic feelings toward traditional maritime images. Upon reaching Lake Champlain, Snedeker records some of these

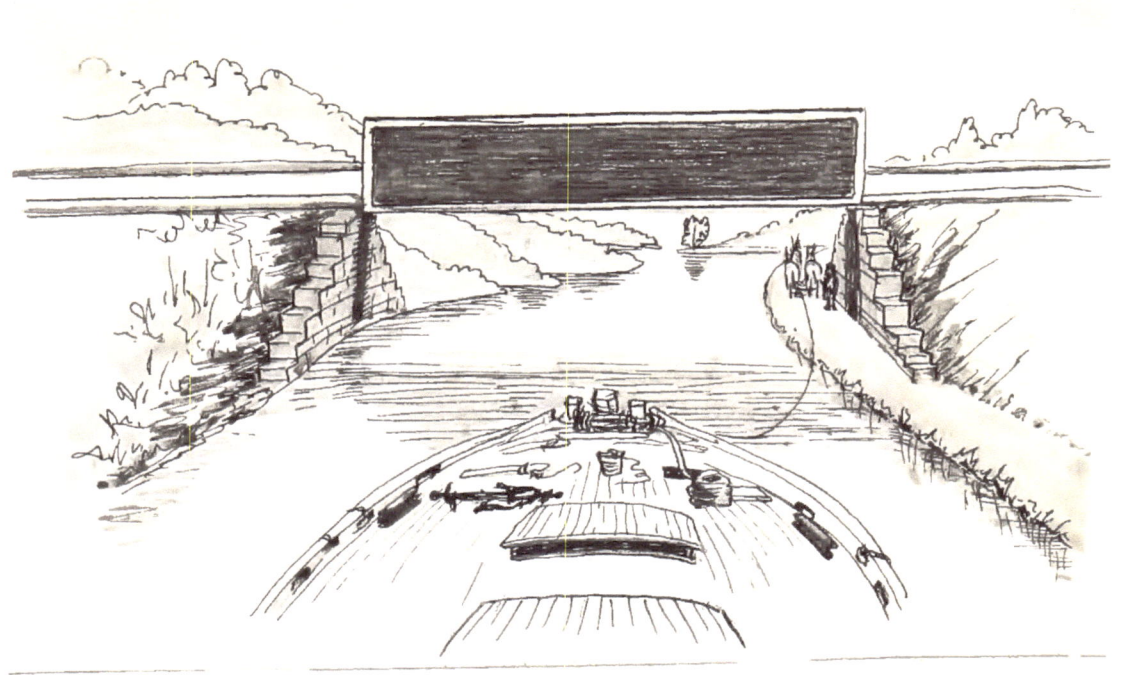

(Figure 4) A sketch by Augusta Brown of their canal boat passing under a bridge on the Champlain Canal, 1895.

sentiments, writing: "Great, empty, silent lake! In the days before railroads, it used to be alive with dockyards, sailors, ships. Now, as we went speeding northward, we saw but one other sail -- that of the lazy ferry-scow laden with meditative cows."[24] Boats that were used for hauling freight, previously seldom noticed and uncelebrated, began to be seen not just as utilitarian, but as quaint, honest, and reminiscent of a maritime heritage that was fading.

It is important to note that these two narratives popularizing canal travel in this era were both written by women. Canal boats, which had been traditionally cramped, dirty, and sometimes even violent spaces in the popular imagination, were not thought of as places of domesticity or enjoyment for women and families. Many of the boatmen themselves felt "keenly that conditions on the boats are not favorable for women and children, giving the following as the principal reasons for their attitude: Congestion in cabins and lack of sanitary facilities, fostering immorality and disease; inaccessibility of schools and doctors; lack of opportunities for recreation; and dangers from fire." In fact, during the first decades of the 1900s, there were even unsuccessful attempts by progressive politicians to make it unlawful for women and children to live on boats in New York State waters.[25]

Nonetheless, tourists of all ages and genders began to travel on these boats in the decades after the Civil War. Canal boats became well adapted as spaces for the "domestic" world –– a term used by this era to refer to any realm that could welcome women, children, or "home life." Journalist William Rideing highlights this during an 1873 journey up the canals: "From the windows of some cabins floods of hospitable light poured, revealing domestic groups at supper, reading and sewing; with the voices of men and women mingled the soft, swelling tones of a parlor organ, and the less musical clicking of several sewing-machines. Contentment and tranquility rested upon these water-homes, a gentle spirit pervaded them, and though they were ever moving, the bonds within seemed permanent and strong."[26]

Comfort and morality, especially when connected to "home life" or "domesticity," were always on the minds of travelers in this era and canal boats naturally satisfied these desires. Many expressed surprise at this new impression of the maritime world: "Our boat was our home -- as cozy and comfortable, as simple and cheery, a home as ever floated on fresh water... so it was as a boat. A magician touched it, and lo! it became a home -- a little floating, windowless cottage."[27] The collective community of canal vessels, which still operated on the waterways in this era, was also a source of novel comfort. Augusta Brown paints a vivid picture of this highly-mobile 1890s canal community in her journal, as Scott McClaughlin shows in chapter four. Upon reaching the area of Port Kent in a large northbound tow, the weather forced the canal boats to take refuge. Brown writes:

> ...so there we lay in a conglomerate mass, a community of boats, -- a canal town, No less than one hundred and fifty souls with their homes about them; "all sorts and conditions of men" women and children, from the free and independent excursionist, the aristocratic canal boat owner and captain, to the cunning baby in arms, and the coal heaver on the open flat boat.[28]

Even children were included as part of this floating domestic world. In fact, boat life was sometimes thought to be safer and cleaner than life in the city for children: "Decks of canal boats make a picturesque but somewhat restricted playground. A baby tethered on a sunny day to the flat, smooth top of a closed hatch is probably as well off as any baby need be, certainly infinitely better off than most city babies shut within four walls."[29]

The vessels themselves, which had always been designed to house a family unit, now became easily adaptable as a space for touring, even as they continued to transport freight. Augusta Brown and friends recounted some of the spatial elements of touring aboard canal boats. For one thing, the vessels appeared highly adaptable for pleasure travel, with a tent being assembled on deck whenever the weather and bridges allowed.[30] The boating community generally seemed very happy to accommodate and entertain travelers. Brown and her four friends spent much time visiting neighboring boats and meeting the families that owned and operated them. They described the wide array of cabin layouts:

> We visited quite a number of the boats, comparing cabins, as we stopped at different places to drop off or take up boats. Though all seemed alike in a general way, some were very much nicer than others. The "B.M.B." had a large room, a bed room and a kitchen while some had the bedroom only curtained off, and others had four rooms, as the "Palisade", with rolling doors between, so that all could open into one in the day time. Most of the boats have awnings over the cabins, with swings and hammocks underneath, the top of which reaches back so as to shelter the steersman from sun and rain.[31]

Some families who operated Lake Champlain's hybrid sailing canal boats were also experimenting with a switch from cargo-hauling to sail touring. A well-known Champlain canal boat, the *O.J. Walker*, normally a working vessel, was recorded to have carried a troupe of musicians aboard for a "grand tour" of the lake in 1884. Twenty-one people traveled aboard on this tour, which included music from a special organ and theater in the hold of the boat, as well as meals provided by the boat's cook.[32] The traditional rig of

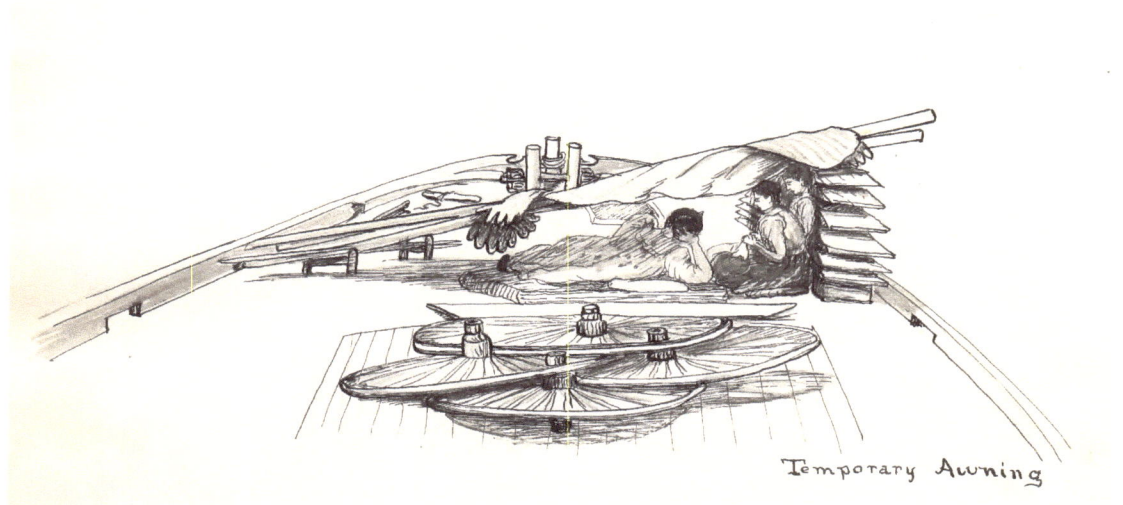

(**Figure 5**) A sketch by Augusta Brown of the "temporary awning" employed to keep canal boat tourists comfortable on deck during their voyages along the Northern Waterway.

the Champlain boats (described simply as "schooners") provided even more of an impetus for touring, since this type of vessel was not restricted to the canal and did not need to be towed by a steam powered vessel. Given the mystique of traditional sailboats, it is possible that these vessels had even more appeal to tourists than traditional canal vessels.

Camps and Canoes on the Northern Waterway

For a large portion of the year, the Northern Waterway is a cold and gray-brown landscape. Much of the waterway freezes, the canal is drained, and water transport ceases altogether. But come summer, the thaw brings not only the ability to travel again, but also the desire among many to enjoy the natural beauty of the Northern Waterway. Outdoor recreation was first popularized in this region of America, with the ease of transportation provided by the canal and its connected systems playing a major role in this development. Included in the early popularity of camping, hiking, and the outdoors was a great interest in boating. Writer William H.H. Murray, often credited with kick-starting American camping culture through his 1869 book *Adventures in the Wilderness,* was also deeply involved in boating culture. After the success of his first book, which set off a tourist rush to the Adirondacks in the 1870s and '80s, Murray lived for a time in Burlington, Vermont, and wrote books and articles touting the recreational opportunities of the Lake Champlain.

Even before Murray began publicizing it, camping in this region was closely associated with recreational boating due to its many lakes and robust water transport. Adirondack traveler Joel Tyler Headley wrote for the *New York Times* in 1858, describing the lifestyle of one of his Adirondack guides: "you travel in boats, go on pleasure excursions in boats, get all your meat, and fish, and vegetables in boats, and finally your milk and butter in boats. Well, a boat with you is a great institution."[33] Boats were everywhere in the lake-filled Adirondacks. But reaching that "wilderness playground" also involved extensive water transportation up the canalway, whether for visitors to the Champlain Valley or for campers and canoeists bound for the Adirondacks.

In many ways, the early canoeing culture was the beginning of private recreational boats on Lake Champlain. As the sport took off, the first organization to support it arose in this region. The American Canoe Association (ACA), which blossomed on Lake George and Lake Champlain in the 1880s and 1890s, knit together paddlers from the U.S. and from Canada and held large seasonal gatherings of canoeists. Called ACA "encampments," four such gatherings occurred on Lake Champlain in the 1880s and 1890s. An event was held in 1887 on North Hero Island, followed by two more encampments held at Willsboro, New York, in 1891 and 1892. These latter two conventions were hosted on the grounds of The Willsborough, a large hotel that stood for around a decade at the northern end of Willsboro Point, on the New York side of Lake Champlain, roughly across from Burlington. A fourth encampment was held at Bluff Point in 1895. Eventually, the enthusiasm of its Canadian contingent seems to have shifted the ACA's meeting northward in the 1890s and after.[34]

Francis Snedeker's account of the 1891 ACA meetup shows that regional travel played a major part in the early days. By the Gilded Age, the ubiquity of railroads also gave boat travel a rustic mystique for travelers, who saw it as a quaint, old-time tradition. Although a majority of travelers did utilize the network of transportation available along the canal corridor, a handful of the most intrepid long-distance "cruising canoeists" like Snedeker and family would make such trips entirely by boat. The ACA encouraged members to avoid modern conveniences and to travel to its gatherings the "authentic way," in canoes via the inland waterways.[35] Some groups made very long journeys. One, named the "Jabberwock Canoe Club," paddled to Lake Champlain from Springfield, Ohio, for the ACA's 1887 meeting, while another made plans to travel to Lake Champlain from Chicago.[36]

Canoeists who made their way to Lake Champlain from the south could hitch rides up the Hudson on canal boats as well as steamboats, which offered novel but flexible travel options. Canoers could pay for tows up the canal for their smaller vessels, just as the commercial vessels did. The Glens Falls feeder canal offered a shortcut for canoeists to reach Lake George, which remained a major destination for canoeing and resorting in the summer months. Many cruising canoeists then took the route from Glens Falls overland to Lake George, over the short portage at famous Ticonderoga, and then onward to Lake Champlain. A number of travelogues were published between the 1870s and 1900 recounting such trips, trying to encourage more people to take advantage of the exciting opportunity to boat and camp recreationally along the Northern Waterway.

In general, it appears that small craft were accustomed to catching tows along the upper Hudson and Champlain Canals, as Augusta Brown reports in her journal: "Now and then a canoe with boys and girls drawing up alongside for a "life", paying "toll" by some cheerful song."[37] Another group of paddlers from Lowell, Massachusetts, in 1883 saw an opportunity to use railroad connection to reach a Lake George meet in a novel direction –- embarking from Vergennes, Vermont, and traveling down Otter Creek before touring the south lake on their way to the event, celebrated that spring in the popular outdoor touring magazine *Forest and Stream*.[38]

Upon arrival at Willsboro in August 1891, Snedeker and family describe a vibrant recreational boating culture on Lake Champlain. Over the course of three weeks, campers from the U.S. and Canada shared in events, dining, and many small boating races in canoes in Willsboro Bay, which included a visit by a large floating model of "Champ," apparently built by one of

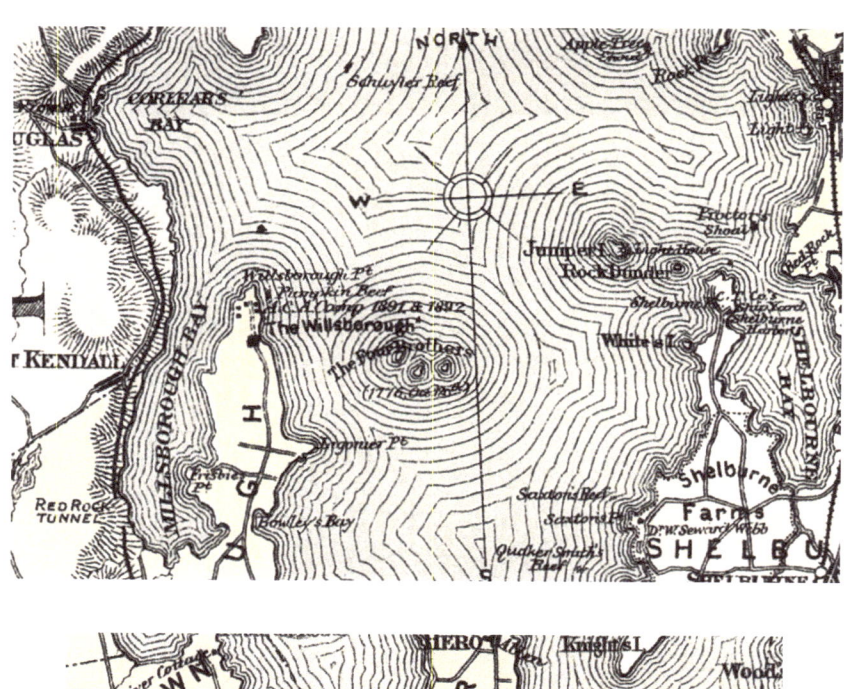

(Figures 6.1 and 6.2) John Stoddard published a detailed map of the Champlain Valley for tourists in 1893, complete with attractions, hotels, and transportation lines and details. The Willsborough hotel and the site of the American Canoe Association camps for 1887, 1891, and 1892 are noted on the map, showing that they were major events within the valley.

the competitors and described by Florence as the "fabled Champlain sea-serpent."[39] It is impressive to find this aspect of Lake Champlain culture so well established as early as the 1890s!

The ACA held one more encampment on Lake Champlain in 1895 before shifting its gatherings farther north to the St. Lawrence Valley and establishing a fixed camping ground there.[40] Snedeker's involvement with the ACA came to a sad end in 1893 when she passed away at age thirty-five. She had given birth to her third child only a month prior. That same month, The Willsborough hotel on Willsboro Point, where she and her family had paddled with her only a few years before, had also burned to the ground.

Despite this shift in organized boating in the region, long-distance "cruising canoeists" continued to make similar trips up the waterway into the early 1900s. Noted maritime artist John A. Noble, famous for documenting the physical decline of New York's maritime docklands, made a long-distance honeymoon trip with his wife, Susan, in a rowboat in August of 1934. They rowed five-hundred miles up the Hudson, through the Champlain Canal and onward to Burlington, Vermont, rowing, catching tows, and recording sketches and drawings along the way.[41]

Overall, though, boating dynamics were never focused on such long-distance travel as Nobel's and Snedeker's stories record. Instead, lake camps, both private and public, became major centers for boating and water recreation in the North Country and were often in historic locations. Camping as recreation was becoming more and more popular by the 1880s, and multiple established summer camps and resorts sprouted up along the lake

The Sea-serpent, Lake Champlain

(Figure 7) Photograph of the model of the Lake Champlain monster created by theatrical artist Lafayette Seavey, towed behind his canoe and presented during sailboat races at Willsboro's Indian Point, during the 1891 American Canoe Association Meeting.

in that decade, catering to the easily accessible New York populations down the Hudson.

Camping and water recreation increasingly became part of the world of childhood too. A network of "sleepaway" camps for youths in the North Country began to develop in the late 1800s, and soon generated lasting enthusiasm for the outdoors and for boating among camp-bound teens. Meant to help youths "master the lake" by swimming and sailing, these institutions built on the new idea that summer outdoor recreation was socially and physically necessary for the health of youths.[42] Such camps originated in New Hampshire, but before long a robust collection of summer camps for boys and girls had developed on Lake Champlain and in the surrounding region. In 1891, the "father of YMCA camping," Sumner Francis

Dudley, settled on Westport, New York, as the permanent site for Camp Dudley, which continues today. This boys' day camp is one of the oldest youth day camps in the country, and would eventually be joined by another campus on the Vermont side of Champlain, Camp Kiniya in Colchester, Vermont.[43]

As the days of commercial freight receded, one summer camp in particular captured the unique blend of nostalgia and outdoor recreation on the lake. A curious pair of youth leaders, Francis and Marion Baker, both veterans of the First World War, established a camp on South Hero Island in 1928, seeking to serve "older boys" who had aged out of other regional summer camps. Francis Baker, a Canadian engineer and mariner who had been affiliated with the American Canoe Association, clearly bought into developing ideas about the benefits of maritime or nautical training for youths.[44] Originally called "Adventurers Summer Boys Camp," this imaginative camp set about building a large fantastical "pirate" vessel called *Aladdin*. The seventy-five-foot-long vessel could berth a crew of more than twenty and became a primary attraction for campers aged fourteen to nineteen. The brochure for the first year (1929) explained the mission this way:

> *We plan to take cruises of short duration to the various parts of this wondrous mountain-rimmed lake, returning at intervals to Dingley Dell for tennis, horse-back riding, lacrosse, soccer, and other sports. A thorough training in coastwise navigation and general seamanship will be given everyone.*[45]

The strange, colorful vessel with multiple masts, topsails, and rainbow-colored sails must have been quite a spectacle for all the boating community of northern Lake Champlain during this era. Baker, the "skipper," and a crew of youths toured the lake each summer, stopping where they pleased, sometimes fishing and foraging for food or anchoring inside the Burlington Breakwater to catch an evening movie. The descriptor "adventure" in the name of the camp was quite literal, as numerous instances of wild scrapes with weather, accidents, and other maritime adversity are listed in the logbooks of *Aladdin* during its decade on the lake. *Camp Aladdin*, as it was quickly renamed, came to an end in 1939, but the remains of the vessel *Aladdin* persisted for some decades on the shore of Beech Bay, South Hero Island, as a beach house and a familiar sight to local boaters and residents. The boat finally burned in 1960.[46] While *Aladdin* seemed most often to voyage north into Canada, it is entirely possible that the southern lake and even the Champlain Canal would have been within reach of the adventurers -- unfortunately, the complete logbooks have been lost. Finally, the transportation route that brought campers to South Hero and indeed to most Champlain Valley camps continued to trace the north-south track of the Northern Waterway.

Yachts and Canal Boosters

By the 1900s, the Champlain Valley had a robust reputation for beauty and history, long a destination for tourists. But the canal and its connection to tourism continued to change, particularly in the nature of the ownership of boats. As commercial canal vessels gradually disappeared from the scene, private recreational boating became the primary maritime activity of the

(Figure 8) The imaginative summer camp vessel *Aladdin* combined the mystique of maritime heritage and lake recreation in the 1920s and 1930s. Though most of its logbooks have been lost, it may well have traveled around the area of the Champlain Canal on its summer voyages.

waterways. This history is the next phase of the canal –- as private ownership of small boats in the mid-1900s allowed for small-scale recreational utilization of the canal and its connected regions.

As already discussed, early environmentalism went hand in hand with outdoor recreation, and boating played a major part in this transition. Organized "yachting" on Lake Champlain began alongside the 1800s canoeing craze, though it centered more on local summer communities rather than the out-of-region canoeists. The Northern Waterway was the incubator for this "canoe culture" in America, and canoes and "yachts" were linked at this time. A prominent early camping enthusiast, the class-conscious North Country paddler George Sears, wrote in 1887:

> The canoe is coming to the front, and canoeing is gaining rapidly in popular favor, in spite of the disparaging remark that "a canoe is a poor man's yacht."... For myself, I freely accept the imputation. In common with nine-tenths of my fellow citizens I am poor—and the canoe is my yacht, as it would be were I a millionaire.[47]

By contrast with canoeing's accessibility to all classes, "yachting" was largely a middle- and upper-class form of recreation. A Victorian-era desire to combine boating and comfort in the "healthful" outdoors led to the development of yacht clubs throughout the Champlain Basin.[48] Many of the first yacht clubs were utilizing craft not unlike the one Snedeker and family traveled aboard. The word "yacht" in this era was much more flexible than it is today. As shown in Sears' quote above, the terms "canoes" and "yachts" could be used interchangeably despite the clear class distinction.[49] Early "yachts" on Lake Champlain appear to have been small boats mostly for local racing rather than regional touring, interchangeable with the "canoes" that were raced at Willsboro in the 1890s by the members of the ACA.

Murray in particular sold Lake Champlain as a prime "yachting" location, for its safety, freshwater, lack of tides, physical beauty, and easy access to the coasts via the canalways. "It is beyond question the safest sailing and cruising ground that the amateur yachtsman can find," he wrote in 1890.[50] Murray founded the Lake Champlain Yacht Club in 1887, the earliest yacht club in the Champlain watershed and originally called the Burlington Yacht Club. The organization's history recounts that the "Lake Champlain Yacht Club, organized on May 16, 1887, grew out of the Sharpie Yacht Club of Burlington, which had been organized in 1886," to encourage the introduction and development of yachting on Lake Champlain. Its leadership consisted of many of the wealthiest residents of the Champlain Valley, in particular William Seward Webb as the first commodore. Murray recounts that as of 1890 the LCYC had a "fleet of nearly forty well-built boats... composed of catboats, sharpies, burgess-modelled sloops, and English cutters; nearly all of them new boats and of much larger size than is generally found in amateur clubs."[51]

"*What fairy fleet flying about us*"

(Figure 9) Illustrations of small boat races on Lake Champlain, from Snedeker, 1891. These boats were referred to as "canoes" but were much more varied in size and design than a "canoe" of today.

Additional yacht clubs formed throughout the twentieth century, including Malletts Bay Boat Club (1936), Split Rock Yacht Club in Essex, New York (1939), Chazy Yacht Club in Plattsburgh (1955), and Diamond Island Yacht Club (1980s). Port Henry and Westport clubs hosted both sail and motorboat races, many of which continue today.[52] Student-led boating also grew. Middlebury College's Dinghy Club, founded in 1939 by future Olympian Stuart Walker, became one of the school's largest clubs, sailing on Kingsland Bay on Lake Champlain.[53] The University of Vermont's competitive sailing team also began around 1946. Both programs faded by the 1960s but were later revived.

To this "yachting set," the northern sections of Lake Champlain were the most attractive, with their wide water and access to sumptuous hotels and the exotic nearby Canadian waters. Murray largely neglects the Champlain Canal and the south lake in his writing, despite the fact that many boaters would have been transiting the route. Working-class towns along the Champlain Canal like Glens Falls and Whitehall were less aligned with elite tourism, despite their important geographic position on the canal.

Even as small boats flourished, interest remained in accommodating larger recreational craft and calls to modernize the Champlain Canal intensified. By the early 1900s, it had been determined that the old canal of the previous century would be expanded for the modern era. The impetus for such a project was apparent to Augusta Brown, who believed that an expanded canal would encourage tourist activity, writing: "When this is accomplished who could resist the temptation of a trip to Canada in a Canalboat?"[54] By 1918, the New York State Barge Canal was completed, enhancing infrastructure across the Erie and Champlain Canals. But its larger scale discouraged small family boats, favoring incorporated barge traffic. The larger modern canal barges lacked the quaint nostalgia of the earlier family-owned vessels, and tourist recreation moved off these unique vessels once and for all as they disappeared from the scene.

Simultaneously, a great increase in interest in motor yachting occurred, with Lake Champlain being an ideal location. Augusta Brown reported on her 1895 canal trip that "we were grounded by a passing yacht which seemed to want the entire channel, by no means broad and deep just there. It took one hour and much labor to get by."[55] Steam yachts had previously plied the canal and lake, but by the early 1900s, private gas-powered vessels were promoted as drivers of tourism. Traveling yachts were first seen as the answer to barge canal tourism, and those with an interest in preserving or reimagining the canal continued to tout it as a route for longer-distance recreation. In 1900, the Lozier Motor Company relocated the production of their early gas-powered engines to Plattsburgh, New York, to take advantage of the busy lake recreation.[56] They promoted the Northern Waterway route to justify their new Plattsburgh location: "Lake Champlain, The Champlain Canal and Hudson River form a continuous water way between Plattsburgh and New York City, and during the summer this trip...is enjoyed by many owners of private yachts."[57] One of the earliest gas-powered yachts, a thirty-one-foot-long vessel called *Beulah,* completed the five-hundred-mile trip from Toledo, Ohio, to Plattsburgh, New York, through the Champlain Canal and to Lake Champlain as part of the Lozier Motor Company's move to Plattsburgh.[58]

(Figure 10) The Lozier Motor Company used stereotyped Native American imagery to sell a nostalgic vision of Lake Champlain to elite buyers. Its Plattsburgh plant stood until 2024.

During conversations about a possible "ship canal" (even larger than the barge canal) beginning in the 1920s, boosters of that plan suggested that the waterway should be an important one for recreational boating. A Mr. Wood, a leader of the Vermont commercial community, presented "two exhibits, one covering the number of documented yachts regarded as potential users of the seaway. Mr. Wood was of the opinion that with the development of a through waterway, it would be used very extensively by pleasure craft... going north and south between the Hudson and the St. Lawrence..."[59] Though this larger project was never undertaken, the aspirations of Mr. Wood and his canal boosters would continue to reverberate.

On Lake Champlain, steamships tried to adapt to the change. The *Ticonderoga*, the last palace steamer to operate on the lake, augmented one of its decks to carry automobiles. By the 1940s, gas-powered ferries designed explicitly for cars were the norm across the lake, outcompeting the older coal-powered steamships. The gradual disappearance of the network of lake steamers was also nostalgic to locals. In 1940, Vermont historian Wallace Lamb repeated nostalgic feelings that extended back a century:

> *...we live in a rapidly changing world, and though it makes us sad to say it, the age of large steamers now seems to be over. No longer will those stately craft crowded with happy tourists, glide through the islands of Lake George, or sweep majestically up and down the broad bosom of Lake Champlain... Because of competition from the automobile, the railroad, and other factors, the Champlain Transportation Company was forced to discontinue its through service after 1932.*[60]

Despite the decline of the steamboat, the advent of private motor yachting and boating presented new opportunities for individuals to travel the length of the lake and to utilize the canal, visiting and sometimes competing on Lake Champlain from points south.[61] Newspapers in 1950 recalled the early 1900s "when 150 to 200 visiting boats would come for the season, attracted by the [Lake Champlain Yacht] Club. They came from Albany, Long Island, New York City, New Jersey points and other distant places."[62] This large number of sail and motor vessels was partially thanks to enthusiasm for nautical activity driven by Americans' participation in the World Wars, the same interest that had driven the development of regional collegiate sailing clubs. But this era also witnessed the beginning of the modern seasonal "Great Loop" route for yachts through the Champlain Canal, traveling south or west along the intercoastal waterway, the Mississippi, and the Great Lakes.

(**Figure 11**) Motor vessels like this one became a primary form of lake recreation in the 1930s and 1940s on Lake Champlain and eventually the waters of the Champlain Canal.

By the time of the construction of the New York Barge Canal, the Champlain Canal's towpath, no longer used by horses or mules, transitioned to an automobile route and remains memorialized through names like "towpath road." By the early twentieth century, automobiles were becoming more and more common. This new technology encouraged better roads, bridges, and ferries to be constructed along the Northern Waterway. Tourism, alongside wider American culture, transitioned to the world of automobiles. The Lozier plant in Plattsburgh gave up its marine engine business in 1906 and left the Champlain Valley to build gas automobile engines.[63]

Although there are a few large ferries or touring vessels left on the lake today, all cater to automobile travel. Cars allowed much more individualistic lake recreation, with boaters transporting their own private craft wherever accessible by road. With the Champlain Canal no longer being the only vector for boats to enter the lake from the south, new environmental concerns arose around invasive species on small craft.

Protecting the Northern Waterway

Despite the changing transportation scene in the twentieth century, tourism and recreation along the Champlain Canal and Lake Champlain continued to increase. As this happened, state oversight shifted from commercial priorities to environmental protection. Rather than concern for commercial interests, the focus switched to protection of the watershed and its unique natural resources. The movement of oil on the Champlain Canal, which had remained the primary example of commercial activity on the canal late into the 1900s, began to attract concern. Barge transport bringing oil to consumers and to federal military based in the valley accounted for "70 percent (335 million gallons) of the total petroleum product consumed in the basin in 1976."[64] The tank farms that supported this industry had a "total storage capacity of about 413 million gallons (106 million gallons in Vermont and 307 million gallons in New York)."[65] A 1970s report cited these facilities, located along the Champlain Canal and Lake Champlain, as a source of potential spills and accidents on canal or lake. Industrial activities on the canal were now presented as a threat to the vital tourism and recreational value of the watershed.

These risks drove a broader transition from commercial use to environmental stewardship. Efforts eventually began to clean up and transform "abandoned" canal-side industrial properties into spaces and resources useful for recreation, both on the Champlain Canal and on Lake Champlain, where affiliated industrial plants were located.[66] This process continues today. Environmental concerns affiliated with the canal also continue today, with evidence of the widespread impact of invasive species entering the Champlain Watershed through the Champlain Canal, as discussed in chapter seven.

By the 1970s, state organizations were continuing to predict growth of recreational use on Lake Champlain, calling "boating (particularly sailing)" the "fastest-growing activity in Vermont," though growth was focused largely on the populous northern section of the lake.[67] Many more boat ramps were recommended to handle this increase and tourism progressed into a primary industry of the Champlain Valley. By the 1990s, a monitoring organization reported that "recreational use of Lake Champlain has increased dramatically over the last decade. Of the total of 12,425 boats on the lake, 62% were motor vessels while 25% were sail, and other small craft the rest."[68] On the south lake, near the northern outlet of the Champlain Canal and farther from major population centers, activity was quieter.

Though it can be hard to see due to the expansive geography of the Champlain Valley, the Northern Waterway continues to host a fleet of small vessels that transit the canal between the Hudson and Champlain watersheds. Recognizing the Champlain Canal's distinct character, New York State promoted it as a separate regional entity from the Erie Canal, which has led to modest improvements to the canal frontages in towns like Mechanicville, Fort Edward, and Whitehall.[69] The Glens Falls Feeder Canal, restored for public use starting in the 1980s, now attracts over 100,000 visitors annually for walking, biking, and paddling, according to its alliance organization.[70] A "Canal Recreationway Commission" was established to encourage further development of recreational resources and infrastructure.[71] As in the early days of recreation, paddling remains popular. The Champlain Canal forms the northern end of the Hudson River Greenway Water Trail, used by long-distance canoeists no longer trailing cargo vessels. A similar Lake Champlain Water Trail, launched in 1988 by the Lake Champlain Committee and Champlain Kayak Club, offers a low-impact recreational corridor with detailed guides on amenities, launch points, and lock navigation.[72] A National Park Service guide supports paddlers along the Champlain Canal route, though a fully continuous bike route—like the Erie Canalway Trail—has not yet materialized along the Champlain corridor as of 2025.[73]

(Figure 12) The Feeder Canal Alliance has restored Glens Falls' 1800s canal for recreational use, attracting summer paddlers—echoing Florence Snedeker's 1890s journey north.

Nonetheless, canal boosterism around recreation continues as it has since the 1870s, promising continued growth. A 1993 New York State report touted the canal's ideal location between New York and Montreal, suggesting strong tourism potential as the only direct waterway between them.[74] Seasonal flows of recreational boats—averaging 100 to 150 per month during peak times—move through the Champlain Canal, nearly all for leisure use.[75] The canal also serves private vessels on "The Great Loop," a long-distance circuit of U.S. and Canadian inland waterways that connects various historically commercial routes.

Looking south from Lake Champlain, the long-term impact of the canal on regional tourism is clear, even if not always along its banks. Recent New York State planning documents call for "repositioning of the Canal as a spine of recreation and tourism," while recognizing limitations of the century-old barge canal.[76] This report concludes by acknowledging that as the canal system "enters its third century, it also stands poised for its third reimagining."[77] Whatever its future form, the region's geography and recreational legacy will continue to shape activity along the Champlain Canal.

Endnotes

1   Seneca Ray Stoddard, *Lake George Illustrated and Lake Champlain. A Book of Today, Twenty-Second Edition*, (S.R. Stoddard, 1892), 109; Florence Waters Snedeker, *A Family Canoe Trip*, (Harper & Brothers, 1892), 47. Thomas Pownall, *A Topographical Description of the Dominions of the United States of America*, (University of Pittsburgh Press, 1949), 50.

2   Nathaniel H. Bishop, *Voyage of the Paper Canoe*, (David Douglas, 1878).

3   W.H.H. Murray, *Lake Champlain and Its Shores*, (De Wolfe, Fiske & Co.,1890), 125.

4   Philip G. Terrie, *Contested Terrain: A New History of Nature and People in the Adirondacks* (Syracuse University Press, 1997), 95; Hallie E. Bond, *Boats and Boating in the Adirondacks,* (The Adirondack Museum, 1995), 12-14, 95.

5   Terrie, *Contested Terrain: A New History of Nature and People in the Adirondacks,* 95; Bond, *Boats and Boating in the Adirondacks*, 12-14, 95.

6   Augusta Woodruf Brown, *Notes of a canal boat trip taken in the summer of 1895,* manuscript in New York State Library, (August Woodruf Brown, 1895), 1.

7   Horatio Gates Spafford, *A Pocket Guide for the Tourist and Traveller, Along the Line of the Canals and the Interior Commerce of the State of New York*, (T. and J. Swords, 1824), iii.

8   Spafford, *A Pocket Guide for the Tourist and Traveller,* 19.

9   Wallace E. Lamb, *The Lake Champlain and Lake George Valleys, Vol. I & II,* (The American Historical Company ,1940), 585.

10   Murray, *Lake Champlain and Its Shores*, 124.

11   Brown, *Notes of a canal boat trip taken in the summer of 1895*, 8.

12   Snedeker, *A Family Canoe Trip*, 135-136.

13   Howard Pyle, "Though Inland Water", *Harpers Magazine*, no.558, vol.92, May 1896, 70.

14   Spafford, *A Pocket Guide for the Tourist and Traveller,* 57.

15   Snedeker, *A Family Canoe Trip*, 53

16   Howard Pyle, "Though Inland Water", *Harpers Magazine*, no.553, May 1896, 73.

17   John R. Bratten, *The Gondola Philadelphia & the Battle of Lake Champlain*, (Texas A&M University, College Station, 2002), 87-89.

18   Snedeker, *A Family Canoe Trip*, 11.

19   Snedeker, *A Family Canoe Trip*, 19.

20   Brown, *Notes of a canal boat trip taken in the summer of 1895*, 9.

21   Brown, *Notes of a canal boat trip taken in the summer of 1895*, 7.

22   Brown, *Notes of a canal boat trip taken in the summer of 1895*, 12.

23   Brown, *Notes of a canal boat trip taken in the summer of 1895*, 8.

24   Snedeker, *A Family Canoe Trip*, p.65.

25   Ethel M. Springer, "Canal-boat Children," Monthly Labor Review, Vol. 16, No. 2 (FEB-RUARY, 1923), 21.

26   William H. Rideing, "The Waterways of New York", *Harper's New Monthly Magazine*, no. 233, vol. 48, Dec. 1873, 7.

27   Howard Pyle, "Though Inland Water", *Harpers Magazine*, no.553, May 1896, 75.

28   Brown, *Notes of a canal boat trip taken in the summer of 1895*, 12.

29   Springer, "Canal-boat Children," 19.

30   Brown, *Notes of a canal boat trip taken in the summer of 1895*, 14-15.

31   Brown, *Notes of a canal boat trip taken in the summer of 1895*, 18. Brown's party of women was a rambunctious group for the 1890s. Pages 21-22 amusingly recounts that one of them with the nickname Snorum "began a lively flirtation with the Captain of a neighbour-ing boat, and never lost an opportunity to cheer him up, as he was a lonely widower. He once told her she reminded him of his first wife. Whether he had been blessed with a second we did not know."

32   "Fun Afloat - A Pleasure Trip by Schooner from Port Henry to Montreal, P.Q. and Re-turns", 63, Newspaper Clipping, 1884, Scrapbook A of the Woodbridge Collection, Sherman Free Library, Port Henry NY. https://www.lcmm.org/the-musicians-of-the-sailing-canalboat-o-j-walker/

33   Kenneth Durant, *Guide-Boats Days and Ways* (Adirondack Museum, 1963), 31.

34   American Canoe Association webpage, https://americancanoe.org/community/his-tory/. C. Bowyer Vaux, History of American Canoeing: Outline Sketches With Pen and Pencil. II-1879 to 1883.

35   Jessica Dunkin, *Canoe and Canvas: Life at the Encampments of the American Canoe Association, 1880-1990*, University of Toronto Press, 2019, 60.

36   Dunkin, *Canoe and Canvas*, 61.

37   Brown, *Notes of a canal boat trip taken in the summer of 1895*, 6.

38   *Forest and Stream*. 1883. Vol. 20. New York, N.Y: [Forest and Stream Publishing Co.]. https://www.biodiversitylibrary.org/page/40326944.

39   D.B. Goodsell, "A Canoeing Reminiscence" (paper in the American Canoe Association Collection, B4, New York State Historical Association, Cooperstown, New York, n.d.), cited in Hallie E. Bond, *Boats and Boating in the Adirondacks* (The Adirondack Museum, 1995), 111; Snedeker, *A Family Canoe Trip*, 107.

40   Dunkin, *Canoe and Canvas,* 41.

41   Erin Urban, *Hulls and Hulks in the Tide of Time: The Life and World of John A. Noble* (The John A. Nobel Collection, 1993), 29-30.

42   Allen F. Davis, *Postcards From Vermont: A Social History, 1905-1945,* (University Press of New England, 2002), 193.

43   "Camp Dudley: 1885 - 1907, The Pioneering Years" - https://issuu.com/campdudley/docs/combined

44   "The Adventurers (A Camp for Older Boys)", Camp Brochure for 1929, in Brett Corbin, *The Pirates of Dingley Dell: A True Swashbuckling Story at a Vermont Boys Camp* (2015), 59.

45   "The Adventurers (A Camp for Older Boys)", in Corbin, *The Pirates of Dingley*, pp58-59.

46   Brett Corbin, *The Pirates of Dingley Dell: A True Swashbuckling Story at a Vermont Boys Camp* (2015), 59.

47   George Sears "Nessmuch", *Woodcraft and Camping*, (Dover Publication, 1963), 87.

48   Maldwin Drummond, *Salt-Water Palaces*, 105; Thomas J. Schlereth, *Victorian America: Transformations in Everyday Life 1876-1915*, (HarperCollins, 1991), 214.

49   Bond, *Boats and Boating in the Adirondacks,* 106.

50   Murray, *Lake Champlain and Its Shores*, 159.

51   Murray, *Lake Champlain and Its Shores*, 159. John A. Williams, Dale Hyestay, Bern Collins. *History Highlights of the Lake Champlain Yacht Club, 1887-2023*. LCYC, 2023. https://lcyc.info/club/history/lcyc-history-1887-present; Davis, *Postcards From Vermont,,* 190.

52   Malletts Bay Boat Club, "Brief History", accessed 3/5/2025, https://mbbc-vt.com/history.asp; Split Rock Yacht Club, accessed 4/5/2025, http://www.sryc.us/ and Morris F. Glenn,

Glenn's History of Lake Champlain, Volume 6, (Morris F. Glenn, Alexandria VA, 1980); Diamond Island Yacht Club, "About DIYC", accessed 4/5/2025, https://diamondislandyc.org/; North Cheever Sailing Club at Port Henry, on facebook, and the Westport Yacht club remains in the form of a restaurant.

53   Editors, *Middlebury College News Letter* 1939-06-01: Volume XIII, Issue 4, 2. Middlebury College, *Middlebury Campus* 1946-04-11 : Volume XLIII, Issue 13, 1.

54   Brown, *Notes of a canal boat trip taken in the summer of 1895*, 45.

55   Brown, *Notes of a canal boat trip taken in the summer of 1895*, 9.

56   The Lozier Motor Co., 1901, Book 7 Catalog, "The Lozier Motor Co., Builders of High Grade Lozier Launches with the Lozier Gas Engine, Plattsburgh, N.Y.", 31. Accessed from Adirondack Experience Library, Control Number 01410, 6/24/2025; Bond, *Boats and Boating in the Adirondacks,* 190.

57   The Lozier Motor Co., Book 7 Catalog, "The Lozier Motor Co.", 31.

58   Bond, *Boats and Boating in the Adirondacks,* 190.

59   Champlain Valley Council, *Minutes, 1928-1930,* 38

60   Lamb, *The Lake Champlain and Lake George Valleys,* 586.

61   Lamb, *The Lake Champlain and Lake George Valleys,* 586-587.

62   John A. Williams, Dale Hyestay, Bern Collins. *History Highlights of the Lake Champlain Yacht Club, 1887-2023.* LCYC, 2023. https://lcyc.info/club/history/lcyc-history-1887-present=

63   The Lozier Motor Co., Book 7 Catalog, "The Lozier Motor Co.", 31.

64   *Shaping the Future of Lake Champlain : The Final Report*. Burlington, Vt: Lake Champlain Basin Study, New England River Basins Commission, 1979. 61.

65   *Shaping the Future of Lake Champlain : The Final Report,* 73.

66   The Lake Champlain-Lake George Regional Planning Board, "The Champlain Canal Corridor Study for the New York State Thruway Authority Canal Recreationway Commission, December 1993", 3.

67   *Shaping the Future of Lake Champlain : The Final Report*, 54.

68   *The Lake Champlain Boat Study Program : Produced as a Technical Report for the Lake Champlain Recreation Management Plan [i.e. Program] and the Lake Champlain Basin Program.* Waterbury, Vt. Vermont Dept. of Forests, Parks and Recreation in cooperation with the New York Office of Parks, Recreation and Historic Preservation and U.S. Coast Guard, 1993. 7.

69   The Lake Champlain-Lake George Regional Planning Board, "The Champlain Canal Corridor Study for the New York State Thruway Authority Canal Recreationway Commission, December 1993", 17.

70   Feeder Canal Alliance, "About Us", accessed 4/20/2025, https://feedercanal.org/about-us/

71   New York Canal Corporation, "Canal Recreationway Commission" accessed 4/20/25, https://www.canals.ny.gov/About/Canal-Recreationway-Commission#legislation-5

72   https://hudsonrivergreenwaywatertrail.org/index.php; Lake Champlain Committee, "Lake Champlain Paddlers Trail, Trail History", accessed 3/15/2025, https://www.lakechamplaincommittee.org/explore/lake-champlain-paddlers-trail/trail-history

73   "Champlain Canal Region Gateway Visitors Center." Accessed June 27, 2023. https://www.hudsonhoosicpartnership.org/gvc/; Parks and Trails New York, "Cycle the Erie Canal" map, accessed 3/15/2025, https://www.ptny.org/bike-canal/map/

74   The Lake Champlain-Lake George Regional Planning Board, "The Champlain Canal Corridor Study for the New York State Thruway Authority Canal Recreationway Commission, December 1993", 11.

75   Justin Bills, Justin A Perry, "Mitigating the Spread of the Invasive Round Goby: Interim Rapid Response Plan for the Champlain Canal System in New York State", (New York Power Authority, Canal Corporation, Department of Environmental Conservation, Update for May 2023), Appendix F-1, 107-111.

76   *Reimage the Canals Taskforce Report*, January 2020, New York, 18.

77   *Reimage the Canals Taskforce Report*, January 2020, New York, 18.

Figure Citations

(Figure 1): Illustration from Snedeker, *A Family Canoe Trip*, 81-82.

(Figure 2): Brown, *Notes of a canal boat trip taken in the summer of 1895*, Sketch "No 10 from page 17," from the collections of the New York State Library, Manuscripts and Special Collections, Albany, New York.

(Figures 3.1 & 3.2): Illustration from Snedeker, *A Family Canoe Trip*, 21, 25-26.

(Figure 4): Brown, *Notes of a canal boat trip taken in the summer of 1895*, Sketch "No 6 for page 9," from the collections of the New York State Library, Manuscripts and Special Collections, Albany, New York.

(Figure 5): Brown, *Notes of a canal boat trip taken in the summer of 1895*, Sketch "No 11 for page 16," from the collections of the New York State Library, Manuscripts and Special Collections, Albany, New York.

(Figures 6.1 and 6.2): Excerpts of John Stoddard 1893 Map, Lake Champlain Maritime Museum Collection.

(Figure 7): Illustration from Snedeker, *A Family Canoe Trip*, 105.

(Figure 8): From Lake Champlain Maritime Museum Collections.

(Figure 9): Illustration from Snedeker, *A Family Canoe Trip*, 89.

(Figure 10): *McClure's Magazine,* Vol. 16, November, 1900, 135.

(Figure 11): From Lake Champlain Maritime Museum, McKelleher Collection.

(Figure 12): Courtesy of the Feeder Canal Alliance and Gene Bowen Photography.

Bibliography

Beach, Bob, "Historical Tour of Basin Harbor" (2016) - https://vimeo.com/174441209

Justin Bills, Justin A Perry, "Mitigating the Spread of the Invasive Round Goby: Interim Rapid Response Plan for the Champlain Canal System in New York State", (New York Power Authority, Canal Corporation, Department of Environmental Conservation, Update for May 2023), Appendix F-1.

Bishop, Nathaniel H., *Voyage of the Paper Canoe*, (David Douglas, 1878).

Bond, Hallie E., *Boats and Boating in the Adirondacks,* (The Adirondack Museum, 1995).

Bratten, John R., *The Gondola Philadelphia & the Battle of Lake Champlain*, (Texas A&M University, 2002).

Brown, Augusta Woodruf, *Notes of a canal boat trip taken in the summer of 1895,* Manuscript in New York State Library, https://nysl.ptfs.com/, (Augusta Woodruf Brown, 1895), Courtesy of New York State Library, Manuscripts and Special Collections, Albany, New York.

Camp Dudley, "Camp Dudley: 1885 - 1907, The Pioneering Years" - https://issuu.com/camp-dudley/docs/combined

"Champlain Canal Region Gateway Visitors Center." Accessed 9/27/2023. https://www.hud-sonhoosicpartnership.org/gvc/.

Champlain Valley Council, *Minutes,* 1928-1930, Carton: 1, Folder: 27. Alfred H. Heininger Papers, mss-979. University of Vermont Libraries, Special Collections. p.38

Corbin, Brett, *The Pirates of Dingley Dell: A True Swashbuckling Story at a Vermont Boys Camp* (Red Barn Books of Vermont, 2015).

Davis, Allen F., *Postcards From Vermont: A Social History, 1905-1945,* (University Press of New England, 2002).

Diamond Island Yacht Club, "About DIYC", accessed 4/5/2025, https://diamondislandyc.org/

Drummond, Maldwin, *Salt-Water Palaces*, NY 1979.

Durant, Kenneth, *Guide-Boats Days and Ways* (Adirondack Museum, 1963)

Dunkin, Jessica, *Canoe and Canvas: Life at the Encampments of the American Canoe Association, 1880-1990*, (University of Toronto Press, 2019).

Editors, Middlebury College News Letter 1939-06-01: Volume XIII, Issue 4. https://archive.org/details/middleburyNewspapers_1939-06-01/page/n1/mode/2up?q=%22sailing%22

Feeder Canal Alliance, "About Us", accessed 4/20/2025, https://feedercanal.org/about-us/

Forest and Stream. 1883. Vol. 20. New York, N.Y: [Forest and Stream Publishing Co.]. https://www.biodiversitylibrary.org/page/40326944.

"Fun Afloat - A Pleasure Trip by Schooner from Port Henry to Montreal, P.Q. and Returns", p.63, Newspaper Clipping, 1884, Scrapbook A of the Woodbridge Collection, Sherman Free Library, Port Henry NY. https://www.lcmm.org/the-musicians-of-the-sailing-canalboat-o-j-walker/

Gilbert, C. L. (ed), *Vermont Odysseys,* (Plume, 1991).

Glenn, Morris F., *Glenn's History of Lake Champlain, Volume 6*, (Morris F. Glenn, 1980).

Goodsell, D.B., "A Canoeing Reminiscence" (paper in the American Canoe Association Collection, B4, New York State Historical Association, Cooperstown, New York, n.d.), cited in Hallie E. Bond, *Boats and Boating in the Adirondacks* (The Adirondack Museum, 1995).

Lamb, Wallace E., *The Lake Champlain and Lake George Valleys, Vol. I & II,* (The American Historical Company, 1940).

Lake Champlain Basin Program, *The Lake Champlain Boat Study Program: Produced as a Technical Report for the Lake Champlain Recreation Management Plan [i.e. Program] and the Lake Champlain Basin Program,* (Vermont Dept. of Forests, Parks and Recreation in cooperation with the New York Office of Parks, Recreation and Historic Preservation and U.S. Coast

Guard, 1993).

Lake Champlain Committee, "Lake Champlain Paddlers Trail, Trail History", accessed 3/15/2025, https://www.lakechamplaincommittee.org/explore/lake-champlain-paddlers-trail/trail-history

Lake Champlain-Lake George Regional Planning Board, The, "The Champlain Canal Corridor Study for the New York State Thruway Authority Canal Recreationway Commission, December 1993"

Lozier Motor Co., Book 7 Catalog, 1901, "The Lozier Motor Co., Builders of High Grade Lozier Launches with the Lozier Gas Engine, Plattsburgh, N.Y.". Accessed from Adirondack Experience Library, Control Number 01410, 6/24/2025, https://adirondack.pastperfectonline.com/library/8B0E4904-DE1E-4D3C-A765-376997357203

Malletts Bay Boat Club, "Brief History", accessed 3/5/2025, https://mbbc-vt.com/history.asp

McClure Co., S.S., "McClure's Magazine", Vol. 16, November 1900, p.135.

McLaughlin, Scott Arthur, "With Their Homes About Them" The World of the Northern Canal Boat Community 1873-1940," Dissertation, (Binghamton University State University of New York, 2011).

Middlebury College, *Middlebury Campus* 1946-04-11: Volume XLIII, Issue 13.

Milne, Graeme J., *People, Place and Power on the Nineteenth-Century Waterfront,* (Palgrave Macmillan, 2016).

Murray, W. H. H., *Lake Champlain and Its Shores*, (De Wolfe, Fiske & Co.,1890).

New England River Basins Commission, *Shaping the Future of Lake Champlain : The Final Report*. Burlington, Vt: Lake Champlain Basin Study, New England River Basins Commission, 1979.

New York Canal Corporation, "Canal Recreationway Commission" accessed 4/20/25, https://www.canals.ny.gov/About/Canal-Recreationway-Commission#legislation-5

New York Reimagine the Canals Taskforce, *Reimagine the Canals Taskforce Report*, January 2020.

New York State Hudson River Greenway Water Trail, accessed 3/15/2025, https://hudsonrivergreenwaywatertrail.org/index.php

O'Hara, John E. (John Edward). *Erie's Junior Partner : The Economic and Social Effects of the Champlain Canal upon the Champlain Valley*, (Columbia University Press, 1951).

Parks and Trails New York, "Cycle the Erie Canal" map, accessed 3/15/2025, https://www.ptny.org/bike-canal/map/

Pownall, Thomas, *A Topographical Description of the Dominions of the United States of America*, (University of Pittsburgh Press, 1949).

Pyle, Howard, "Though Inland Water", *Harpers Magazine*, no.553, May 1896.

Rideing, William H., "The Waterways of New York", *Harper's New Monthly Magazine*, no. 233, vol. 48, Dec. 1873.

Schlereth, Thomas J., *Victorian America: Transformations in Everyday Life 1876-1915*, (Harper-Collins, 1991).

Sears, George, *Woodcraft and Camping by "Nessmuk"*, (Dover Publication,1963), https://www.gutenberg.org/files/34607/34607-h/34607-h.htm#Page_87

Snedeker, Florence Waters, *A Family Canoe Trip*, (Harper & Brothers, 1892).

Spafford, Horatio Gates, *A Pocket Guide for the Tourist and Traveller, Along the Line of the Canals and the Interior Commerce of the State of New York*, (T. and J. Swords, 1824). https://www.google.com/books/edition/A_Pocket_Guide_for_the_Tourist_and_Trave/S40rAAAAYAAJ?hl=en&gbpv=1

Slip Rock Yacht Club, accessed 4/5/2025, http://www.sryc.us/

Springer, Ethel M., "Canal-boat Children," *Monthly Labor Review*, Vol. 16, No. 2 (February, 1923).

Stoddard, Seneca Ray, *The Adirondacks: Illustrated,* (Weed, Parsons & Co., 1874).

Stoddard, Seneca Ray, *Lake George Illustrated and Lake Champlain. A Book of Today, Twenty-Second Edition*, (Glens Falls, 1892).

Sweeney, Martin A., "The Trials and Tribulations of Homer's Circus Owner, Sig Sautelle", *New York History Review Blog*, April 9, 2020 - https://newyorkhistoryreviewarticles.blogspot.com/2020/04/the-trials-and-tribulations-of-homers.html

Terrie, Philip G., *Contested Terrain: A New History of Nature and People in the Adirondacks* (Syracuse University Press, 1997).

Urban, Erin, *Hulls and Hulks in the Tide of Time: The Life and Worl of John A. Noble* (The John A. Nobel Collection, New York, 1993)

Vaux, C. Bowyer, *History of American Canoeing: Outline Sketches With Pen and Pencil.* II-1879 to 1883.

Williams, John A., Dale Hyestay, Bern Collins, *History Highlights of the Lake Champlain Yacht Club, 1887-2023,* https://lcyc.info/club/history/lcyc-history-1887-present, (Lake Champlain Yacht Club, 2023).

CHAPTER 6

Canal, Water, and Environment

Unintended environmental consequences of the canals: aquatic invasive species impacts

Meg Modley Gilbertson
Healthy Ecosystems and Aquatic Invasive Species Management Coordinator, Lake Champlain Basin Program/NEIWPCC

Ryan Mitchell
Education and Outreach Coordinator, Lake Champlain Basin Program/NEIWPCC

The Champlain Canal opened September 10, 1823, providing water connectivity between the Champlain and Hudson drainages for the first time. This new hydrologic pathway provided a trade route between the Hudson and Lake Champlain. This connection also opened the opportunity for aquatic invasive species, nonnative species that can cause harm to the environment, economy, and human health, to swim, float, or be entrained by boats using the system to move across the watershed divide. While there are a number of ways that aquatic invasive species may be introduced to new bodies of water, including overland transport on boats and trailers, baitfish trade, aquarium release, and water garden escape, the Champlain Canal represents the largest vector of Lake Champlain aquatic invasive species introductions.[1]

The Lake Champlain Basin Ecosystem

Lake Champlain is more than 120 miles long, 12 miles wide at its widest point, and more than 400 feet deep. The lake drains north from Whitehall, New York, at its southern end to the Richelieu River, St. Lawrence River, and eventually to the Atlantic Ocean.

Lake Champlain provides high-quality drinking water for many residents and supports many recreational opportunities, including cold-, cool-, and warm-water angling. Fish from the lake may be consumed as part of a healthy diet when consumption advisories are followed. With 587 miles of shoreline, the lake provides swimming opportunities at more than forty public beaches. The Lake Champlain Basin is home to rich cultural heritage resources, including underwater shipwrecks and historic forts on the hillsides.

Resource managers in New York, Vermont, and Quebec have invested in research and habitat restoration to support the Basin's native, rare, threatened, and endangered species. Water quality monitoring helps to target restoration efforts where they are most needed. The removal of dams and improvement of culverts at road crossings are helping fish and other wildlife migrate more freely on streams and rivers to access cold-water habitat and spawning grounds. Scientists are monitoring the lake's fish forage base and investing in control of parasitic sea lamprey to support the lake's fishery.

These efforts are yielding results. Recent increases in the number of breeding pairs of common loons, the removal of the bald eagle from the Vermont Threatened and Endangered Species List, and widespread detection of American eel throughout the lake are indicators of the health of the Basin's ecosystem. Impacts of sea lamprey on lake trout and landlocked Atlantic salmon from 2021 to 2023 were the lowest on record, and below the management target rate for Atlantic salmon. Fisheries managers stopped stocking lake trout in spring 2025 because wild-born populations have rebounded to the point that they are self-sustaining. They also report an increasing trend in bass size and catch rate.

Aquatic Invasive Species in the Lake Champlain Basin

As of 2025, Lake Champlain is home to 51 known aquatic nonnative and invasive species. Aquatic invasive species (AIS) are nonnative plants, animals, and pathogens that cause or are likely to cause harm to the economy, environment, or human health.[2] Just over a dozen of the nonnative species present in Lake Champlain are considered invasive.

Most water bodies in the Lake Champlain Basin are free of aquatic invasive species and their impacts. Early detection and education and outreach programs help to prevent new introductions and the spread of existing invasive species. Once aquatic invasive species become established it is much more expensive to contain and control populations than prevent their introduction. The burden of all of these measures falls primarily on local entities like lake associations in partnership with state and federal funding support.

The Lake Champlain Long-Term Water Quality and Biological Monitoring Project and volunteer aquatic invasive species survey programs work together to report new introductions of species to Lake Champlain. The fishhook waterflea, an invasive crustacean, was detected in Lake Champlain in 2018 during routine phytoplankton monitoring at established sites in the lake. In late 2024, golden or basket clam, was detected in the southern end of Lake Champlain by a trained volunteer AIS monitor. Resource managers are evaluating the golden clam's status to determine the extent of its presence, and if established, would be the fifty-second nonnative species in Lake Champlain. Other key AIS in Lake Champlain include the zebra mussel, water chestnut, Eurasian watermilfoil, alewife, sea lamprey, and spiny waterflea.

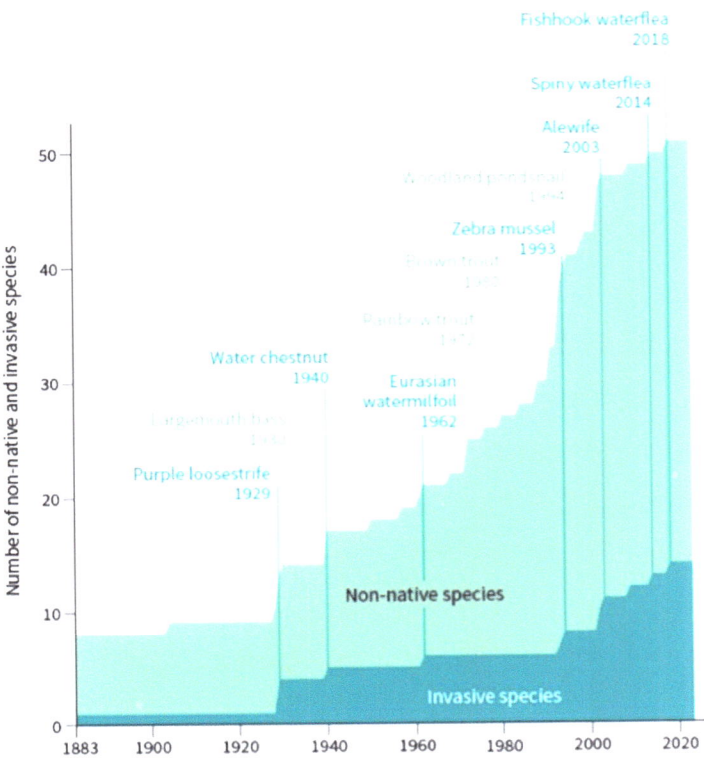

(Figure 1) Number of introduced aquatic non-native and invasive species in Lake Champlain.

The primary source of aquatic invasive species in North America is ballast water taken on in ports around the world and then released into the Great Lakes. Once species become established in the Great Lakes, they can spread quickly to other regions.

Lake Champlain has fewer nonnative and invasive species than surrounding water bodies, likely as a result of its isolation from commercial traffic. But Lake Champlain is connected by canals to the Great Lakes and other water bodies that have a greater number of aquatic invasive species. The Chambly Canal, which connects Lake Champlain north to the St. Lawrence River, and the Champlain and Erie Canals, which connect south to the Hudson River and Great Lakes, pose some of the greatest threats of AIS introduction to Lake Champlain. These canals were originally built to accommodate trade and commerce and are now used primarily by recreational watercraft.

Humans also often unintentionally move aquatic invasive species overland on boats and trailers or in bait buckets. Accidental introductions may occur during extreme rainfall and flooding events with escapes from private ponds and water gardens. State agency regulated and prohibited species lists provide guidance on which species to avoid planting or stocking, and pets and aquarium species should never be released into the wild. Some nonnative species present in Lake Champlain were intentionally introduced, such as largemouth bass and rainbow and brown trout.

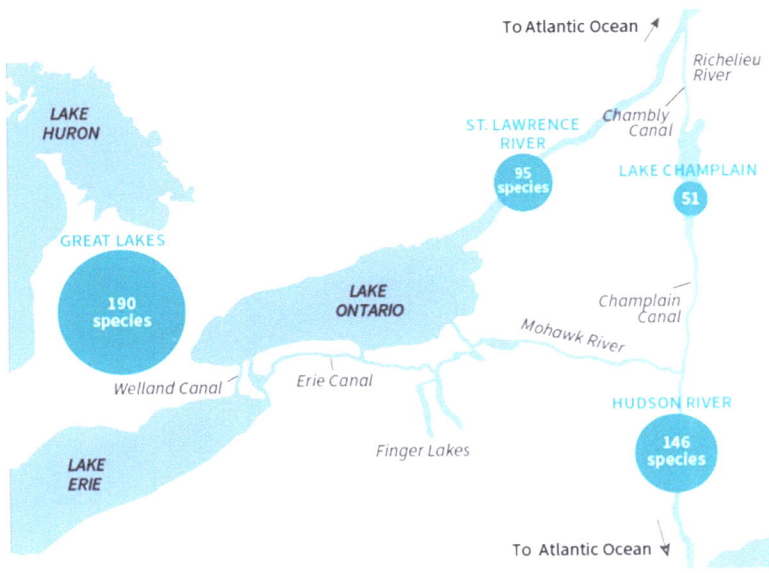

(Figure 2) *Nonnative species in Lake Champlain and connected waterways.*

Economic Impacts of AIS

The Office of Technology Assessment (OTA) of the U.S. Congress estimated nationwide economic and ecological damages from seventy-nine harmful aquatic and terrestrial invasive species to agriculture, forestry, fisheries, utilities, building, natural areas, and other water uses to be $97 to $137 billion between 1906 and 1991.[3] Specifically concerning aquatic invasive species, the OTA report assessed close to two-hundred species of fish and molluscs to identify those that have had high negative impacts. The cumulative loss to the U.S. between 1906 and 1991 for three harmful fish was $467 million and $1.2 billion for three aquatic invertebrates. The list of particularly high impact aquatic species in the report includes sea lamprey, zebra mussels, and Asian clam (now referred to as golden or basket clam), all of which are present in Lake Champlain. Other research estimates environmental and economic damage and control costs for the U.S. to be $137 billion per year due to harmful non-native species.[4]

Heavily natural-resource dependent, the economy of the Adirondack Park and the Lake Champlain region in Vermont is also threatened by aquatic invasive species. Home to more than eighty species of fish, Lake Champlain is a world-class angling destination. State and federal fish and wildlife agencies in Vermont and New York stock high-priority game fish species to support the Lake's sport fishery. The economic impact of aquatic invasive species to the fishery and other aspects of water bodies in the region is difficult to quantify precisely. Invasive fish such as alewife and sea lamprey outcompete native fish species and can affect the health of key sportfish. Recreational fishing in Lake Champlain generates about $474 million in economic activity annually.[5] A significant nuisance to anglers, fishhook and spiny waterflea foul fishing lines and downriggers, causing them to need to be removed or replaced. Invasive species also impair boating on Lake Champlain, which is a significant driver of local economies. Recreational boating brings $426.4 million to Vermont annually.[6]

A study of the direct impact of four terrestrial and four aquatic invasive species in the Adirondack Park approximates $468 to $893 million in economic losses. The study estimated $46 to $51 million per year in direct visitor spending in the recreational and tourism sector which includes activities like boating, swimming, angling, and fall tourism. Another $2 million was expected in agriculture and primary forest production. The largest cost comes from loss of property value due to water quality impacts and the presence of Eurasian watermilfoil which is estimated at $420 to $840 million.[7]

Each aquatic invasive species has unique impacts on the economy. Eurasian watermilfoil and water chestnut form mats on the water's surface, impairing boating, fishing, and swimming. These plants negatively affect the desirability of property on or near water bodies and reduce property values in some areas. Lower property values, in turn, reduce local government revenue. Dense beds of Eurasian watermilfoil, water chestnut, and Japanese knotweed can also increase the likelihood of flooding and associated costs by reducing the capacity of channels to carry floodwater.

Other species, such as zebra mussels and golden clams, clog water intake pipes used for irrigation, water supply, fire protection, and manufacturing. Zebra mussels attach to hard substrates like rocks, manmade infrastructure, and other zebra mussels. Colonization of pipes constricts flow and reduces water intake into motors, heat exchangers, and cooling systems, which can foul and damage equipment. Zebra mussels also threaten underwater shipwrecks in Lake Champlain by encrusting and destroying sensitive cultural resources.

Controlling established populations of aquatic invasive species in Lake Champlain comes at significant economic cost. State and federal management partners have worked to reduce sea lamprey and water chestnut populations for decades. These agencies spend an estimated $1.7 million annually on sea lamprey control to support the recovery of landlocked Atlantic salmon, lake trout, and lake sturgeon in Lake Champlain.[8]

(Figure 3 & 4) Angler retrieving from Lake Champlain with fishing lines fouled by thousands of fishhook waterflea

Mechanical harvesters and hand pulling crews combat water chestnut in Lake Champlain at a cost of roughly $800,000 each year.

Local organizations and agencies commit significant resources to contain, control, or eradicate aquatic invasive species and their impacts. A 2013 survey showed that eighty-eight organizations spent $3.56 million on invasive species management in the Adirondack Park alone, 85 percent of which was spent on aquatic invasive species management (mostly Eurasian watermilfoil).[9]

Ecological Impacts of AIS

Aquatic invasive species can cause extinctions of native plants and animals and reduce biodiversity by competing for limited resources, altering habitats, and impairing water quality. Over 40 percent of the species listed as threatened or endangered under the Endangered Species Act are considered at risk due to invasive species competition and predation.[10] In Lake Champlain, Eurasian watermilfoil and water chestnut outcompete native plants; they have greater tolerance for a range of water temperatures and are often the first seeds to germinate. These invasive plants get an early growth start and shade out native plants as they compete for food, light, and space. When these plants top out at the water's surface they impair habitat for waterfowl, fish, and other wildlife. Water chestnut forms dense mats that limit light penetration for native plants that produce oxygen through photosynthesis and when mats die back in the fall and decompose, oxygen levels are further reduced for fish and other wildlife.

Spiny and fishhook waterflea are voracious predators that can alter the base of the food web by competing with native zooplankton and small fish for food. Scientists have documented reductions in the density of some key native zooplankton species and seasonal shifts in their population peaks during summer months in Lake Champlain. Pre- and post-invasion of spiny and fishhook waterflea showed deep water shifts in the zooplankton community structure.[11]

The introduction of zebra mussels to Lake Champlain in the early 1990s resulted in a measured decrease in phytoplankton biovolume.[12] This species is listed by the U.S. Fish and Wildlife Service (USFWS) as injurious wildlife.

They have colonized most areas of Lake Champlain and grow in water depths up to sixty meters. Each zebra mussel can filter over a liter a day, which can alter the nutrient cycle in the lake. Zebra mussels have been found growing on top of threatened native mussel species, outcompeting them for food and limiting their ability to move and feed.

Parasitic adult sea lamprey prey on popular sportfish in Lake Champlain, favoring lake trout and landlocked Atlantic salmon. Sea lampreys attach to the side of host fish and feed on their bodily fluids, leaving the fish weak and injured or dead. Annual management of the juvenile stage of sea lamprey with lampricides in the lake's tributaries is critical in reducing wounding rates on lake trout and landlocked Atlantic salmon.

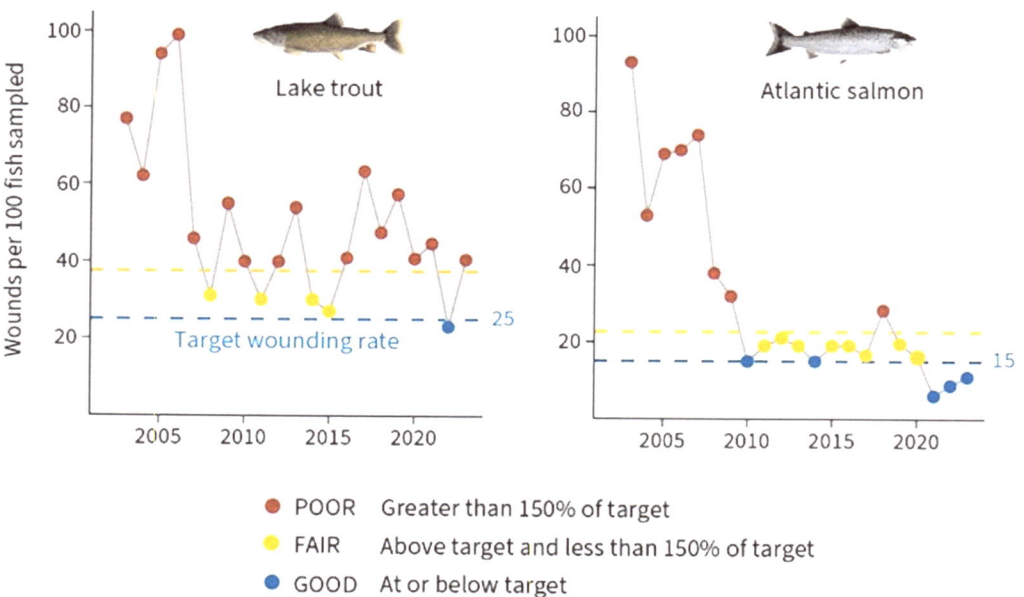

(**Figure 4**) Sea lamprey wounding rates in Lake Champlain.

Nonnative and invasive fish continue to be a challenge in Lake Champlain. Invasive alewives disrupt the food chain by outcompeting native rainbow smelt, the primary food source for lake trout and Atlantic salmon. Some sportfish prey on alewife, but a diet rich in alewife can cause elevated levels of thiaminase enzyme in lake trout and Atlantic salmon. This enzyme can prevent the uptake of thiamine in salmonid eggs, leading to early mortality in fry.

Human Impacts of AIS

The primary human impacts of aquatic invasive species in the Lake Champlain Basin are the limitation of recreation opportunities, including boating, fishing, and swimming—and the loss of property value in areas that are choked with aquatic plants. Dense beds of invasive aquatic vegetation may also aid in the spread of disease by causing water to stagnate and support breeding mosquitos. Fishing lines fouled by fishhook and spiny waterflea that need to be replaced or cleaned are a nuisance to anglers. Zebra mussels that encrust rocks near the shorelines and water chestnut seeds that wash up on shorelines often cut the feet of swimmers.

The cost of managing the impacts of aquatic invasive species is a burden that is shouldered by taxpayer dollars through federal and state programs, and local residents and lake associations. Preventing the introduction of aquatic invasive species is more cost-effective than the long-term, annual costs of managing and reducing infestations once they become established.

AIS Spread Prevention

Management partners in the Lake Champlain Basin have been working for decades to address sources of aquatic invasive species introduction and spread. Aquatic invasive species transport laws and watercraft inspection and decontamination programs help to reduce overland transport of aquatic hitchhikers on watercraft, trailers, and recreational equipment. The designated noxious weeds list in Vermont and prohibited and regulated invasive species in New York regulates the possession, transport, importation, sale, purchase, and introduction of select invasive species. These regulations address, for example, the transport and sale of invasive plants and animals in commercial garden, aquarium, water garden, and live food markets. Baitfish regulations help prevent both intentional and unintentional introductions by requiring the purchase of certified, disease-free species and limiting transport of harvested bait species. Partners are working to address the threat posed by canals, which provide an open pathway for movement of aquatic nonnative and invasive species.

Champlain Canal and AIS

Canals played a pivotal role in the economic development and geographic expansion of the United States, but they have also been unintended pathways for fish, plants, crustaceans, and pathogens to move across watershed divides. When the Champlain Canal was cut through a short expanse of low-lying land between Waterford and Whitehall, New York, it linked the previously unconnected Hudson and Lake Champlain watersheds. This link opened New York City markets to Lake Champlain timber and other products. It also unleashed a wave of aquatic invasive species introductions.

Water levels in the Champlain Canal are maintained with water sourced from upstream in the Hudson River that travels through the Glens Falls Feeder Canal to the height of the Champlain Canal between Locks C8 and C9. From there, the Hudson River-sourced water flows downhill and south back into the Hudson River *and* downhill and north into the southern end of Lake Champlain.

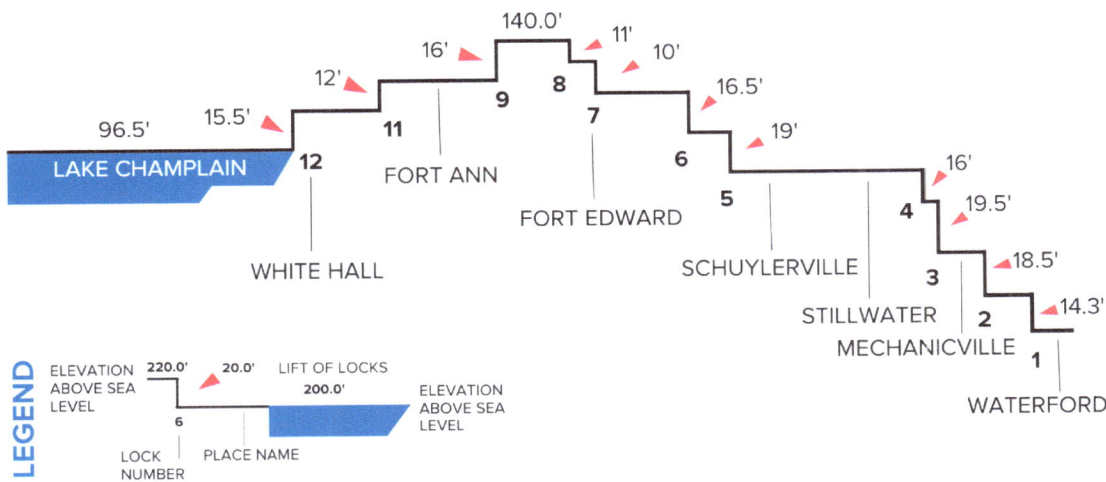

(Figure 5) Champlain Canal elevation profile.

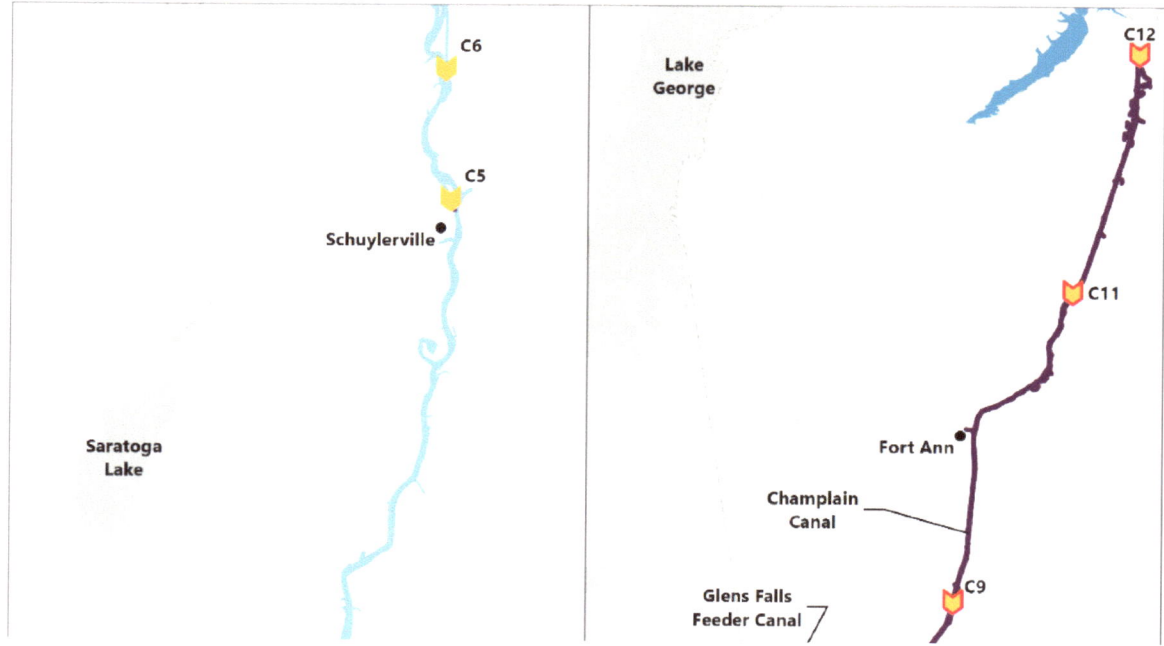

(Figure 6) Upper Hudson and Champlain Canal locks, New York Power Authority and Canal Corporation.

The historic impact of the Champlain Canal's construction on Lake Champlain's water quality is unclear, but poor water quality in the canal may have prevented AIS introductions in the past. Improvements to water quality in recent decades may be aiding new introductions. The number of new documented species in Lake Champlain increased in the 1990s, potentially because of improved water quality in the canal as well as increased sampling effort and recreational use.

An estimated twenty species—more than half of species for which a source can be confidently identified—have entered the lake by canals; at least twelve of these used the Champlain Canal. These organisms include sea lamprey, water chestnut, zebra mussel, and white perch.[13]

Scientists have been tracking the movement of invasive spiny waterflea basket clams, and round goby in the Champlain Canal. Sampling of dewatered locks and the Champlain Canal channel between 2008 and 2011 found half of the fish, mollusc, plant, and crustacean species were nonnative to one or both of the connected watersheds. Half the fish species collected showed evidence of reproduction, which suggests that not only is the Champlain Canal an open pathway for invasions, but it contains self-sustaining fish populations. Many other species in the hydrologic network connected to the canal, including the Erie Canal, could still enter Lake Champlain by this route.[14] Harmful invasive species such as the round goby, quagga mussel, and hydrilla that are not yet present in Lake Champlain have been detected in multiple locations in the Erie canal.

Since 2014, scientists have documented the movement of round goby from the Great Lakes through the Erie canal eastward to the confluence of the Mohawk and Hudson Rivers.[15] The arrival of this aquatic invasive fish to the Hudson River system has alarmed resource managers and fish biologists. The round goby is a bottom-dwelling fish that can outcompete and displace native fish species. Round goby are aggressive egg predators and could threaten lake trout recovery and the thriving bass fishery in Lake Champlain. They are known to carry a harmful fish pathogen, viral hemorrhagic septicemia, that can infect many freshwater fish and is not present in Lake Champlain. As of June 2025, round goby has not been found north (upstream) of Lock 1 in the Champlain Canal; however, there have been a few environmental DNA detections above Lock C2.

(Figure 7) Round goby.

Quagga mussels, small bivalve mussels that are very similar to zebra mussels, but that have the potential for greater economic and environmental impacts and are listed as injurious by the USFWS have been detected in multiple locations in the Erie Canal. Quagga mussels have outcompeted zebra mussels in the Great Lakes ecosystem and can reproduce more frequently and grow at greater depths. Impacts of quagga mussels are similar and more significant than zebra mussels, including removal of phytoplankton from the water column and altering the food web and biofouling infrastructure.

(Figure 8) Quagga mussels.

Additionally, hydrilla, an invasive aquatic plant, listed as a noxious weed by the U.S. Department of Agriculture, has been detected in the Erie Canal. This aquatic invasive plant grows aggressively, displacing beneficial native vegetation, and obstructing boating, fishing, and swimming.

(Figure 9) Hydrilla.

Tench, a nonnative fish first detected in Lake Champlain in the early 2000s, has spread throughout Lake Champlain and is now caught in increasing number and size. Tench escaped during a flood event in the 1980s from a stocked pond into the Richelieu River in Quebec and may have entered Lake Champlain via the Chambly Canal. It is likely that Tench will soon be considered invasive in Lake Champlain. Tench are a potential threat to the Hudson River system where they are not yet present. It is possible they could utilize the Champlain Canal to enter the Hudson drainage.

Management response to AIS in the Champlain Canal

Scientists first raised concerns about the spread of aquatic invasive species through the Champlain Canal in 1989.[16] In 1995 a Lake Champlain Sea Grant report identified and reviewed six possible options for addressing AIS in the Champlain Canal, including taking no action, installing a physical/mechanical, behavioral, chemical, or biological barrier, and closing the canal altogether.

The Water Resources Development Act (WRDA) of 2007 provided federal recognition of the threat of AIS in the Champlain Canal, when it authorized the U.S. Army Corps of Engineers to determine the feasibility of a dispersal barrier to prevent the spread of aquatic nuisance species. The legislation also calls for the construction, maintenance, and operation of a project at full federal expense.

Management partners initiated the first step to identify a solution when they supported a U.S. Army Corps of Engineers study in 2017 to evaluate aquatic invasive species spread alternatives in the Champlain Canal. The study, conducted in partnership with New York State Department of Environmental Conservation (NYSDEC), New York State Canal Corporation (NYSCC), U.S. Fish and Wildlife Service, Vermont Agency of Natural Resources, and Lake Champlain Basin Program/New England Interstate Water Pollution Control Commission, was funded under WRDA Section 542. Lake Champlain Watershed Assistance Program. It identified priority solutions that would prevent all taxa from moving through the system, including recreational boat lifts with watercraft decontamination and a physical berm to prevent water and species from moving from one watershed to the other.[17] Additional studies will be necessary to optimize a selected solution; conduct hydrologic, topographic, boundary, and canal traffic surveys; and conduct the National Environmental Policy Act environmental review process.

The Lake Champlain Aquatic Invasive Species Rapid Response Task Force, composed of resource managers and experts from New York, Vermont, and Quebec and coordinated by the Lake Champlain Basin Program, is engaged in early detection monitoring and preventing the spread of round goby and other aquatic invasive species to Lake Champlain. The task force worked with NYSDEC and NYSCC to develop a plan that identifies response actions that may be taken if the species advances through the Champlain Canal. Immediate interim measures, such as leaving canal lock gates closed unless preparing to move watercraft through the system, double flushing locks before passing traffic, and scheduled locking, are measures in the response plan that have been implemented to prevent goby movement north through the Champlain Canal. Resource managers are also evaluating the use of an electrical barrier as a potential interim measure. However, the long-term all-taxa solution to prevent aquatic invasive species from passing through the Champlain Canal will be the responsibility of the U.S. Army Corps of Engineers.

Conclusion

The spread of aquatic nonnative and invasive species through the Champlain Canal continues to be a significant threat to Lake Champlain. A variety of spread prevention measures have helped reduce the number of introductions to Lake Champlain in recent years, but several key invasive species are on our doorstep, and dozens more are in waters farther away but still hydrologically connected to the lake. A barrier to the movement of AIS on the canal will be necessary to prevent further economic and ecological harm to Lake Champlain and the Hudson River.

Balancing this threat with the canal's historical and cultural significance and its current recreational use poses a challenge for resource managers. The Champlain Canal was a major economic driver until the 1970s; today it is primarily a recreational amenity for boaters and a valued cultural resource for members of the communities through which it flows. As awareness of the economic and ecological impacts of aquatic invasive species grows, resource managers must find a solution that balances the ecological integrity of our waterways and the social values placed on this historic infrastructure. Solutions exist that will keep recreational traffic moving through an intact ecosystem. The future will prove how long it will take to implement a solution that meets stakeholder needs.

Endnotes

1   J. Ellen Marsden and Bret J. Ladago, "The Champlain Canal as a Non-Indigenous Species Corridor," *Journal of Great Lakes Research* 43, no. 6 (2017), https://www.sciencedirect.com/science/article/abs/pii/S0380133017301259, 1173.

2   *Executive Order 13112 of February 3, 1999: Invasive Species*, Federal Register 64, no. 25 (February 3, 1999), President of the United States, 6183.

3   Office of Technology Assessment, U.S. Congress, *Harmful Non-Indigenous Species in the United States*, OTA Publication OTA-F-565 (Washington, DC: U.S. Government Printing Office, 1993), 72.

4   David Pimentel et al., "Environmental and Economic Costs Associated with Non-indigenous Species in the United States," *BioScience 50* (2000), 53.

5   A. H. Gilbert, "Benefit Cost Analysis of the Eight-Year Experimental Sea Lamprey Control Program on Lake Champlain" (VTDFW, 1999), 39.

6   National Marine Manufacturers Association, Vermont Economic Impact Infographic, 2023, https://www.nmma.org/statistics/publications/economic-impact-infographics.

7   Yellowwood Associates, Inc., *The Actual and Potential Economic Impact of Invasive Species on the Adirondack Park: A Preliminary Assessment*, 2014, 3.

8   U.S. Fish and Wildlife Service, *Title of Report* (City: Publisher, 2024). *(Replace with accurate report title and publication details.)* https://www.fws.gov/project/sea-lamprey-control-lake-champlain-basin

9   Yellowwood Associates, Inc., *The Actual and Potential Economic Impact of Invasive Species on the Adirondack Park: A Preliminary Assessment*, 2014, 5.

10   David S. Wilcove et al., *Quantifying Threats to Imperiled Species in the United States: Assessing the relative importance of habitat destruction, alien species, pollution, overexploitation, and disease* BioScience 50 (1998), 609.

11   Z. A. Cutter, T. B. Mihuc, and L. W. Myers, "Invasion of *Bythotrephes longimanus* and *Cercopagis pengoi* in Lake Champlain: Impacts on the Native Zooplankton Community," *Diversity* 15, 1112 (2023), 2.

12   T. Mihuc et al., "Long-Term Patterns in Lake Champlain's Zooplankton: 1992–2010," *Journal of Great Lakes Research* 38 (2012), 50.

13   J. Ellen Marsden and Michael Hauser, "Exotic Species in Lake Champlain," *Journal of Great Lakes Research* 35, no. 2 (2009), https://www.sciencedirect.com/science/article/abs/pii/S0380133009000562, 250.

14   Marsden and Ladago, "The Champlain Canal as a Non-Indigenous Species Corridor," *Journal of Great Lakes Research* 43 (2017), 1178.

15   George et al., "Eastward Expansion of Round Goby in New York: Assessment of Detection Methods and Current Range," *Transactions of the American Fisheries Society* 150, no. 4 (2021), 259.

16   Malchoff et al, "Feasibility of Champlain Canal Aquatic Nuisance Species Barrier Options," Lake Champlain Sea Grant NOAA (2005), 4.

17   USACE, New York District, "*Champlain Canal Aquatic Invasive Species Barrier Study Phase 1 Report* (New York District: USACE, Princeton Hydro, LLC, and HDR, 2022), iii.

Figure Citations

(Figure 1) Lake Champlain Basin Program, *2024 Lake Champlain State of the Lake and Ecosystems Indicators Report. Grand Isle, VT* June, 2024.

(Figure 2) Lake Champlain Basin Program, *State of the Lake,* 2024.

(Figure 3) Lake Champlain Basin Program, *2024 Lake Champlain State of the Lake and Ecosystems Indicators Report. Grand Isle, VT*, 2019.

(Figure 4) Lake Champlain Basin Program, *State of the Lake,* 2024.

(Figure 5) NYPA/Canal Corporation and NYSDEC, *Mitigating the Spread of the Invasive Round Goby: Interim Rapid Response Plant for the Champlain Canal System in New York State*, May, 2023.

(Figure 6) NYPA/Canal Corporation and NYSDEC, *Mitigating the Spread of the Invasive Round Goby,* 2023.

(Figure 7) Peter van der Sluijs, Wikimedia.

(Figure 8) Ellen Marsden, UVM.

(Figure 9) University of Florida.

Bibliography

Cutter, Z. A., and T. B. Mihuc. *Champlain Canal Aquatic Invasive Species Barrier Study Phase 1 Report.* New York District: USACE, Princeton Hydro, LLC, and HDR, 2022.

Cutter, Z. A., T. B. Mihuc, and L. W. Myers. "Invasion of *Bythotrephes longimanus* and *Cercopagis pengoi* in Lake Champlain: Impacts on the Native Zooplankton Community." *Diversity* 15 (2023): 1112.

George, Amanda, Matthew J. Snyder, Zachary L. Lane, and Donald E. DeGolier. "Eastward Expansion of Round Goby in New York: Assessment of Detection Methods and Current Range." *Transactions of the American Fisheries Society* 150, no. 4 (2021).

Gilbert, A. H. *Benefit Cost Analysis of the Eight-Year Experimental Sea Lamprey Control Program on Lake Champlain.* Waterbury, VT: VTDFW, 1999.

Grigelis, Julie, and James Caudill. *Conserving, Restoring and Enhancing America's Fisheries and Aquatic Resources: The Economic Contributions of the U.S. Fish and Wildlife Service Fish and Aquatic Conservation Program*, 2025.

Lovell, Sabrina J., and Susan F. Stone. *The Economic Impacts of Aquatic Invasive Species: A Review of the Literature.* U.S. Environmental Protection Agency, National Center for Environmental Economics, Working Paper #05-02, 2005.

Marsden, J. Ellen, and Michael Hauser. "Exotic Species in Lake Champlain." *Journal of Great Lakes Research* 35, no. 2 (June 2009). https://www.sciencedirect.com/science/article/abs/pii/S0380133009000562.

Marsden, J. Ellen, and Bret Ladago. "The Champlain Canal as a Non-Indigenous Species Corridor." *Journal of Great Lakes Research* 43, no. 6 (December 2017). https://www.sciencedirect.com/science/article/abs/pii/S0380133017301259.

Mihuc, T., F. Dunlap, C. Binggeli, L. Myers, C. Pershyn, A. Groves, and A. Waring. "Long-Term Patterns in Lake Champlain's Zooplankton: 1992–2010." *Journal of Great Lakes Research* 38 (2012): 49–57.

Mills, Edward L., James H. Leach, James T. Carlton, and Carol L. Secor. "Exotic Species in the

Hudson River Basin: A History of Invasions and Introductions." *Estuaries and Coasts* 19, no. 4 (1996): 814–823.

Office of Technology Assessment, U.S. Congress (OTA). *Harmful Non-Indigenous Species in the United States.* OTA Publication OTA-F-565. Washington, DC: U.S. Government Printing Office, 1993. http://www.wws.princeton.edu:80/~ota/disk1/1993/9325_n.html.

Pimentel, David, Lori Lach, Rodolfo Zuniga, and Doug Morrison. "Environmental and Economic Costs of Nonindigenous Species in the United States." *Bioscience* 50, no. 1 (2000): 53–56.

Pimentel, David, Sarah McNair, Sandy Janecka, Jeff Wightman, Christine Simmonds, Caroline O'Connell, Emily Wong, et al. "Economic and Environmental Threats of Alien Plant, Animal and Microbe Invasions." *Agriculture, Ecosystems and Environment* 84 (2001): 1–20.

Smith-Root, Inc. *Conceptual Report: Fish Repelling Barrier at Lake Champlain Canal.* Compiled for New York State Department of Environmental Conservation, 1993.

Strayer, David L. "Alien Species in the Hudson River." In *The Hudson River Estuary*, 296–310. 2006.

Yellowwood Associates, Inc. *The Actual and Potential Economic Impact of Invasive Species on the Adirondack Park: A Preliminary Assessment*, 2014.

A Canal Re-examined

As we close this anthology, the Champlain Canal appears not as an antiquated remnant of 1800s infrastructure, but as a dynamic thread woven through two centuries of transformation. From the outset, the canal reshaped the Champlain Valley—altering landscapes, livelihoods, and even ecologies. Its effects, though sometimes subtle, have been lasting and profound.

Together, these chapters challenge the traditional south-to-north framing of Champlain Canal history. This shift in perspective allows us to see the canal not as a minor offshoot of the Erie, but as a central and active force in a cross-border region from our perspective in the Champlain Valley. For builders and legislators in the 1820s, it was a bold assertion of economic connectivity. For nineteenth century boat families, it was a working highway—and for many, a home. For early boosters of tourism in Vermont and Adirondack New York, it was a stage for recreation and reinvention. And today, the Champlain Canal remains a source of both environmental challenge and recreational opportunity.

If this book accomplishes anything, we hope it reminds readers that the canal is not just a story of the past. It remains a vector of transit, ingenuity, and conflict—about the complex interweaving of human and environmental histories. Even two hundred years after its opening, the Champlain Canal invites us to consider what it still has to offer residents of the Champlain Valley and beyond. Its future, like its past, will be shaped not only by decisions we make tomorrow, but by what we imagine today.

The funding for this project was provided by the Champlain Valley National Heritage Partnership under a Special Programs Grant. We are grateful to all the writers who contributed to this project, and especially to Brad Utter for research and source suggestions, and to the New York State Library, Manuscripts and Special Collections for primary resources access. Thanks to the Glens Falls Feeder Alliance for use of their images, to Kaitlin Buerge and Middlebury College Special Collections for research help, and to University of Vermont Special Collections and the Center for Research on Vermont for providing support and counsel in the early phases of this project. Thank you also to the patient folks at Onion River Press and the staff at the Lake Champlain Basin Program, who have remained flexible through the changing timelines of this project. In some very few sections in Chapter Five and in this conclusion, an AI tool was used to massage passages for ease of reading, but all foundational writing and research has been entirely a human endeavor!

www.ingramcontent.com/pod-product-compliance
Lightning Source LLC
Chambersburg PA
CBHW041452120626
46547CB00003B/428